The Presidency Reappraised

The Presidency Reappraised

Edited by
Rexford G. Tugwell
and Thomas E. Cronin

PRAEGER PUBLISHERS
New York • Washington

Portions of "War Powers: A Need for Legislative Reassertion," by Louis Fisher, appear in chapters 6 and 7 of the author's *President and Congress* (New York: The Free Press, 1972).

"Congress and the Making of American Foreign Policy," by Arthur Schlesinger, Jr., is reprinted by permissison from *Foreign Affairs*, October, 1972. Copyright 1972 by Council on Foreign Relations, Inc.

"The President and the Press," by Daniel P. Moynihan, is reprinted by permission of the author from *Commentary*, March, 1971. Copyright 1971 by Daniel P. Moynihan.

Published in the United States of America in 1974
by Praeger Publishers, Inc.
111 Fourth Avenue, New York, N.Y. 10003

Second printing, 1974

Library of Congress Cataloging in Publication Data

Tugwell, Rexford Guy, 1891–
  The Presidency reappraised.
  Includes bibliographical references.
  1. Presidents—United States—Addresses, essays, lectures. 2. Presidents—United States—History—Addresses, essays, lectures. 3. Executive power—United States—Addresses, essays, lectures.
I. Cronin, Thomas E., joint author. II. Title.
JK516.T82   353.03'13   73-6201

Printed in the United States of America

Contents

I

Introduction

1

The Presidency:
Ventures in Reappraisal

Rexford G. Tugwell and Thomas E. Cronin

This collection of essays is about the American Presidency—its powers, limitations, and responsibilities in a democratic society. The central theme is the ability of the Presidency, in an increasingly complex and interdependent world, to furnish needed leadership while remaining, at the same time, responsive to the will of the people. Each essay gives its own interpretation of the Presidency and evaluates, in historical context, how the office has evolved from its original conception.

The Presidency has been subjected to a rising volume of criticism for several decades—indeed, since the end of the nineteenth century—with, sad to say, remarkably little effect. Woodrow Wilson and like-minded Progressives saw that, through the unification and industrialization of the nation and its move toward international involvement, the condition of the United States had changed markedly, but its government had not. Certain experiments and *ad hoc* reforms have been tried since, almost all moving toward a strengthened or at least expanded Presidential Establishment. With the coming of the age of television and nuclear weapons, the Presidency has become a focal point for criticism. It is there that decision-making has tended to lodge, little by little, without much serious concern for the consequences of centralization.

This is changing. The Presidency is now deep in controversy. There is no doubt that it has been ignoring the rule of self-restraint implicit in the Constitution. The silences of the Constitution present ambiguites and wide opportunities for aggrandizement by all the branches. These invitations to disregard the niceties expected of all concerned have been freely taken advantage of, and Presidents have been notable offenders. Presidential aides have been even worse offenders, especially those who act on the premise that the "President *is* the Government" and believe, mistakenly, that what is good for the President is inevitably good also for the country.

Some critics would curtail the functions and authority of the Presidency, because they regard incumbents as increasingly possessors of too much power, arrogant and inclined to an imperial style. Others no longer trust Presidents on a variety of specific issues, such as war-making and control over public communications. Still others would limit Presidential powers for their own benefit or for that of certain special interests with whom they, for reasons good or bad, are allied.

On the other hand, there are many analysts who reject much of the criticism. The Presidency, they say, is subject to limitations and constraints too readily overlooked. They suggest that, in recent decades, primary attention has had to be given to national security. Because of this, the office has become inadequate for decisive priority setting and for leading in the attainment of domestic goals. They suggest that the "other Presidency" —the one charged with improving the quality of life and revitalizing human and social development—has not been succcessful because the institution itself is ill equipped, distrusted, or weak. That there ought to be two or more Presidents is a tempting conclusion to draw from many serious discussions.

There is substantial agreement that the checks and balances of the Constitution have operated more effectively on the legislative and judicial branches than they have on the Presidency. Concentration of information, secrecy and sometimes deceit, war-making without consultation, increasing reliance on executive privilege, executive agreements, impoundment and reprograming are disquieting developments. Concentration on public relations, with subordination of substance to style, is another subject of critical concern. The adversary and critical role of the press and the electronic media is necessary to the very existence of democracy in the crowded and busy nation; but, in spite of their extensive coverage, too many gross deceptions have not been prevented. They sooner or later come to light, of course, and the office has suffered from each exposure.

Both a continuing study and a broader appreciation of the Presidential office are needed. This collection of essays, emerging from various conferences at the Center for the Study of Democratic Institutions, and supplemented by two previously published contributions, is intended to appraise the existing Presidency, influenced by past developments and itself influencing future ones. Each author writes about a different aspect of the Presidency, and, hence, each emphasizes problems and possibilities quite different from those discussed by others. Paradoxes, ambiguities, and unsettled questions are so characteristic of the institution that no reader should expect an agreed assessment or easily achieved solutions for the acknowledged problems. It is in the nature of the Presidency that there should be sharp differences among its critics and defenders.

By way of preface, we may, however, call attention to several general considerations. The increasing tendency to concentrate decision-making in the Presidency is one of these. Crises, both foreign and economic, have enlarged the office. When there has been a need for decisive action, Presidents have had to supply it. The situation of the nation in a suddenly compacted world is involved; so, too, is the existence of armed forces capable of undertaking the missions of enforcement often involved in bargaining. There is also our economy, and its interdependence with those of other nations; there are the special complications of international trade and monetary arrangements. These lead to secret negotiations and innumerable executive agreements and often give rise to crises that must be met without public discussion.

The legislature, of course, is formally expected to develop national policies and establish priorities. Yet, Congress is usually divided and is clearly ill designed for taking the lead in most areas of policy. The increasing complexity of society and the tasks that government must perform have confused the numerous and sometimes inexpert lawmakers and exposed their inability to meet their expected duty. Few members are able to compete with specialists in the executive branch, who are chosen for their capabilities. The legislators' impermanence in office, their ties to local interests, their dispersal of authority through committees—and perhaps the character of those who offer themselves for office—make their claims to national leadership increasingly empty.

Legislators are expected to legislate in the national interest, but have no encouragement for doing so. It has been suggested, with reason, that, if some part of the Congress should be elected at large, it might supply this lacking incentive. The House of Representatives is particularly at fault; no sooner is a member seated than the next election commands his attention. He must claim, almost at once, that he has extracted various benefits from Washington for his district. Each member establishes a kind of service organization for his constituents, and most of his staff attends to these errands; he himself works for projects favored by his supporters; and measures of interest to the nation are considered, if at all, only as they affect his re-election. This is a constitutional defect. The numerous small districts and the short terms originated with the Framers and have never been revised.

Concentration of powers and responsibilities in the White House has occurred because Congress has allowed—even willed—it. If a national controversy exists, Congress is likely to debate it for a while, then turn to the President and charge him to produce a solution with plans, legislation, and annual reports on the subject. Each new assignment to it enlarges the Presidency, requires a larger staff, and causes more frequent resort to executive privilege. The result, of course, is a Presidential Establishment with a staff of thousands, able to expand at once on demand and able, also, to avoid inconvenient accountings. Hence, it is true, as Justice Jackson said in his Steel Seizure opinion, that the power to legislate for emergencies belongs in the hands of Congress—but only Congress itself can prevent power from slipping through its fingers.

The Framers relied on self-restraint to keep each branch of government from too much interference in the responsibilities of the others. But each, in turn, has found reasons for expansion. Each has enlarged its scope and sought to make the enlargement permanent. Checks were supposed to operate automatically, but they have not; and the President has become almost immune. The power of the purse and possible impeachment have proved unusable. In foreign affairs, he can make momentous commitments without being seriously opposed. When adventures prove disastrous, there may be criticism, but there are no penalties. It is apparent that Presidents no longer recognize self-restraint as a virtue applicable to their office, and will go as far as public tolerance will permit.

What can be done? Can Congress be revitalized or reconstituted? Can there be a legislative reassertion of the war powers? Ought there to be some type of impeachment of a policy, somewhere short of impeaching the President himself? Or is there needed some sort of drastic overhauling, considerably more extensive than is proposed by the contributors here, one that would reassign duties and invent national institutions more appropriate for our age and the requirements of an open, responsive, and representative democracy?

There are recurring complaints that Presidents have become very like emperor-kings, dominating public communication, determining national priorities, and removing themselves from criticism and even, sometimes, from public protest. As F. G. Hutchins and George Reedy describe it, this is an imminent threat to democracy. Indeed, it has always been disconcerting that a single chief executive was required in the first place, given a fixed term of four years, and, once decided on, endowed with reverential patriotism. It all began, of course, with the nationalist Framers. Hamilton, explaining it, said that "Energy in the Executive is a leading character in the definition of good government. It is essential to the protection of the community against foreign attacks; it is not less essential to the . . . administration of the laws."

Freedom of information is so necessary in a democracy that there can be no objection to its protection. When a President becomes an advocate and uses his control over the media as an adversary weapon in public matters, he does so not to inform but to demand support for Presidential preferences in crucial decisions. Likewise, the convenience of secrecy has denigrated the democratic process; as a rule, secrecy creates insulation and remoteness, which, in turn, help Presidents in the concealment of mistakes, deviousness, and capriciousness.

On the other hand, the media too often prosper from sensationalism and depart from the canons of reliable reporting to qualify as the sole shapers of public policy. This dilemma—the undesirability of official control and the unreliability of the commercial media—is not an easy one for a democracy struggling with the developments of technology, radio and television. An idea of the dimensions of the dilemma and the problems involved is suggested in the essays by Moynihan and Cronin. Still, it should be possible to elevate the standards of communication so essential to government by the people.

It is true that part of the problem here is the increasing tendency to personalize the Presidency; and television has made the problem worse. Aggrandizement and endless search for personal credit are encouraged by appearances on the screen. The cult of the hero in the White House discourages citizen participation. A deliberately developed skepticism or even cynicism concerning the Presidency and its accomplishments might have a good effect, but, in itself, it would not be a sufficient antidote for the traditional, romanticized view of Presidents. Political scientist William Crotty's warning is appropriate and even urgent:

> *The office of the presidency has been the target of assassins because of its power and visibility as the kingpin of American government. A depersonalization of the office and its incumbent would be helpful as would an emphasis on the complex responsibilities of competing centers of governmental power—the Congress, the state capitals and the mayors' offices.*

Several lessons can be derived. Presidential omnipotence is not desirable; and a sprawling bureaucracy in the executive office of the President, created because Presidents need help and protection, has its own problems. A swollen public-relations corps has actually diminished Presidential credibility. Large staffs create conflicts, make line administrators more distant, and attract more duties to the White House than can be administered effectively. A strong Presidency, ideally, should be a lean and candid one. It should be accessible to Congress and the Cabinet alike and should not speak—or be listened to—as a mouthpiece in the manner of a shrewd public-relations agency.

It is necessary, also, to consider the selection process and the accountability of those selected. Becoming President and being President may well be antithetical. The style and skills needed to advance in the on-deck circle of candidates may actually unfit a person to be President. On the one hand, to run for the Presidency requires the avoidance of issues; a candidate must please the fat cats and political bosses. Everyone has known, for a century, that the choosing of a President is a kind of state- and city-bosses' game, the object of which is to find for the country the leader best suited to their needs rather than those of the nation. As for the recruitment of Vice Presidents—eight of whom have succeeded to the Presidency because of death—they are more often than not picked for no better reason than that they may help to carry a doubtful region.

There is little intense scrutiny of character and competence during the process. There has been a tendency recently to choose Presidential nominees from the Senate, and hence men about whose executive talents very little is known. A senator has no responsibility for organizing, managing, or directing large-scale enterprises. The Presidency requires a highly skilled executive adept in the art of delegating responsibility to people often superior to the chief executive himself in specialized matters. In addition, however, a President must be a shrewd partisan educator and coalition-builder.

Instinctive democratic leadership and dynamic executive talents are rarely joined in any one person; and, even then, the one set of qualifications can easily destroy the other. Moreover, we simultaneously demand a President to be a national unifier and, as priority setter and party leader, a national divider.

Most Presidents have struggled courageously with these dilemmas. None, however, has succeeded in resolving them. If it seems cruel to put a person in a position where it is nearly certain that he will fail, and then pillory him for not succeeding, it is what the United States invariably does to its Presidents—and, sad to say, with little understanding, pity, or even decent tolerance. When the risks of finding incompetence or the "wrong man at the wrong time" are well known and no one cares, then are we really entitled to turn on the incumbent, as recent Presidents have been turned upon? Those who complain most bitterly about the inadequacies of Presidential performance are often the same ones who dismiss out of hand suggestions for recasting selection procedures and reassigning constitutional responsibilities.

Finally, there is the problem of keeping Presidents responsible. Political parties no longer function well enough for this purpose, and perhaps they seldom, if ever, did. One reason, of course, is that issues and events come and go so rapidly that elections increasingly serve less effectively for communicating the public's preferences to their leaders. It is not an exaggeration to say that the election process is, at present, little more than a personnel-selection device.

The Constitution fixes a four-year term; what means are there to ensure accountability between elections? The difficulties of guidance by referendum or poll-taking are obvious, and no other extraconstitutional processes will ensure sustained responsiveness. What can be done? What *should* be done? Can the political parties be overhauled and revitalized? Can election reform remedy the situation? If so, what kinds of electoral reforms? What about the role of the press: Must it be neutral? Can it be expected to inform the electorate better? Can confrontation between and among institutions solve the problem? Is a collegial or restructured Presidency a possible resolution? And what about Congress? Questions concerning the deficiencies of Congress appear in almost all of these discussions, and so they should.

These, then, are some of the questions and critical considerations posed and explored in the following essays. Admittedly, there are other issues not discussed here. Space limits and the availability of research dictate that this will always be the case in such ventures in re-evaluation. We are not in agreement with some of the views incorporated in these essays, but we think that, on balance, the reappraisals suggested do furnish a useful starting place for assessment of the American Presidency as this nation celebrates its two-hundredth anniversary. Indeed, in some sections we have deliberately included contrasting opinions to sharpen the focus on the office. Special mention should be made of the contribution by Adolf Berle. This is, we believe, the last article written by that brilliant counselor of Presidents. He was always a stubborn and determined individualist, and his contribution here manifests such traits even to the point of, as he put it, espousing the unpopular and the countercontemporary.

Above all else, it is hoped that these essays may stimulate an urgently needed reappraisal of an inherited but seemingly essential institution fast becoming inconsistent with cherished democratic ideals.

2

The President's Constitutional Position

C. Herman Pritchett

The Presidency looms so large in our national history, and we are so accustomed to the President as a necessary and familiar fact of life, that it is difficult to conceive of any other way we could institutionalize the executive power. For that reason, it may be helpful to the reader to begin this survey of current constitutional problems with respect to *Presidential powers* by returning to 1787 and reviewing the alternatives as the Founders saw them and the proposals from among which they made the choices that created the Presidency.

What were the attitudes toward executive power in the Founding period? The fear of monarchy was basic to all considerations of the executive office. The shadow of George III was heavy on the land. Executive authority was symbolized by the royal governors. As Corwin says, "The colonial period ended with the belief prevalent that 'the executive magistracy' was the natural enemy, the legislative assembly the natural friend of liberty."[1] The Virginia constitution of 1776 stipulated that the executive powers of government were to be exercised according to the laws of the commonwealth, and that no power or prerogative was ever to be claimed "by virtue of any law, statute, or custom of England." The intention was to cut the executive power off entirely from the resources of the common law and of English constitutional usage.

But, between 1776 and 1787, there was enough experience with state legislatures to destroy naïve assumptions about their inherent goodness. Madison was critical of the state constitutions, which, in their concern with the "over-grown and all-grasping prerogative of an hereditary magistrate," did not realize the "danger from legislative usurpation, which, by assembling all power in the same hands, must lead to the same tyranny as is threatened by executive usurpations." [2] Gouverneur Morris, reversing the earlier pattern, saw the executive as the protector and the legislature as the threat, saying the "Executive Magistrate should be the guardian of the people, even of the lower classes, agst. Legislative tyranny, against the Great & the wealthy who in the course of things will necessarily compose—the Legislative body." [3]

The principal theoretical writers with whom the Founders were familiar likewise supplied support for a strong executive. Particularly impressive is Locke's description of "prerogative" in chapter 14 of his *Second Treatise of Government,* which argues that

> . . . *the good of the society requires that several things should be left to the discretion of him that has the executive power. . . . For the legislators not being able to foresee and provide by laws for all that may be useful to the community, the executor of the laws, having the power in his hands, has by the common law of Nature a right to make use of it for the good of the society.*

Montesquieu's doctrine of the separation of powers, holding that the three departments of government must be kept separate and that each must be able to defend its characteristic functions from intrusion by either of the other departments, provided another source of defense for the executive against legislative supremacy.

The problem, then, as the Founders saw it, was how to secure an executive power capable of penetrating to the remotest parts of the Union for the purpose of enforcing national laws and bringing assistance to the states in emergencies of domestic disorder, yet avoiding, at the same time, stirring up the widespread popular fear of monarchy.

THE DECISIONS THAT ESTABLISHED THE CONSTITUTIONAL DIMENSIONS OF THE PRESIDENCY

Rejection of a collegial executive or a council. The one decision about the executive that was basic to all others was that it should be a man and not a board or committee. Some thought a one-man executive would be too much like a monarch. In the discussions at the Convention, Sherman said that the number of the executive should "not be fixed, but . . . the legislature should be at liberty to appoint one or more as experience might dictate." Randolph then proposed an executive council of three men, contending that "unity in the Executive magistracy" would be the "foetus of monarchy." But Gerry thought that, in military matters, a plural executive would be a "general with three heads." [4]

James Wilson was the leader of the strong executive faction. He wanted a "single magistrate, as giving most energy, dispatch, and responsibility to the office." [5] Unity in the executive would be the "best safeguard against tyranny." As chairman of the Committee of Detail, Wilson had the opportunity to incorporate his conception of the office into the draft. In Articles VI and X of the Committee's report of August 6, the issue was settled in favor of a single executive.

There was still the issue of restraining the executive by a Council. On September 7, while discussing the provision for the President to require the opinion in writing of the heads of departments, Mason said that, in rejecting a Council to the President, "we were about to try an experiment on which the most despotic Governments had never ventured—the Grand Signor himself had his Divan." He proposed a Council of State for the President, made up of six members—two from the Eastern, two from the Middle, and two from the Southern states —with a rotation and duration of office similar to those of the

Senate, and appointed by Congress or the Senate. Franklin approved; he thought a Council "would not only be a check on a bad President but be a relief to a good one." Morris replied that the Committee had considered a Council and rejected the idea; "it was judged that the President by persuading his Council—to concur in his wrong measures, would acquire their protection for them." The proposal was defeated, three to eight.[6]

Rejection of election by the legislature. Election of the President by the legislature, which was very nearly adopted, would inevitably have made the Presidency a much different institution. There was a close relationship between the method of election and the term of office. If the executive were to be chosen by Congress, then a fairly long term, with no re-eligibility, was favored, to reduce the possibility of intrigue with Congress for a second term. If the President could be chosen in some other fashion, then re-eligibility was not objectionable, and a shorter term was possible.

The Virginia Plan called for a national executive to be named by electors chosen by Congress. Sherman wanted the executive to be only an "institution for carrying the will of the legislature into effect," and consequently executive officials should be "persons . . . appointed by and accountable to the legislature only."[7] Early discussion by the Committee of the Whole left the Virginia Plan unchanged.

Choice of the President by electors chosen by the people was proposed by Wilson on June 2 and defeated eight to two. Morris again proposed popular election on July 17, at which time Mason made his famous comment that "it would be as unnatural to refer the choice of a proper character for chief Magistrate to the people, as it would, to refer a trial of colours to a blind man."[8] The popular-election plan failed, and the Convention then reaffirmed legislative election unanimously. But Morris and Madison contended that the executive should be independent of the legislature. The convention then switched to electors, but provided for their choice by the state legislatures.

On July 24, the Convention flopped back to the original scheme for legislative election, with a seven-year term and no re-eligibility. In this posture, the matter went to the Committee of Detail, which had to decide how Congress would vote for President. Would the houses vote separately (they might not agree) or jointly (the larger states would dominate)? Joint election was adopted on August 24, but an effort to have the votes cast by states, each with one vote, failed by a six-to-five margin. Here, Morris again urged popular election and lost only by six to five. The matter was so completely in dispute that it was turned over to the Committee of Eleven, including Morris. This committee proposed the plan that was finally adopted—electors equaling in number senators and representatives from the states and appointed by the states.

A broad appointing power for the President. The appointing power went to the President only after prolonged opposition. The Virginia Plan called for the election of judges as well as the President by the Congress, but the judicial provision was soon eliminated. On June, Wilson argued for appointment of judges by the President. "A principal reason for unity in the Executive was that officers might be appointed by a single, responsible person."[9] Madison inclined toward appointment of judges by the Senate, as the more stable and independent branch of the legislature.

On July 18, Gorham's proposal for executive appointment, with Senate advice and consent, was rejected by a tie vote. Senate appointment was reaffirmed on July 21, and the decision then went to the Committee of Detail. Its report gave the general appointing power to the President, but left judges and ambassadors with the Senate. The Committee of Eleven, reporting on September 4, gave the appointment of Supreme Court justices and ambassadors, and all other officers of the United States whose appointment was not otherwise provided for, to the President, with Senate advice and consent. This formula was accepted by the Convention on September 7.

The grant of power as Commander in Chief to the President and the power to declare war to Congress. In giving Congress the power to declare war, the Convention clearly intended to vest the power to embark on a war in the body most representative of the people, in contrast to the power of the British sovereign to initiate war on his own prerogative. In the draft that came from the Committee of Detail, the language was that Congress should have the power to "make" war. This clause remained in its original form in the Committee drafts for several weeks after other foreign relations powers had been transferred from the whole Congress to the Senate and then to the President.

On August 17, Pinckney opposed the vesting of this power in Congress—"its proceedings were too slow." He thought the "Senate would be the best depositary, being more acquainted with foreign affairs." Butler was "for resting the power in the President, who will have all the requisite qualities, and will not make war but when the Nation will support it." But Gerry said he "never expected to hear in a republic a motion to empower the Executive alone to declare war." [10]

It was Gerry and Madison who moved to substitute "declare" for "make," "leaving to the Executive the power to repel sudden attacks." Mason supported the change; he was against "giving the power of war to the Executive, because [he could] not (safely) . . . be trusted with it." King pointed out that the phrase "make war" might be understood to mean "conduct war," which was clearly an executive function—an argument Ellsworth found convincing. The change was made by a vote of seven to two. [11] Thus, the purpose of the change from "make" to "declare" was by no means to limit the role of Congress to a declaratory formality; the intention was to vest in Congress the full power and responsibility of initiating war.

The power of the President to act as Commander in Chief was not much discussed, according to Madison's notes. There is no evidence that it was thought of as a source of power for the President. Since the clause contains nothing to indicate the purposes for which the President may exercise the power thus granted to command the troops, these purposes must ultimately be found in other provisions of Article II. According to Hamilton, in No. 69 of the *Federalist,* the power "would amount to nothing more than the supreme command and direction of the military and naval forces, as first General and admiral of the Confederacy."

The power to make treaties. The draft of the Constitution, as reported by the Committee of Detail on August 6, gave the

Senate the power to make treaties as well as to appoint ambassadors and judges of the Supreme Court. On August 15, Mercer
objected. The power of treaties, he contended, "belonged to the
Executive department," adding that "Treaties would not be final
so as to alter the laws of the land, till ratified by legislative
authority." Madison, on August 23, agreed, saying "that the
Senate represented the States alone, and that for this as well as
other obvious reasons it was proper that the President should
be an agent in Treaties." [12]

On September 4, the Committee of Eleven reported the new
language giving the President the power to make treaties by
and with the advice and consent of the Senate, with a two-thirds
vote required. It was adopted on September 7, unanimously,
after the Convention voted down, one to ten, Wilson's proposal
that treaties be approved by the House of Representatives also.

*The President's power to take care that the laws be faithfully
executed.* The most general statement of Presidential power to
come from the Founders was the provision that the President
should take care that the laws be faithfully executed. Obviously,
the executive had to have some general authorization to enforce
the laws. The only question was how this grant of power was
to be phrased. The original Virginia Plan gave the national
executive a "general authority to execute the National laws,"
as well as the "Executive rights vested in Congress by the Confederation." [13] On June 1, this language was amended in the
Committee of the Whole to read "with power to carry into
execution the national laws." The additional provision, "to execute such powers, not legislative or judiciary in their nature,
as may from time to time be delegated by the national legislature," was voted down.[14] The subsequent change to the present
language was a change in style, not in content or intention.

THE GRANT OF EXECUTIVE POWERS IN PRACTICE

How did these key textual decisions of the Convention pertaining to executive powers work out in practice?

1. The establishment of a single President is, of course, the
foundation on which the entire subsequent development of the

executive office rests. A collegial executive surely would have collapsed almost immediately. Under President Washington's wise and responsible exploration of Presidential powers, fears of an executive monarchy gradually faded away. While the institution of the Cabinet developed, it hardly filled the role of a Council to the President that some had urged in the Convention. Executive responsibility rested solely on the President, and each incumbent has had ample opportunity to re-create the office in his own image.

2. The system of electing the President, which the Convention made as close to a system of popular election as seemed feasible at the time, proved to be rather readily adaptable to a system of full popular election (with the necessary qualifications that the electoral college system requires). The direct link between the President and the national electorate must be regarded as the primary condition of Presidential power, providing him with a legitimacy possessed by no other official of the government. This legitimacy is slightly diminished when the President is elected with less than 50 per cent of the popular vote, or when the margin between the two leading candidates is very narrow. It would be seriously eroded if, in a future election, the workings of the electoral college awarded the Presidency to a candidate who actually secured fewer popular votes than his opponent.

3. The appointment power is the President's most important instrument for effectuating his control of the executive branch and ensuring that the laws are faithfully executed. The principal limitations on this power derive from the necessity of securing Senate confirmation for his appointments to a very large number of offices, a number extending far beyond positions with substantial policy-forming powers. Normally, however, the great bulk of these appointments are confirmed routinely.

The occasional Senate rejection of a Presidential appointee takes place under two circumstances. First, nominees who are to fill positions in a state may be rejected because a senator from that state announces to the Senate that the nominee is personally obnoxious to him, in which event the rule of senatorial courtesy almost invariably results in rejection of the nomination. Second, a majority of the Senate may reject a nominee because he is deemed unqualified for the post or, for some other reason, personally unfit or politically undesirable. Examples are the rejections of Nixon nominees Clement F. Haynsworth and G. Harrold Carswell for the Supreme Court, Kennedy nominee Francis X. Morrissey for the federal district bench, and Eisenhower nominee Lewis B. Strauss as Secretary of Commerce. Such rejections are embarrassing defeats for the President, but they occur very rarely.

Another technique Congress might employ to limit Presidential discretion in appointments has been used very seldom, and that is to specify qualifications that nominees for a position must have. Thus, members of federal regulatory commissions must come from both parties, and members of the boards of the Federal Reserve Banks must come from certain occupational areas. The various proposals that have been made to require the President to appoint only men with prior judicial experience to the Supreme Court have all failed.

Attempts to limit the President's power of removal have led to some classic and well-known constitutional arguments, but any restraints imposed as a result are of greater theoretical than practical significance. The requirement that the Senate be consulted on removals as on appointments was declared unconstitutional by Chief Justice Taft in *Myers* v. *United States* (1926). An exception for officials in quasi-judicial positions, where Congress had manifested an intention that they be removable only for cause, was created by the Court in *Humphrey's Executor* v. *United States* (1935), an exception extended in *Wiener* v. *United States* (1958) to all positions created by Congress with quasi-judicial duties, whether or not the legislature specified removal only for cause. While these rulings suggest to the President a certain caution in removing members of the regulatory commissions, their practical effect on the President's control over personnel is otherwise negligible.

4. The power that the President has asserted as commander in chief would have been most surprising to the Founders. The Hamiltonian view, that this provision merely placed the President at the top of the military hierarchy, was endorsed half a century later by Story, who interpreted this power in his *Commentaries* as "to give orders and have a general superintendency"

over the armed forces. In a Supreme Court opinion by Chief Justice Taney (*Fleming* v. *Page* [1850]), the Court spoke of the President's duty and power as "purely military."

Corwin describes the transformation that occurred in 1861, as Lincoln met the secession crisis:

> *The sudden emergence of the "Commander-in-Chief" clause as one of the most highly charged provisions of the Constitution occurred almost overnight in consequence of Lincoln's wedding it to the clause that makes it the duty of the President "to take care that the laws be faithfully executed." From these two clauses thus united, Lincoln proceeded to derive what he termed the "war power," to justify the series of extraordinary measures that he took in the interval between the fall of Fort Sumter and the convening of Congress in special session on July 4, 1861.*[15]

In World War I, no such reliance had to be placed on the Commander-in-Chief power, since the war was initiated by a congressional declaration, and Congress provided authority to the President to conduct the war either by substantive legislation or by broad delegation of legislative power. Even so, Wilson called on his power as commander in chief to create such war agencies as the Committee on Public Information, the War Industries Board, and the War Labor Board. He invoked the same authority at the outbreak of the war in closing German wireless stations and subjecting communications companies to regulation with respect to messages received from or going abroad.

The World War II situation was similar, but the emergency started before the declaration of war and extended further beyond it. The destroyer deal with Britain, on September 3, 1940, was directly in violation of at least two statutes and represented an exercise by the President of a power specifically assigned to Congress; but it was defended by Attorney General Jackson as based on the President's powers as Commander in Chief. During the war, President Roosevelt created not fewer than thirty-five executive agencies, generally invoking as authority his powers as "Commander-in-Chief in time of war." In only one case, involving the War Labor Board, was the constitutional legitimacy of these agencies questioned, and then unsuccessfully.[16]

When the President uses American armed forces abroad in the *absence* of a congressionally declared war, his reliance on the Commander-in-Chief power is even more crucial. It seems likely that the Framers never intended troops to be used outside the country without congressional consent. Since neither a standing army nor a navy was contemplated, naturally any military operations abroad would necessarily require congressional participation in securing the troops and providing the funds. However, the availability of a navy made possible three undeclared naval wars—the war with France (1798–1800) and the first (1801–5) and second (1815) Barbary wars. But Jefferson forbade the navy to attack Tripoli in 1801 on the ground that Congress had not declared war; and Madison, in 1812, refused to retaliate against British provocations until Congress declared war.

By the latter half of the nineteenth century, it had become a well-established Presidential practice to use troops abroad for the purpose of protecting American lives and property. In the present century, both Roosevelts, Wilson, Truman, Eisenhower, Kennedy, Johnson, and Nixon have all moved American troops into action or across national frontiers with little or no effort to secure advance congressional assent. Since 1950, there have been Presidential moves into Korea, Lebanon, Cuba, the Dominican Republic, Vietnam, Cambodia, and Laos, as well as distant naval operations, undercover plots, military advisory programs, and aerial overflights of foreign countries that risked conflict—all with no opportunity for congressional review.

The two major examples of undeclared wars are of course the Korean war (1950–53) and the Indochina war (1964–73). In the Korean war, justification for the executive action was provided by the U.N. resolution condemning aggression by North Korea. In 1955, President Eisenhower secured from Congress a joint resolution authorizing his employment of the armed forces, if required, to protect Taiwan from Chinese attack. Again, in 1957, he requested from Congress authorization to use force against Communist aggression in the Middle East when asked to do so by a victim of such aggression. Under Democratic leadership, the

Senate concluded that it would be constitutionally improper to "authorize" the President to take action he already had power to take as Commander in Chief, and so changed the language to read that, "if the President determines the necessity thereof, the United States is prepared to use armed forces" on behalf of nations requesting assistance against armed aggression.

These precedents were used by President Johnson in 1964. At a time when there were only 20,000 American troops in Vietnam, and after alleged North Vietnam torpedo boat attacks on two U.S. destroyers in the Gulf of Tonkin, the President asked Congress for a joint resolution of support to strengthen his hand in dealing with the Vietnam situation. Almost unanimously, Congress adopted the Tonkin Gulf Resolution, approving and supporting the "determination of the President, as Commander-in-Chief, to take all necessary measures to repel any armed attack against the forces of the United States and to prevent further aggression." This is the way, as Corwin puts it, that the "President's power as Commander-in-Chief has been transformed from a simple power of military command to a vast reservoir of indeterminate powers in time of emergency." [17]

5. Naturally, it has made a great difference that the President, and not the Senate, negotiates treaties. However, the requirement that treaties secure ratification by a two-thirds vote of the Senate has been a substantial limitation on the President's power. To a considerable degree, Presidents have met this challenge by the extensive use of executive agreements, which have the same legal effect as treaties. The principal limitations on their use are political in nature—the degree to which it is wise to exclude the Senate from this constitutional foreign-policy role. Prior to the war in Indochina the most serious congressional flare-up over executive domination in the foreign-affairs field was the abortive but serious drive for the Bricker Amendment in the early 1950's, which sought to do two things: One was to prevent the use of executive agreements as alternatives to treaties; the second was to prevent treaty commitments from becoming effective until embodied in ordinary legislation.

6. The power to take care that the laws be faithfully executed was, as already noted, joined by Lincoln to the Commander-in-

Chief power at the outbreak of the Civil War to justify his emergency acts. Standing alone, this power also has been the subject of significant reliance in supporting Presidential action; and it is a principal reliance for the theory of Presidential implied powers.

That the President possesses not only the specific powers mentioned in the Constitution but also the powers necessary and proper for the performance of the executive function finds the broadest support in the first sentence of Article II: "The executive power shall be vested in a President of the United States." It has always been a nice constitutional question whether these words constitute a grant of power or are a mere designation of an office. The former interpretation is consistent with the Lockean notion of executive power as "residual," and it is also supported by the so-called decision of 1789, in which the First Congress relied on the "executive power" provision in deciding that the President already had the power of removal under the Constitution without any authorization by Congress.

The "faithful execution of the laws" clause was authoritatively interpreted by the Supreme Court in the well-known case of *In re Neagle* (1890), where it held that the "laws" that the President was to execute included not only statutes enacted by Congress but also "any obligation fairly and properly inferrible from [the Constitution], or any duty . . . to be derived from the general scope of . . . duties under the laws of the United States." The President's duty to see that the laws are faithfully executed, the Court went on, is not "limited to the enforcement of acts of Congress . . . according to their express terms," but includes also "the rights, duties and obligations growing out of the Constitution itself, our international relations, and all the protection implied by the nature of the government under the Constitution."

The same position was taken by the Court in *In re Debs* (1895), where it upheld the power of the President to order his Attorney General to secure a court injunction against the Pullman railroad strike despite the fact that there was no explicit statutory basis for the injunction.

The principal Supreme Court ruling limiting the implied

powers of the Presidency is the famous Steel Seizure case (1952), in which President Truman's seizure of the steel mills to prevent a strike that would impair the flow of munitions to the troops in Korea was invalidated. That decision, however, turned on the special circumstances of the case and should not be read as imposing any serious limitations on the President's emergency powers. It was the fact that Congress, in passing the Taft-Hartley Act, had specifically considered giving seizure powers to the President and decided against it (though adopting no language at all on the subject) that convinced the swing justices, Jackson and Frankfurter, that this nonaction had stripped the President of powers he might otherwise have had.

Balance Sheet on Presidential Power

The conventional wisdom on the American Presidency, confirmed by our review of the decisions made by the Framers in 1787, is that the Presidency was intended to be an office of great power, and that the successful operation of the American constitutional system requires that this power be used. Presidents who do not use their powers vigorously are condemned as weak and as failures in office. The unity, dispatch, and national outlook of the President are contrasted with the divisiveness, the delay, and the parochialism of the legislature. Let us attempt to appraise the character and extent of Presidential power in the principal executive roles and determine whether the effective performance of these roles requires any changes in Presidential powers.

Head of state. The President gains support for his other roles from his status as symbolic and ceremonial head of the nation. On the other hand, his performance as head of state is handicapped because he is a partisan for whom almost half the electorate, and often more than half, did not vote. No practical plan has ever been suggested for providing the Republic with a nonpartisan chief of state, leaving the President with his other executive duties. Thus, the ultimate symbols of unity have to be inanimate objects—the flag and the Constitution.

Opinion molder. The President occupies incomparably the

"best bully pulpit" in the land, particularly as supplemented by ready access to television. Certainly, nothing could or should be done about this. If he appears on the tube too often, over-exposure will bring its own redress. The principal problem is to provide some balance in presentation of opposing views, a matter on which the networks have recently begun to develop a policy. One issue is: Who speaks for the opposition when it has no recognized national leader?

Legislative function. Clearly Congress has failed to live up to the original constitutional expectations in the field of legislative performance, encouraging the President to assume a greater role than was anticipated in formulating legislative programs. Presidential success in the legislative arena, however, has been limited by factors such as the following:

- Separation of powers makes it possible for the opposition party to be in control of one or both houses.
- There may be substantial opposition to the President within his own congressional party, and he may not even be on particularly good terms with his party's leadership in Congress.
- The seniority system gives committee chairmen the powers of small-time monarchs.
- The unwieldly size of the House and the principle of unlimited debate in the Senate do not facilitate expeditious action.
- The effectiveness of both majority and minority party leadership in both houses is often quite limited.

Efforts to reform legislative procedures or to achieve party responsibility in Congress have repeatedly failed. Similar failure has marked proposals for institutional changes which would strengthen the President vis-à-vis Congress—for example, giving the President the item veto on appropriation bills or providing four-year terms for members of the House with the purpose of making it more likely that a majority of representatives would be from the President's party. Separation of powers has thus left the responsibility for adopting coherent legislative programs thoroughly confused.

Chief administrator. The President's position as administrative chief is guaranteed by his control over personnel, organization, and funds. As we have seen, the Senate's role in confirmation of appointees is troublesome to him only on rare occasions, while the power to remove presidential appointees is practically unlimited.

As for organization of the federal establishment, Congress has largely abdicated to the President by a series of reorganization acts giving the President power to set up new organizational structures or arrangements. Such authority was used, for example, by President Nixon to create the Office of Management and Budget. Congress retains only the power to refuse to approve reorganization plans.

In the area of fiscal policy, Congress by the Budget and Accounting Act of 1921 gave the President responsibility for preparation of the budget, and congressional efforts to control or even effectively to review the budget have been progressively less successful. Even such fiscal autonomy as Congress has preserved was challenged by President Nixon in a full-scale assault on the integrity of legislative spending decisions when between 1971 and 1973 he sought to impound some $25 billion in appropriations for projects he disapproved or in amounts which he deemed unwise. This assertion of executive power was too blatant, however, and was partially countered by judicial decisions and legislative reaction.

In spite of the constitutional powers and position of the executive, all recent Presidents have found it difficult to exercise policy control over the federal establishment because of its size, bureaucratic rigidity, and ties to protectors and sponsors in Congress. Beginning with the development of the Executive Office of the President under Franklin Roosevelt, efforts have been made to achieve a greater measure of executive control, without marked success. Again it remained for President Nixon to make a frontal assault on the problem by greatly increasing the Executive Office staff and by an unprecedented concentration of administrative control in the White House by the appointment as Cabinet members of men who had no independent political base, by placing in key positions in the departments and independent

agencies men who had proved their loyalty to the President in
service on the White House staff, and by setting up four super-
department heads directly under the President. The initial effectiveness of this wide-ranging program was subsequently reduced
in considerable measure by the Watergate affair.

Party leader. This is an extraconstitutional role. The President
is, by virtue of his election, the leader of his party, but this does
not guarantee that he will perform the function effectively. Moreover, he will make trouble for himself if he seems to be giving
priority too consistently to partisan motives.

THE PRESIDENCY AT HOME VERSUS THE PRESIDENCY ABROAD

This summary view of the powers of the President in and
through his different roles affords some measure of understanding of his resources for performing his domestic functions. His
great powers of leadership, initiative, and action are balanced by
countervailing forces inherent in the separation-of-powers system. No President is ever able to develop a domestic program
without working within this system. Roosevelt was able to get
what he wanted from Congress, without fighting for it, only during the first hundred days of his New Deal Administration.
Nixon's artfully planned and vigorously implemented effort to
maximize executive power and subordinate or ignore Congress
would no doubt have encountered increased resistance even if
Watergate had not intervened.

When we consider the President's foreign-policy functions and
his access to the war power, however, the situation becomes quite
different. Here, there is real basis for concern whether the system is in balance, for events have repeatedly demonstrated that
Presidential powers of initiative are greater and the possibilities
of restraint fewer. Some of the reasons for this contrast are suggested in the following summary:

- The President monopolizes the sources of information about
  foreign affairs to a much greater degree than he does the
  sources of domestic information; and much of it is not made

public, so that the President can always contend that his actions are based on data not available to Congress or the public.

- The President directs diplomatic negotiations, which must proceed largely in secret.
- The necessity for emergency action, not permitting consultation, is much greater, the ultimate example being the need to counter a threatened nuclear attack.
- As Commander in Chief, the President is in control of a vast engine of force that can move into immediate operation on his command, as compared with the civil establishment, which the President can put in motion or redirect much more slowly, and sometimes not at all.
- Recommendations for military action come up to the President through a military hierarchy that typically presents specific and coordinated policy proposals, compared with the conflicting and uncoordinated advice he usually receives on domestic matters.
- The doctrine of political questions generally prevents the Supreme Court from reviewing any challenges to the constitutionality of executive action in the field of foreign affairs, in contrast to the full power of judicial review over domestic controversies.

In certain foreign-policy matters, Congress does participate fully, and admittedly its record is not always one to inspire great confidence in congressional capacity. The Senate's action, or inaction, in the ratification of treaties has been a long-standing cause for complaint. The annual foreign-aid appropriation is another field where Congress has not been reluctant to substitute its judgment for that of the President. There are matters with domestic ramifications, such as the closing of military posts, where Congress has often reversed Presidential judgment. On the other hand, appropriations for the CIA are hidden completely from the public and from most members of Congress, and the general appropriations for military supply and procurement are seldom seriously questioned.

A reconsideration of executive-legislative relationships induced by the undeclared war in Indochina suggests the following principles:

1. Because of the inherent differences between domestic and foreign problems, the President may legitimately claim greater freedom of action in the foreign field, particularly the power to take emergency measures in the use of military forces.

2. The broad claims for executive autonomy in the use of military forces, based on the commander-in-chief power, in other than emergency situations find support in the practices of the past hundred years, but are not justified by the intentions of the Framers and are not consistent with the American system of representative government and checks and balances.

3. Congress has the right and the obligation to use its appropriating and legislating power to fix outer limits for American foreign and military policy, and to review and revise ongoing foreign and military commitments.

4. Under present conditions, the congressional declaration of war, which was relied upon so strongly by the Framers as a limitation on the executive, is probably obsolete; for it encourages what is no longer acceptable—the use of unlimited force. Limited war is all that can now be contemplated, and the determination of those limits is a matter for joint action by the President and Congress. Development of such machinery may require adaptation in present procedures, particularly for emergency actions. When longer-range policies are involved, it would seem feasible for Congress to set limits on Presidential autonomy by the normal processes of legislation and appropriation.

NOTES

1 Edward S. Corwin, *The President: Office and Powers, 1787–1957* (New York, 1957), pp. 5–6.

2 *The Federalist*, No. 48.

3 Max Farrand, *The Framing of the Constitution of the United States* (New Haven, 1913), vol. II, p. 52.

4 *Ibid.*, vol. I, pp. 65, 66, 97.

5 *Ibid.*, p. 65.

6 *Ibid.*, vol. II, pp. 541–542.

[7] *Ibid.,* vol. I, p. 65.
[8] *Ibid.,* vol. II, p. 31.
[9] *Ibid.,* vol. I, p. 119.
[10] *Ibid.,* vol. II, p. 318.
[11] *Ibid.,* p. 319.
[12] *Ibid.,* pp. 297, 392.
[13] *Ibid.,* vol. I, p. 21.
[14] *Ibid.,* pp. 63–64.
[15] Corwin, *op. cit.,* p. 229.
[16] *Ibid.,* p. 243.
[17] *Ibid.,* p. 261.

II

The
Expanding Presidency
and the Role of Congress

3

Presidential Autocracy in America

F. G. Hutchins

The tyranny of the legislature is really the danger most to be feared, and will continue to be so for many years to come. The tyranny of the executive power will come in its turn, but at a more distant period.
　　　　　　　　　　　—Thomas Jefferson, *letter to James Madison, March 15, 1789.*

The American Presidency has today become the "tyranny" that Jefferson foresaw. The executive branch, the Cinderella of the Constitution of 1789, which fell into such disrepute and inconsequence in the nineteenth century that Lord Bryce felt compelled to explain "Why Great Men are not Elected President," has in the twentieth century come into an inheritance greater than that ever enjoyed by her two sister branches of government.

The triumph of the Presidency was accomplished without constitutional alteration, because the federal government, from the beginning, was a system of separation of power, but fusion of function. Each of the separate branches of government—the Congress, the Presidency, the Court—was assigned legislative, executive, and judicial functions. The "strengthening of the

Presidency" has resulted not simply from the growth in the importance of executive authority in an increasingly complex, developed society, but, more importantly, from the fused growth of the legislative, executive, and judicial authority of the Presidency. This has not appeared to involve usurpation of functions from the other two branches, because the constitutional framework did give the Presidency a foothold in all three areas from which to develop.

The image of the President as an elective monarch had been present in the minds of the Founding Fathers from the beginning. Monarchy—enlightened or otherwise—was the normal pattern of governance in the eighteenth century, and the availability of a suitable candidate in the person of George Washington made the notion of elective monarchism—articulated most forcefully by Alexander Hamilton—the pattern of the constitutional Presidency. This idea, latent in the Constitution, never died completely. For the time being, however, the expansion of Presidential power was eclipsed in 1801, when Jefferson, a Presidential minimalist, succeeded Adams. Jefferson was effective as President, but his *purpose* as President was to further the independence of individuals rather than to establish and consolidate an autocratic form of government.

Lincoln expanded the powers of the Presidency in practice; but this expansion did not survive, because Lincoln did not develop a rationalization for the retention of these expanded powers. Lincoln expanded his powers because the nation was threatened by an emergency; he increased the *executive* powers of the Presidency because decisions needed to be centralized in wartime. Lincoln was willing to do almost anything to save the Union. But the Union Lincoln wanted to save was a land of free yeomen, and in this land there was no room for an institutionalized monarchy. Lincoln viewed his actions as extraordinary. He took extreme measures under the press of circumstances without trying to build these actions into permanent Presidential prerogatives, and without conducting himself as licensed, in his representative capacity, to articulate newly discovered general principles. The Emancipation Proclamation was viewed as exceptional by Lincoln himself, and its moralistic phraseology was urged upon him by others.

The methodical consolidation of Presidential supremacy required more than monarchical instincts or the *de facto* expansion of powers under the press of emergency. The institutionalization of Presidential supremacy required a theory, and this was not developed until the twentieth century, when the Progressives concluded that the President could wield best all three of the traditional functions of government.

The legislative, executive, and judicial powers of the President have not only been expanded but also used to justify one another. Enthusiasts stress the representative character of the Presidency; the role of Presidential leadership in foreign and domestic affairs; and the judgmental power of the President, who, because of his special representativeness and responsibilities, as well as his special advantages of position and access to advice, is able to arbitrate issues in a uniquely judicious way. The Presidency, in short, is three branches in one. The definition that the Presidency gives to each of these functions is not, however, identical with the definition of these functions traditionally upheld by the other branches. The President's apologists have defined the prime functions associated with the other branches in ways that make it appear that the President is better suited to pursue them than the originally constituted branch.

The most grandiose conception of the President's representativeness was that first articulated by Woodrow Wilson, that the President represents all the people. If the Presidency could be made to seem more truly representative of the "people" than was the Congress, where arguably only "interests" were represented, then the Presidency could, in the name of the people, exercise ultimate power with righteous vigor. If the President really, effectively represents everybody, then the Congress, in opposing the President, may seem to represent nothing more than selfishness. Legislators have themselves helped strengthen this impression by their willingness to accept a role as little more than lobbyists for their constituents, exerting influence in the bureaucratic labyrinth on behalf of their constituents, thereby appearing, in fact, to represent nothing that cannot be rightfully subordinated to a larger national interest. If the President is the only true representative institution, or even only a representative institution that is somewhat preferable to the Congress, then there is logically no reason why the President should feel bound by the Congress; the moral pressure, indeed, moves in the opposite direction.

In 1885, Woodrow Wilson, in his book *Congressional Govern ment,* argued that America needed majestic leadership, and that the Congress was not supplying it. At this time, with the power of the American President at its nadir, and with the brilliant parliamentary duels of Gladstone and Disraeli fresh in Wilson's mind, the remedy for the sorry state of Congress that recommended itself to Wilson was a form of Cabinet government for America on the British model. It was only later, after Theodore Roosevelt had demonstrated in practice the Presidency's potential as a platform for strong leadership, that Wilson finally found the proper solution for America. In 1908, he paired his denunciation of Congress with a eulogy for the President: "The nation as a whole has chosen him, and is conscious that it has no other political spokesman. His is the only national voice in affairs. Let him once win the admiration and confidence of the country, and no other single force can withstand him, no combination of forces will easily overpower him. His position takes the imagination of the country. He is the representative of no constituency, but of the whole people. When he speaks in his true character, he speaks for no special interest. If he rightly interprets the national thought and boldly insists upon it, he is irresistible; and the country never feels the zest for action so much as when its President is of such insight and calibre." [1]

The Wilsonian conception of the Presidency has triumphed far beyond Wilson's wildest imaginings. The President, representing all the people, can act in his executive capacity in response to his representative capacity. He need not think of himself as the executive of the Congress; he is the executive of the people. He does not need a law upon which to base his actions. Actions can be justified by reference to the President's "constitutional powers," which means, in effect, his direct representativeness. In 1973, President Nixon, for example, defended his bombing of Cambodia as an exercise of his "inherent authority" as commander in chief and pointed to his re-election margin of 1972 to refute the apparent constitutional requirement of congressional authorization for military initiatives. Originally, the President's constitutional powers meant little more than the power to enforce the laws approved by Congress. Being commander in chief did not seem initially a license to use force if the President, exercising his personal judgment, deemed it necessary. Now, the President's constitutional power is defined to mean the power to make and enforce decisions in response to a direct popular mandate. The Congress is frequently urged to pass laws that amount to little more than the authorization of administrative discretion in new areas. Many other laws passed by the Congress contain saving clauses stating that they can be set aside by the President in response to some "emergency." The President in fact is considered derelict by the public if he does not himself initiate the bulk of legislation placed before Congress. The President may use Congress's laws with discretion and further has innumerable direct discretionary powers.

Most recent Presidents have seemed to take literally the Wilsonian aspiration to "represent all of the people all of the time." John Kennedy, however, while still a senator, defended the election of the President by the electoral college against the proposal that the college be abolished in order to ensure a more representative Presidency, on the grounds that the President represented the industrial North to a greater extent than other parts of the country, under the present arrangement, and that this was desirable because other parts of the country were better represented in other parts of the government. Since the Congress was a stronghold of Southern strength, the slight advantage the North had in the contest for the Presidency was important to preserve, in Kennedy's eyes. This argument implied a conception of representation that included the entire government, in which the Presidency was seen as a competing representative institution, representing a part of the whole, while the Congress represented another part.

While few Presidents have advanced such an explicit argument as Kennedy made, all Presidents feel representative of a primary constituency as well as of the people as a whole. One's primary constituency may be only characterized vaguely as "the forgotten man" or "the silent majority," or its existence may be denied altogether. The significant consideration, however, is that the direct, fractional representativeness of the President is not thought to make it impossible for him to be, when necessary, also the representative of all. The President may feel that the better half of the nation that supports him is also more representative of the nation's future, and that, in responding to it, he is thereby responding to the interests of all, properly and prospectively defined.

The representativeness of the Presidency is inherent and desirable. What and whom the President actually represents is important and affects the decisions he makes. It is consequently possible to argue about the impact of the President's constituency on his decisions. The President's ability, in individual cases, to decide whether or not to act as a representative of his constituency, and to alter the definition of the group he will consider himself representative of, suggests the other half of the story: The President is a representative not only of the people but also of the inherent power of the Presidency in his dealings with the people.

The complexity of the meaning of the Presidency, answerable and yet not answerable to the people, is similar to the complexity inherent in the medieval concept of dual sovereignty, according to which sovereignty resided both in the King and in the people. The King was both God's representative on earth and the representative of all the people. The "confusion" of legal texts on the issue of sovereignty, as perceived by later, more logical generations, was no more than the confusion of reality, a complex balance in which neither the King nor the people claimed exclusive rights. It was only the eventual breakdown of this confused but viable system that necessitated the location of sovereignty in either King or Commons, in the seventeenth century. The medieval King ruled by virtue of his divine position, but only in the way in which a divinely sanctioned monarch was supposed to rule. Beyond the bounds of conventionally sanctioned behavior, the King might seem to be acting nakedly, without the divinity that hedged him—but also hedged him in. The people could not rule without the King, but a bad King could be replaced, though, of course, only to be followed by another King.[2]

The people might have a role in protesting the conduct of

the King, or the state of the kingdom, but once the act of confirming a new King had been completed, the people were expected to settle down and watch the new King address himself
to the country's problems. The people could hope that the new
King would remedy their problems and be different from his
predecessor, but all they could do was wait and see. And the
active process of selecting a new King determined nothing about
the set of personal advisers he might choose—quite possibly the
same ones who had surrounded his hated predecessor. The new
King might have witnessed the old King's fate but have concluded that the hatred directed against him was now expended
and that it would be safe for him to act in precisely the same way
—certainly safe for a period.

The practice in America is not too different. The President
is chosen by the people, more or less, and can be removed by
the normal process of election, by the extraordinary process of
impeachment and conviction for high crimes and misdemeanors,
or by the illegal action of assassination. Once chosen, however,
he is the President. There is only one President at a time. Certain
things can be done only by Presidents. Thus, as in the Middle
Ages, the exercise of popular sovereignty is circumscribed.

The American people are involved in the exhausting process
of substituting one President for another. But the range of substitutes available is limited, and the degree of popular control
that can be exercised on the President in the day-to-day performance of his duties is also limited. The new President may choose
as his deputies the same people, or the same kind of people, used
by his predecessor. The Constitution provides that the Senate,
representing the people, should have a role in the screening of
Presidential advisers, but even the formality of Senate confirmation is now frequently evaded by the utilization of special Presidential assistants not subject to Senate approval for duties once
performed by Cabinet officers.

Some feel that the President, though freed from most congressional and popular restraints, is nonetheless still effectively
controlled by the groups who helped put him in office. This is
true only with qualification. Presidential candidates are selected
by powerful coalitions in American society who hope to sustain
their power by association with a person who may become the

legitimate President of all Americans. Every four years competing coalitions offer alternative candidates, and the acquisition
of the largest number of votes is accepted as proof of constitutional legitimacy. The President is then able, if he acts with
circumspection, to dispense with the services of the coalition
behind him. Once in office the office is his, and he belongs to
the office, not to his backers. Only the sustained opposition of
the nation as a whole—not the withdrawal of the support of his
backers—can bring him down. He is now motivated by his own
sense of who he is—a person placed in a historic office who will
be judged in retrospect in terms of his ability to radiate the full
majesty of that office. The President tries to act as the legitimate
spokesman of an entire people. As a spokesman, he speaks not
only to the people but also to history. By history, he means the
court of future public opinion that will assign him his rank.
Speaking to the court of history, the President is speaking to his
own moral conscience, to his own conviction that certain values
will be shared by future generations. In speaking for the people,
the President also hopes to retain his legitimacy in the eyes of
the present generation of voters, from whom he must secure
re-election.

Being above politics is the best, the only politics for a legitimate
President. If being above politics means that the President must
dissociate himself from some of those who put him in office, he
will do so.

Once installed, a President is hedged by the divinity of his
office. Although selected by a coalition and elected by the people,
once sworn in he is also the representative of the Constitution,
from which stems the Presidential line. The President must
safeguard the source of his legitimacy by identifying himself
with his precursors in this office, an office which only its holders,
so they say, can understand. By convention there are areas in
which the President's sole responsibility is respected; in recent
decades, foreign policy has been championed as one such. By
convention there are other areas—primarily domestic—in which
the President is conceived as relatively helpless. In these areas,
continual defeats for the President will not damage his dignity,
because here the dual sovereignty of the people is recognized.

The people, through Congress, have a right to settle directly for themselves certain matters affecting their fate, just as the President has a right to the unfettered exercise of his power in certain other matters, not so directly affecting people in his country. When the President ventures beyond the hedge of his office, he is naked. Defeats within the hedge will not damage his image; victories beyond it may be ruinous.

The Presidency's insulation from popular pressure in specified areas has not discouraged Presidents from trying to expand their room for maneuver by pushing the hedge of their divinity outward. Presidents, like others, create wishing worlds. Presidents may find themselves, for example, tantalized by the thought that the deference they inspire in a self-selected circle of sycophants abroad might be replicated at home.

A supposedly representative leader is naturally interested in appearing to be responding to "demands" in taking a given action, even if this means orchestrating the demands to order. If a demand comes from a source beyond the immediate familiarity of those the President is addressing, they will not know how to refute the assertion that a demand has been received from this other source. A President may make a claim to be responding to invisible parts of the electorate or to the higher imperatives of the office he holds, just as he may pretend to be responding to foreign obligations—and to have no choice but to do so. A President elected in the purest democratic manner with no evident way of pretending to be the representative of any group other than the electorate will be tempted to build up foreign alliances to create obligations to which he may respond if he wishes to act in opposition to a popular mandate. Such obligations, the electorate will be told, are obligations of the Presidential office, and hence of the nation as a whole; failure to fulfill them would disgrace the nation. In reality, they may have been created by Presidential pump-priming and may be used to disguise arbitrary actions the President wishes to take for his own purposes.

Presidents who grasp the potential of their office have seldom had difficulty being re-elected, even if opposed on specific issues by a majority of the people. The President can easily hold out against transitory opposition. A President may not even claim to represent more than a plurality; even if he claims to represent the people as a whole, he will not think of himself simply as their representative, with no choice but to bend to every public pressure. The President thinks of his representativeness as an attribute compatible with, but subordinate to, his other attributes, as leader and rational decision-maker. The President, as a representative institution, wants to be representative enough to be re-elected; but as an executive institution, he wishes to do grand things worthy of his office.

Montesquieu contended that the governing principle of a constitutional monarchy is honor, whereas that of a republic is virtue. The leader of a republic, Montesquieu suggested, is satisfied with the existence in it of many individually virtuous men. A monarchy, whether elective or hereditary, is concerned with grandeur, with putting all its subjects to tasks of appropriate magnitude, with justifying the awe in which it is held abroad by acting in accordance with the dignity of its power.[3] In advocating a step-up in military activity in Vietnam, Presidential adviser McGeorge Bundy, for example, argued that America's power imposed an obligation. In a memorandum to President Johnson written on February 7, 1965, Bundy noted "that in all sectors of Vietnamese opinion there is a strong belief that the United States could do much more if it would, and that they are suspicious of our failure to use more of our obviously enormous power." [4]

The concentration of power in the President's hands, which has permitted him to indulge in international exploits in a manner befitting a powerful monarch, was first urged, ironically, by liberals attempting to replace conflict for conflict's sake with regulation for regulation's sake. Governing institutions, standing above others, it was felt, would not need to engage in petty competition with those below them and would be able to govern in the interest of all. The Presidency was to be the one place where all competing interests would be viewed from a superior "vantage point," to use Lyndon Johnson's phrase. Since no one had his perspective, no one could be entirely sure that the President's judgment was flawed; everyone consequently ought to be expected to give the President the benefit of the doubt. But the

President's liberal eulogists did not succeed in placing above the chaos of competition a single individual who was liberated from the amibitions that drove men placed lower. Rather, they succeeded in elevating a single man driven by the same passions as others into a position in which the only way he could gratify his passions was in a vastly more dangerous arena. The man who was supposed to act in the public interest, because it was at his personal disposal, became a man who could subordinate the public interest to his personal drive for glory. It was, in fact, tempting to the man exalted above others to endeavor to fulfill his particular drive for recognition by utilizing all his citizens in a competition with powerful enemies. James MacGregor Burns has noted that "for a man with Theodore Roosevelt's need for personal fulfillment it was a sort of tragedy that he had no war—not even a Whiskey Rebellion." [5] President Kennedy referred to the week of the Cuban missile crisis as a week in which he "really earned his pay." This was pre-eminently the week in which Kennedy felt that his conception of his proper activity as President of all Americans was fulfilled; the power of all Americans was pitted against a worthy antagonist in a way that permitted him to test his leadership ability. Kennedy saw the Presidency as a position of great power; he defined his personal challenge as the holder of that office as the grasping of opportunities to exemplify "grace under pressure." In planning the strategy of the Vietnam conflict, Lyndon Johnson felt that a large group "with 100 people sitting around was not the place . . . to build a military effectiveness. . . . I want to put it off as long as I can, having to make these crucial decisions. I enjoy this agony." [6]

Ruling, as President, as a neutral arbiter of lower conflicts among his subject has not afforded equal gratification. Only Eisenhower, of recent Presidents, has come close to the conception of a neutral Presidency, and this was clearly a reflection of his life-stage, as a man of proven skill in grand combat now in semi-retirement.

Montesquieu was right: If you make a man a King he will begin to think in terms of glory. How could proponents of the enhancement of Presidential power not have anticipated that a great leader armed with great discretion would seek glory rather than goodness? They failed to anticipate this result because they had also written into the drama a role for themselves. The President, subordinating representativeness to the imperatives of executive leadership of a great power, in turn was to subordinate executive leadership to the directives of a "rational" decision-making process. A judicious President, exercising discretion wisely, would be guided at every juncture by the expert advisers at his side.

The original purpose of the Constitution was to give necessary power to officials hamstrung by legal strictures. As Herman Melville put it, "If there are any three things opposed to the genius of the American Constitution, they are these: irresponsibility in a judge, unlimited discretionary authority in an executive, and the union of an irresponsible judge and an unlimited executive in one person." [7] The rule of laws, not men, meant that, though men would rule, they could not rule as idiosyncratically as they would wish. Implicit in the contemporary vision of Presidential government, in contrast, is a vast role for discretion. Centralized action is obviously more efficient; if it can be claimed that it is also more just, then the old fears of the Founding Fathers can be dismissed as out of date.

A judicious President, it is argued, can act with speed, flexibility, and on the basis of expert advice. Is not the President the best-informed person, the best-situated person to make a decision? Actually, the availability of expert advice has served to isolate the President. Whether advised by an elite of independently accomplished men, or by specialists on his own payroll, the President is trapped by those trying to help him. The President may be the worst-informed person in the country if he is systematically shielded from the normal experience and outlook of citizens. Akbar the Great of India and Henry V of England used to disguise themselves as ordinary men and wander freely amongst their subjects to learn what was really going on. Surrounded by sycophants and specialists, these monarchs went to their lowly subjects in search of unbiased views on the needs of the kingdom. A President who honors his advisers with the highest possible praise—his trust that their presentation of this country's need makes him well informed—is the most pathetic of captives, a bear on a string.

The myth of the judicious President is not only factually inaccurate, it is deeply destructive of the character of the occupant of the office. The President, we are told, is a different sort of person from the generality of Americans. As he has a special nature, so he has special duties. He alone, for example, can determine when his political opponents are endangering "national security" and giving "comfort to America's enemies." His special duties necessitate his possession of special privileges—picturephones, jet airplanes, summer and winter palaces, and a prescriptive right to impound the consciences of the highest and lowest members of his realm. The Watergate affair demonstrated graphically that a surprising number of Americans of high patriotism felt unable to refuse a request from "the White House" that they break the law of the land.

A structure wrought to ensure rational decision-making has instead hopelessly entangled private whims with national needs. A President, freed to do as he wishes, is expected to be right; in fact, he is permitted no defense against his own fallibility. He is routinely tempted by the logic of false determinism; having made a decision, he is likely to say, and come to believe, that he had "no choice" but to make the decision he did. George Reedy has argued that, with the possible exception of Franklin Roosevelt, recent Presidents have been ordinarily unable to profit from their mistakes. In Reedy's view, a person who enters the Presidency with normal, or even above-normal, intelligence and political sensitivity will soon start making political blunders which would make a ward-heeler blush.[8] Together, the forces around and within the President are likely to destroy even the elementary political sensitivity of men who show enormous subtlety in their march to the throne.

No person can rule without help; no sane person can come to believe he is infallible without frequent testimony to that effect from others. The President is unlikely to experience a rude awakening at the hands of his staff. In fact, the greater effort he makes to surround himself with apparently distinguished, independent, accomplished professionals with standing in their own fields, the greater may be the resulting delusion that their praise is accurate. Independent American intellectuals have offered their services to the President to ensure the rationality of his decisions;

ironically, their willingness to serve negates the goal they seek. Their availability feeds the vanity of the President and offers no obstacle to his ability to toy with them for his own purposes, while they remain subject to the delusion that the President values them for their wisdom. A King and his courtiers feed one another's vanity. Pride in servility for the adviser, pleasure in adulation for the King: both are satisfied by a mutually corrupting relationship.

Many observers have been puzzled by the reluctance of the President's "independent" advisers to resign when the President disregards their advice. Yet, if they sense their impotence within the inner circle, they also realize that they would be even more powerless outside of it, capable only of making appeals to "public opinion." A class of notables may put pressure on the person they advise if, as a class, they possess independent bases of power and regulate admission to their class—and if the class is not very large. If a group of would-be advisers lacks cohesion, the task of selecting favorites who will identify with the King rather than the class from which they are drawn will be child's play. A regulating class, such as the Barons at Runnymede or, on rare occasions, the British Prime Minister's Cabinet colleagues, even in the best of circumstances, purchases its power of regulation at a high price. It can only perform a restraining function, pinning the King down. It cannot actively advise the King on the positive manner in which he should conduct his affairs in those areas which remain his prerogative. Its preference for defiance is a self-denying ordinance, tying its hands from accepting a position as a trusted ally of the King. An adviser can only influence an autocrat in a positive manner by presenting himself as a person who presumably advises the autocrat to do what is in his own interest —who claims to be putting the interest of his master above the retention of his class affiliation. He may use his class identity to present himself to the autocrat as an analyst of his class, an interpreter of the way in which it can be best exploited by the autocrat, but he cannot act as a spokesman for his class. In a sense, the most salient question is the simplest: Who rewards his services? [9]

A President needs different sorts of advisers from different backgrounds. A President's advisers are drawn from many sources —business, the professions, politics, the bureaucracy. In their new role, however, they become the President's agents in his dealings with these estates, and they most probably will remain in this role, even if they formally return to the estates from which they came. A high government official who returns to his bank or airplane factory or university may well remain informally a member of the President's staff, even though he is now only engaged in a rear-guard action of defending his past actions.

The King's men are not likely to provide him with the corrective advice that might shake his confidence. Even the designation of a devil's advocate within the inner circle may only reinforce the impression that all possible objections have been anticipated and can be coped with. Beyond the circle of Presidential appointees, however, there remain the great bureaucratic establishments, which have, on occasion, been portrayed as an immovable "fourth branch of government," fiercely resistant to Presidential prodding. In fact, this tenured establishment can only rarely provide a corrective to the President. Bureaucrats have even less independence than private advisers. The bureaucrat is an employee who must look up to the President and his agents as the embodiment of the public interest he has sworn to serve. In this sense, even a merit bureaucracy becomes, to a degree, a personal household staff. The bureaucrats' job is not to analyze reality, but to make their presentation of reality one that will appeal to their superiors. The simple fact that a bureaucrat is right is no guarantee of his credibility in the eyes of his superiors. The bureaucracy is not a class capable of limiting the President's freedom of action; it is a group of servants dependent on his attention.

A sizable bureaucracy is naturally difficult to control, but by making careful appointments and promotions, the President can usually drive opposition underground, whatever the organizational structure of the bureaucracy may be. In dealing with obstructive agency heads, he can threaten the creation of competing policy-making units within the White House. The State Department in recent years, for example, far from "influencing" the President, has had to acquiesce in the concentration of for-

eign-policy–making in the White House. This lesson has not
been lost on other bureaucratic establishments. It has seemed
far safer to be accommodating than to oppose and then be circumvented. Even those apparently indispensable and autonomous
specialized agencies, the CIA and the FBI, have found it difficult
to withstand pressure to perform unwelcome tasks set by the
White House when threatened with the possible establishment
of competing units within the White House. J. Edgar Hoover—
a uniquely powerful bureaucratic fixture—did prevent the creation of a White House "crime" unit desired by President Nixon,
but lesser men have ordinarily been unwilling to risk their agencies' prospects by defying clear White House preferences. Far
from encouraging open deliberation of policy alternatives, the
President's elevation has only intensified Presidential arrogance
and bureaucratic servility.[10]

What, finally, can be said of the effect of the myth of the
judicious President on the morale of the public at large? The
President's superhuman prerogatives ultimately rest on the assumption that it is in the interest of all of us to have a person
who is pure and high-minded, and who consequently must be
presented publicly as such even if there are good grounds for
believing differently. The feeling persists that something dread-
ful would happen to all of us, and to the entire structure of government from which we benefit so substantially, if anybody acted
publicly on the basis of his private knowledge of the personal
character of the President. If all avert their eyes, the President
will not be in danger of damaging his image by walking around
naked. The myth of the Presidency is the creation of people who
know better but who are appalled by the prospect of having to
consider the alternatives. We cling to the hope that a person,
even though an ordinary man to all appearances, when supplied
with a magical apparatus, can bring about a complete change
in the entire polity. The irony is, we know that the President's
magic is manufactured and maintained by our own efforts and
that a man riding on a wish is not really a magician; he is a
confidence artist. We supply him with the confidence that makes
him look like an artist. You can't fool all the people all the time;
but can all the people fool themselves all the time?

The myth of the magical President is of relatively recent origin. The contemporary phenomenon of Presidential autocracy was created by the strengthening of one of the three constituted branches of government, a strengthening resulting not from necessity but from choice, the considered preference of idealists for a kind of decision-making that somehow seemed more just because it was made on high by one man. Today many people recognize that the system has not worked as hoped but are uncertain why that is, and how it might be remedied. The most natural response is to assume that there is nothing wrong with the basic approach but only with its implementation. The easiest argument is that all that is lacking for the system to function as planned is the right individual. If all our troubles can be said to stem from the tragic unsuitability of the individuals catapulted into office by a series of historical accidents, why is it not reasonable to hope that all will be set aright through one more swing of the pendulum?

As in the Middle Ages, so in America today, much political discourse ranges between two poles, from romantic optimism to grim pessimism, from hope for the succession to the throne of a truly good King, to tyrannicide. This discourse, as in the Middle Ages, is limited by the assumption that the extent of political change possible is to replace one monarch by another—by natural or surgical means. Such a preoccupation with the possibility that the replacement of one man with another will produce a total transformation in the policy and posture of government is as intense as it would be in any divine-right monarchy; the basis for such a preoccupation is so fragile as to be pathological. Like any entrenched pathology, it is an effort to adjust to the presence in the organism of a searing disease and may consequently be stabilizing in the short run. Since the effort to adjust cannot halt the progress of the disease, however, the effort at adjustment only makes things worse in the long run. Intense hope in the magical transformation that a change of regime will produce turns to appalling disillusionment when that change occurs and nothing happens. The engine of hope is once again revved up. Attention focuses once again on the next succession and the high-minded, pure people whose elevation will make all the difference.

And yet, as the cycles of hope and disillusionment expand their duration and intensity, they begin to overlap, and people become increasingly aware of the similarity between the new vain hope and the last blasted hope.

The answer lies not in pursuing the present course to the end but in changing course. Instead of attempting to remove the human need to demonstrate adequacy by wielding power, one should attempt to neutralize the danger of wielding power by restricting the scope of possible conflicts. Placing men above ambition simply releases them from normal restraints and forces them to invent new and more reckless forms of moral testing. To attempt to institutionalize virtue is to guarantee disaster.

The President should be respected for what he is—a man representative of the forces that put him in office—not what it is hoped he may become once in office, through the magic of disinterestedness or the brilliance of his advisers. If the President ceases to pretend that he does not represent some more than others, he will be a more candid, more effective person. He will be less deferential to his predecessors in office, who represented other coalitions, and by his candid partisanship, he will make it easier for ordinary citizens to recognize him for the significant, partial person that he is. A series of Presidents with alternating constituencies would make it possible for each President to pursue an active policy of representing primarily the interests of some, with the implicit understanding that others would have their turn. This could be said to be the situation currently in existence in Great Britain. In Britain, the representative and executive functions are formally consolidated in one man, the Prime Minister. The Prime Minister, in fact, does represent little more than one-half of the electorate, and the country is governed by two halves, each taking turns at the exercise of substantial, directly representative executive power.

A second alternative would be to establish a purer division of legislative and executive power, in which the Congress decided policies and the President merely implemented them. Firm lines of division between functions embodied in separate institutions do not offer much promise on the basis of past performance. The classic example of a clear-cut division between executive and legislative bodies is in the meeting of the French Estates-General, which led to the outbreak of the French Revolution. The monarchy and the Estates-General were so completely out of touch that inevitably each was driven to try to govern without resort to the other. First the monarchy tried to get along without the Estates; then the Estates tried to get along without the monarchy. The American system has never been characterized by the separation of legislative and executive powers ascribed to it, and there seems little reason to hope for improvement by making that separation a practical reality. The balance of *power* between legislative and executive branches should be redressed more favorably to the Congress, but a viable system would retain fused functions in each of the branches of government. The Congress thus should increase its legislative and executive roles, while those of the Presidency should be diminished.

One should be cautious, in strengthening the Congress, that one is, in fact, strengthening it in the name of an alternative vision of governmental functioning. There is an ominous tendency, for example, to speak of the strengthening of Congress by providing congressmen with longer terms and more staff and amenities. It is possible that the Congress might, in consequence, be strengthened in relation to the President, and that both these branches would then be even more isolated from the citizenry. The Congress should not be strengthened to make it more like the present Presidency; the current appeal of Congress is in the fact that it shares many of the hardships experienced by ordinary citizens. Television viewers of the Senate's Watergate hearings saw a disorderly, contradictory human spectacle—in contrast to the cut-and-dried imperial pronouncements from the closed Presidential suite to which the American public had become so accustomed. The Senate's hearings were accessibly, persuasively inefficient.

The main direction of congressional reform should be to bring Congress even closer to the ordinary citizen, by eliminating the rigidities in the internal structure of the Congress that make it most representative of the public opinion of twenty or thirty years ago. A strict seniority system for selecting committee chairmen is ludicrous in a body such as the House of Representatives that the Constitution directed should be freshly elected once every two years.

One may safely assume that the main structural outlines of the American political system will remain: that an individual will continue to be selected by powerful coalitions and accepted by the general public as a legitimate ruler because of their minimal role in his final ratification. One may safely assume that the uniqueness of the office will continue to hold a fascination for its occupant, and that he will never be simply a creature of those who put him in a position where he can dispense with their services. There is no great reason to hope for significant change from the assembling of a new coalition of interests for the purpose of putting a new man into this unique office. The only hope of significant change in the nature of Presidential conduct lies in the alteration of the expectations a President is supposed to live up to, an alteration in the constraints on his actions in office rather than in the obligations he may assemble on his way to the office. Such constraints would have to be reflected in popular expectations of what a good President would be like. Such expectations would have to be clear and deep enough to impress every President with the belief that they will still be around when history puts him in his place.

What constitutes greatness in a President? Is a great President one who permits the gigantic bureaucracy he heads to occupy itself in vindicating his special privileges and powers? Is a great President one who patterns his personal life and public conduct after Louis XIV? Is a great President one who, like monarchs of the past, engages in warfare to preserve personal vanity, to avoid, for instance, being the first President to lose a war? (Countries can usually survive the loss of a war; Presidents cannot.) Can one not conceive of a country that insisted that its President did not have a special nature, did not have a special wisdom stemming from his vantage point and number of advisers? Such a country's President would not be permitted to pretend to infallibility; if he spoke with pious smugness or implied that his policy was inevitable, he would be laughed at.

Citizens are too sensible to want to concern themselves all the time with everybody else's business, but the President in

Washington should be made aware that citizens want public men directing the polity politically, with the force of argument, not administratively, with the assistance of advertising. Citizens should demand responsible leaders and not settle for covert controllers.

NOTES

[1] Woodrow Wilson, *Constitutional Government in the United States,* quoted in James MacGregor Burns, *Presidential Government* (Boston: Houghton Mifflin, 1965), p. 96.

[2] See Donald Hanson, *From Kingdom to Commonwealth* (Cambridge, Mass.: Harvard University Press, 1970).

[3] Baron de Montesquieu, *The Spirit of the Laws,* trans. Thomas Nugent (New York: Hafner, 1962).

[4] *The Pentagon Papers* (New York: Bantam Books, 1971).

[5] Burns, *op. cit.,* p. 66.

[6] *The Pentagon Papers,* p. 496.

[7] Herman Melville, *White-Jacket* (New York: Russell and Russell, 1963), p. 178.

[8] George Reedy, *The Twilight of the Presidency* (New York: New American Library, 1970). This book provides an excellent insider's account of the "court" atmosphere of the contemporary White House.

[9] For a heroic but ultimately unpersuasive effort to formulate a procedure which will encourage "rational" Presidential decision-making by a rearrangement of the President's advisory establishment, see Alexander George, "The Case for Multiple Advocacy in Making Foreign Policy," *American Political Science Review,* September, 1972.

[10] Concerning Hoover's opposition to Nixon, see Nixon's statement, *New York Times,* May 23, 1973. The Watergate hearings turned up elaborate evidence of White House pressure on the CIA and the post-Hoover FBI and of the reluctance of their senior officials to oppose or report to the public illegal requests made by White House aides.

4

War Powers: A Need for Legislative Reassertion

Louis Fisher

More by tradition and pre-emption than from a reading of the Constitution, foreign policy has tended to become a Presidential preserve. For the past several years, this historic shift of power has been challenged by an unusual alliance, including conservatives and liberals, Republicans and Democrats. Indeed, it is the "high-flying prerogative men," to use Edward S. Corwin's term, who have recently become the most vociferous critics of Presidential war powers.

Arthur Schlesinger, Jr., for instance, in an address before the American Enterprise Institute in 1966, counseled that "something must be done to assure the Congress a more authoritative and continuing voice in fundamental decisions in foreign policy." In February, 1967, Henry Steele Commager appeared before the Senate Foreign Relations Committee to urge that there be a "reconsideration of the relationship of the executive and the legislative branches," particularly the President and the Senate in the conduct of foreign relations. In March, 1969, at the Congressional Conference on the Military Budget and National Priorities, scholars and scientists from both parties called upon Congress to reassert its control over defense spending and the scope of international commitments. Senator J. W. Fulbright, who had written, in the fall, 1961, issue of the *Cornell Law Quarterly*, that "for the existing requirements of American foreign policy we have hobbled the President by too niggardly a grant of power," soon found himself in the forefront of those who are trying to place limits on the President.[1]

The time is certainly long overdue for reassessing Congress's role in the war power and in foreign policy generally. Holbert Carroll, in his study on Congress and foreign affairs, estimated that the proportion of bills concerning international matters, in 1925, was not more than one in twenty-five. The situation since World War II has been radically different, with more than half the standing committees now playing some role in international affairs. Not only the Senate but also the House must assume new responsibilities. Dean Acheson once remarked that the "time has passed when the Senate monopolized the congressional function in this field, since it is the execution of policy, calling for legal authority, funds, and men, which is the ultimate test of success or failure." [2]

If the President chooses to ignore Congress while acting in external affairs, his domestic and foreign programs become targets for reprisal. The feeling among legislators that President Johnson overreached himself in Southeast Asia, and failed to treat Congress as a coequal branch, produced a voting record marked by negativism and defiance. The Senate's rejection of Clement F. Haynsworth, Jr., and G. Harrold Carswell also reflected a reassertion of legislative prerogatives. And yet, the confirmation power is used with reluctance, taken off the shelf on occasion to prevent rusting, but not wielded with full firmness as a legitimate constitutional weapon.

The claims by recent Presidents to a virtual free hand in conducting foreign affairs owe much in constitutional law to a landmark Supreme Court decision of 1936, *United States* v. *Curtiss-Wright*. Justice Sutherland, speaking for the Court, said that legislation in the international field must often accord the President a "degree of discretion and freedom from statutory restriction which would not be admissible were domestic affairs alone involved." All that was necessary, in this particular case, was for the Court to uphold the right of Congress to delegate embargo powers to the President. Instead, Justice Sutherland added several pages of *obiter dicta* on the far-reaching dimensions of executive power in international affairs, referring to "this vast external realm, with its important, complicated, delicate and manifold problems," and stating that the President, not Congress, has the "better opportunity of knowing the conditions which prevail in foreign countries, and especially is this true in time of war." [3]

These sweeping assertions have since been used to justify an expansion of Presidential war powers, based not on new powers delegated by Congress but rather on inherent executive powers. In fact, however, Sutherland's remarks should be taken as *dicta* and nothing more. Their source is not in the Constitution but in Sutherland's own political philosophy. He had earlier served on the Foreign Relations Committee and was a forceful exponent of the use of American power abroad. His biographer, Joel Francis Paschal, has written that Sutherland had "long been the advocate of vigorous diplomacy which strongly, even belligerently, called always for an assertion of American rights." Many of the arguments in Sutherland's book, *Constitutional Power and World Affairs* (1919), were to appear two decades later in the Curtiss-Wright decision. [4]

Sutherland's ironclad distinction between foreign and domestic problems seems increasingly artificial to most observers today. Actions taken on behalf of "national security" can easily overwhelm basic domestic freedoms. It was Justice Jackson, in the 1950 *Knauff* v. *Shaughnessy* decision, who said that "Security is like liberty in that many are the crimes committed in its name." More recently, in the 1971 *New York Times* decision, Justice Black joined with five members of the Court to strike down the government's effort to prevent publication of the Pentagon Papers. "The word 'security,' " he wrote, "is a broad, vague generality whose contours should not be invoked to abrogate the fundamental law embodied in the First Amendment. The guarding of military and diplomatic secrets at the expense of informed representative government provides no real security for our Republic." [5]

In addition to retaining this artificial distinction between foreign and domestic affairs, we attribute to the executive branch a number of imaginary qualities. The properties of the executive anticipated by the Founding Fathers—unity, expertise, secrecy, and speed—are not always to be found in our sprawling bureaucracy today. Instead of "unity," we find the apparatus for foreign-policy–making splintered within the State Department as well as between it and other executive agencies competing for control. The interservice rivalries of the postwar period were supposedly remedied by "unification" of the military services and by the coordinating apparatus of the National Security Council, yet scholars pointed to the type of logrolling and vote-trading that persisted within the executive branch. Arthur Maass, in studying how the Budget Bureau conferences resolved policy and legislative disputes, concluded that the conferences "avoid the basic issues and compromise, through a game of give. and take." Samuel P. Huntington observed that "Just as Congress often wrote tariff legislation by giving each industry the protection it wanted, the N.S.C. and the Joint Chiefs make decisions on weapons by giving each service what it desires." [6]

Henry Kissinger, in *No More Vietnams?*, spoke of a "sort of blindness in which bureaucracies run a competition with their own programs and measure success by the degree to which they fulfill their own norms, without being in a position to judge whether the norms made any sense to begin with." A vivid example of what Kissinger had in mind came to light in June, 1969, when former Budget Director Charles Schultze appeared before the Joint Economic Committee. He described the effort of the Budget Bureau to select an optimum continental air-defense system. Various alternatives were studied before selecting the system that was "more effective at slightly lower cost than most." An impressive exercise in program budgeting, and yet what the Budget Bureau had failed to ask, Schultze said, was whether we needed an air-defense system of that magnitude at all. Other basic questions, such as the need to spend $5 billion a year on the Chinese contingency, also received far too little attention.[7] Although it has been customary to regard the Budget Bureau as the unifying, coordinating element in the executive branch, it is evident that military spending has received less scrutiny than domestic spending.[8]

The foreign-policy bureaucracies, in the view of many congressmen and federal officials, have often become juggernauts, each operating on its own momentum, sustained by its own special-interest constituency, and propelled toward narrow objectives. Decisions on defense spending offer the most graphic illustration of this. In hearings before the House Government Operations Committee, in April, 1969, an air force colonel admitted that evidence of cost-overrun problems on the C-5A cargo plane had been withheld from Congress. For what reason? Because disclosure might have jeopardized the contractor's position in the financial market.[9] In another example of public operations acquiring a quasi-private character, five air force officers who had worked on the Minuteman missile contract for the government later retired and went to work for the contracting company.[10]

Thus, instead of an adversary relationship between the Pentagon and private contractors, with the buyer seeking the lowest cost and the seller the highest profit, officers and contracting personnel have been operating under the "team concept"—apparently a euphemism for collusion. Gordon W. Rule, a top-ranking procurement official for the Navy, put the matter bluntly to the Joint Economic Committee in June, 1969: "We play games. We know that if we tell the DOD [Department of Defense] across the river how much something is really going to cost, they may scrub it. And they know that if they tell the Congress how much it is really going to cost the Congress may scrub it. So you start in with both sides knowing that it is going to cost more. And that is not an overrun, because we know." [11] Because of his penchant for telling the truth to Congress, Rule was threatened with dismissal in 1973.

How easy it is now to understand Hubert Humphrey's prescient and ironic warning in the July, 1969, issue of *Foreign Affairs*. Congress, he wrote, could not submit to the executive will even if it wanted to, because "there is not one executive will, but a number of conflicting wills which have not yet surrendered to the authority of an overriding national purpose." If modern Presidents have often been unable to master their own bureaucracies, there is ample reason for concern and re-assertion by Congress of its own lapsed constitutional powers.

A close look at the administrative record in defense procure-ment and military operations justifies the skepticism of the Sen-ate Foreign Relations Committee when it speaks of the "cult of executive expertise." [12] Although the executive branch has access to vast quantities of information, there are too many instances in which it resorts to "selective declassification" or outright doctoring of information in an effort to sustain its position. A series of deceptive announcements and maneuvers helped dis-credit the Johnson Administration: conflicting and contradictory explanations of the Tonkin incident and the Dominican inter-vention; a host of unreliable estimates on Vietnam spending, civilian casualties, and the number of refugees; a dreary succes-sion of various "turning points" and "lights at the end of the tunnel." Executive expertise did not prevent blunders in the production of Cheyenne helicopters and Main Battle Tanks, nor did it eliminate gross mismanagement in the Minuteman and C-5A programs. Executive officials may be "expert" and at the same time deceptive. Moreover, it is the strong and often justified suspicion of many congressmen that the deceptions are used to conceal incompetence. Testimony by executive officials before congressional committees betrays a lack of that professional ob-jectivity that is the hallmark of true expertise.

In the October, 1969, issue of *Foreign Affairs,* Representative Jonathan Bingham offered a revealing story of how the Pentagon juggled figures in trying to exaggerate the extent of the Soviet threat. In a presentation comparing Soviet and U.S. strengths in submarines, the navy deducted a certain percentage from the U.S. figure to allow for vessels confined to home port at any given time. When a civilian systems analyst asked what percentage had been deducted from the Soviet figure for the same reason, the "answer was that no deduction had been made; the incredible excuse was that 'we don't know what their lay-up percentage is.'" [13] Senator Proxmire disclosed how the air force shifted figures in an effort to conceal the magnitude of the cost overruns on the C-5A.[14] Sophisticated cost-benefit studies can be manipulated simply by underestimating the cost of a weapons system and overstating its benefits.

This brings up another vaunted property of the executive branch: "economy and efficiency." During the past few years, Congress has unearthed some bizarre practices in military procurement: Department of Defense personnel harassed by their superiors for telling Congress about fuel pilferage in Thailand and cost overruns on the C-5A (as payment for his candor and expertise, the Pentagon abolished A. E. Fitzgerald's job); billions of dollars of government plant and equipment used by private industry for commercial purposes instead of for work on defense contracts; a perennial fleecing of the government in its procurement of small parts; and estimates of "fat" in the military budget from $10 billion and up. The theory of executive "expertise" suffered an ignominious setback in 1969, when the Gore subcommittee conducted its own analysis of the Safeguard ABM system. Under the pressure of informed and vigorous questioning, the Administration was forced to correct claims of Russian first-strike capability, continually revise its cost estimates, admit to less warning time in the event of attack, and manufacture new rationales as earlier ones were exploded.[15]

American Presidents have historically invoked three main doctrines to justify waging war on their own initiative: the doctrines of self-defense, protection of American lives and property, and hot pursuit. The first of these rationales, that of "defensive war," knows few boundaries today, however well defined a concept it may have seemed in 1787. An attack on the United States includes our bombers in constant flight, ships in the Mediterranean and Pacific (as well as Tonkin Gulf and Wonsan Bay), and other elements of our far-flung defensive system.

In a note to the Philippine Foreign Secretary in 1954, Secretary of State Dulles said that our air and naval installations in that country were such that an "armed attack on the Philippines could not but be also an attack upon the military forces of the United States. As between our nations, it is no legal fiction to say that an attack on one is an attack on both." In a 1964 communiqué, President Johnson maintained that "any armed attack against the Philippines would be regarded as an attack against United States forces stationed there and against the United States and would instantly be repelled." [16] The Dulles and Johnson language, giving a unilateral executive guarantee, seems an extension of the earlier Senate-approved language of the North Atlantic Treaty, which provides that an armed attack against one or more of the parties in Europe or North America "shall be considered an attack against them all." The Rio Treaty extends a similar kind of commitment to the nations of the Western Hemisphere. In both of these cases, a President's right to wage defensive war has been given great scope.

The decision of the Johnson Administration, in 1964, to transfer B-57 bombers from the Philippines to Bien Hoa, in South Vietnam, was followed by Vietcong mortar attacks on that air base. The result: substantial damage to U.S. troops and aircraft and a further upward twist in the escalation of the Vietnam war. Some of our bases agreements elsewhere, the Senate Foreign Relations Committee warns, form a "kind of quasi-commitment, unspecified as to their exact import but, like buds in springtime, ready, under the right climatic conditions, to burst into full bloom." [17]

The geographical sweep of "defensive war" was dramatized by several crises of the past decade. In 1962, President Kennedy announced the sending of additional U.S. forces to Thailand. He claimed that a threat to Thailand was of "grave concern to the United States" and emphasized that the sending of U.S. military forces was a "defensive act." After the discovery of missile sites in Cuba, he declared that the Western Hemisphere ("as far north as Hudson Bay, Canada, and as far south as Lima, Peru") was in danger. He gave notice that the launching of any nuclear missile from Cuba, against any nation in the Western Hemisphere, would be regarded "as an attack by the Soviet Union on the United States, requiring a full retaliatory response upon the Soviet Union." [18]

When President Johnson requested the Tonkin Resolution two years later, he maintained that a threat in Southeast Asia "is a threat to all, and a threat to us." A number of congressmen elaborated on that theme, calling Southeast Asia our first line of defense and arguing that enemy attacks on American forces in that region were essentially the same as enemy attacks on America itself.[19] Under such generous definitions, the President's power to wage defensive war is virtually open-ended.

Another open-ended prerogative—the right to use armed force to protect American lives and property—has been invoked by Presidents four major times in the past sixteen years. Protection of life provided a semblance of constitutionality for our military intervention in Lebanon in 1958. President Eisenhower announced that U.S. forces were being used to "protect American lives and by their presence there to encourage the Lebanese government in defense of Lebanese sovereignty and integrity." When President Johnson ordered troops into the Dominican Republic in 1965, he was able to claim later, despite the Administration's fears of a Communist take-over, that "99 percent of our reason for going in there was to try to provide protection for these American lives and for the lives of other nationals." [20] On April 30, 1970, President Nixon explained that he was sending troops into Cambodia because enemy actions "clearly endanger the lives of Americans who are in Vietnam now and would constitute an unacceptable risk to those who will be there after withdrawal of another 150,000." [21] On February 8, 1971, after the Nixon Administration had provided support for the South Vietnamese invasion of Laos, the State Department justified the action, in part, on the ground that it would "protect American lives." [22]

Even after a peace settlement was signed January 27, 1973, followed by the withdrawal of U.S. armed forces and the return of American prisoners of war, the Nixon Administration continued to bomb Cambodia. A statement prepared by the State Department argued that the bombing was justified as an "interim action" needed to preserve the right of self-determination of the South Vietnamese people.[23]

The doctrine of "hot pursuit" offers yet another opportunity for the President and his military commanders to initiate war or expand hostilities without congressional approval. In the Korean war, the original objective of the United States was defined by the Security Council resolution of June 25, 1950, which called for North Korean forces to cease hostilities and withdraw to the 38th parallel. Later, after the North Koreans had been pushed back and the *status quo* was restored, the Administration enlarged the objective to seek the establishment of a "free, independent and unified" Korea.[24] General MacArthur's push into North Korea was followed by Chinese intervention and the start of a much broader, longer-lasting conflict. In the Vietnam war, U.S. troops crossed the Laotian border from South Vietnam in hot pursuit of the enemy—or what the Pentagon called "protective reaction" missions.

Disillusioned with the Vietnam war, and reacting to the dubious constitutionality of executive military initiatives abroad, Congress has for several years been reasserting its responsibilities in foreign affairs. An important—if largely symbolic—bench mark was the National Commitments Resolution, adopted by the Senate in June, 1969, by a solid margin of seventy to sixteen. Though not legally binding on the President, the resolution was intended as a restraint on his power to dispatch troops abroad without congressional approval.

A war-powers resolution, passed by the House of Representatives in November, 1970, recognized that the President "in certain extraordinary and emergency circumstances has the authority to defend the United States and its citizens without prior authorization by the Congress." Rather than try to define when the President could, and could not, act, the resolution sought to introduce new procedures. First, the President should consult with Congress "whenever feasible" before involving U.S. forces in armed conflict. And second, in the event that the President committed U.S. forces without prior authorization of Congress, he was to report to Congress on the circumstances that necessitated his action, as well as the constitutional, legislative, and treaty provisions authorizing his action, together with his reasons for not seeking specific prior congressional authorization. The Senate, however, did not act on the measure.

Both Houses passed war-powers legislation during the 92d and 93d Congresses, going beyond reporting requirements to impose limitations on Presidential emergency powers. The House acted most recently on July 18, 1973; the Senate on July 20, 1973.

The House of Representatives, following its earlier efforts, did not try to define or codify Presidential war powers. It directed the President in "every possible instance" to consult with Congress before committing U.S. forces to hostilities or to situations where hostilities may be imminent. In the event that he is unable to do so, he is to submit a report to Congress within 72 hours, setting forth the circumstances and details of his action. Unless within 120 days Congress declares war or specifically authorizes the use of U.S. forces, the President shall terminate the commitment and remove the forces. Congress may also direct disengagement by passing a concurrent resolution at any time prior to the end of the 120-day period.

Under the House bill, a President could so firmly commit the nation's forces and prestige—during the 120-day grace period—that it might be politically and militarily impossible for Congress to reverse the process. What began as marginal or contrived could deteriorate into a genuine emergency, compelling congressional support. Furthermore, once engaged in hostilities, the President would be able to draw upon constitutional authority to protect U.S. forces. Could such authority be curbed in any way by a congressional directive to disengage or by a refusal to extend the President's power beyond 120 days?

In contrast to the House bill, the Senate attempted to spell out the conditions under which Presidents can take action prior to congressional authorization. Armed forces could be used in three situations: (1) to repel an armed attack upon the United States, its territories, and possessions; to take necessary and appropriate retaliatory actions in the event of such an attack; and to forestall the direct and imminent threat of such an attack; (2) to repel an armed attack against U.S. armed forces located outside the United States, its territories, and possessions, and to forestall the direct and imminent threat of such an attack; and (3) to rescue endangered U.S. citizens and nationals located in foreign countries or on the high seas.

Presidential action would have to cease unless Congress, within 30 days, specifically authorized the President to continue. A separate provision would allow the President to sustain military operations beyond the 30-day period, with or without congressional authorization, if he determined that "unavoidable military necessity respecting the safety" of the armed forces required their continued use for purposes of "bringing about a prompt disengagement."

The Senate proposal carries a number of risks. Is it possible to anticipate and codify all of the circumstances under which Presidents may act without advance congressional approval? If the grounds for executive initiative are made broad and ambiguous, Presidents would be able to justify military adventures under the cloak of "defensive war," life-and-property actions, and other vague categories. In an effort to restrict the war powers of the President, Congress may inadvertently widen them by sanctioning initiatives under ill-defined categories.

Moreover, as the 30-day deadline approaches, Congress is very likely to "rally around the flag" rather than independently debate the wisdom and merits of the President's action. Once again Presidential power would be broadened. And lastly, by passing a generic piece of legislation, Congress might wrongly conclude that it had discharged its responsibility for "reassertion," whereas what is needed is the daily grind of overseeing Administration policies, passing judgment on them, and behaving as a coequal branch.

If Senate and House resolutions turn into mere parchment barriers because of inescapable ambiguities in our language, what concrete actions are needed for legislative reassertion in foreign affairs? Congress must first of all take part in the early stages of foreign-policy–making, when options are still open and positions have yet to harden. At the time of the Tonkin crisis in 1964, Congress could do little else than follow along in the footsteps of the President. The time for influence was during the prior decade, when our involvement in Vietnam was beginning to take shape and when Congress was appropriating the funds to make that involvement possible.

It could, of course, have used its power of the purse to withhold funds at that time. But the long-prevailing faith in executive "expertise" in the field of national security, combined with the postwar tradition of "bipartisan" foreign policy, had accustomed the legislature to accept rather uncritically most Presidential definitions of military need. Moreover, a legislator could not cast a vote against the war without appearing to abandon American fighting men and prisoners of war. As the U.S. Court of Appeals for the District of Columbia observed, in a March 20, 1973, decision, a court cannot be "unmindful of what every schoolboy knows: that in voting to appropriate money or to draft men a Congressman is not necessarily approving of the continuation of a war no matter how specifically the appropriation or draft act refers to that war. . . . An honorable, decent, compassionate act of aiding those already in peril is no proof of consent to the actions that placed and continued them in that dangerous posture." [25]

Short of slashing executive fund requests, Congress can and should participate more than it traditionally has in the formation of specific foreign policies. I am not suggesting that it participate in every detail of executive policy-making. Yet it will have to ignore the traditional division of labor that limits itself to "broad-policy" questions while delegating "day-to-day" decisions to the executive branch. Congress must monitor policies *and* operations. Day-to-day decisions, upon accumulation, have a way of forming policy—what the Senate Foreign Relations Committee has called a "process of commitment by accretion." [26] Congress will have to organize itself to influence policy at the formative stage and maintain close review thereafter.

A recent example of this is the series of hearings held by the Symington Subcommittee on U.S. Security Arrangements and Commitments Abroad. During the 91st Congress, the two-man staff of the Subcommittee traveled to twenty-three countries for on-the-scene investigations. Subsequent hearings examined U.S. policies and operations in thirteen countries, plus NATO. The Subcommittee pressed the executive bureaucracies to defend and explain their policies, secured the declassification of much nonsensitive information that an overzealous officialdom had labeled "secret," and was able to shed new light on some of the 2,200 U.S. bases overseas in thirty-three countries. A number of these bases, the hearings suggested, were products of bureaucratic inertia, anachronistic relics dating back to the 1940's but unnecessary to the 1970's.

On December 2, 1970, Senator Clifford Case introduced a bill to require that all international agreements, other than treaties, be transmitted to Congress within 60 days of their execution. If an executive agreement is one whose immediate disclosure would prejudice national security, it is to be transmitted to the Senate Foreign Relations Committee and the House Foreign Affairs Committee, under an injunction of secrecy removable only by the President. As reintroduced in the 92nd Congress, the Case bill became law on August 22, 1972.

To tighten congressional control still further, Senator Ervin introduced a bill on April 11, 1972, to provide that executive agreements shall come into force 60 days after being transmitted to Congress, unless both Houses pass a concurrent resolution within that period disapproving the agreement. Extensive hearings were held on the bill that spring. As reintroduced in the 93d Congress, the Ervin bill was cleared at the subcommittee level and readied for action by the Senate Committee on the Judiciary.

Structural and procedural reforms are needed *within* the legislative branch, however, before Congress can begin to achieve the greater effectiveness in foreign affairs that it seeks. Much of the legislative decline in influencing foreign policy, James A. Robinson has written, "must be attributed to the profound change in the requirements of public policy-making and to the failure of Congress to alter its organization to cope with the new demands made upon it." [27]

For instance, it is clear that the crowded schedules of senators and representatives do not permit effective supervision of Administration policies. The late Senator Dirksen, at one time a member of more than a dozen committees and subcommittees, claimed that he needed roller skates to get to all the meetings. It is not at all unusual for a senator to have two or three committee meetings scheduled at the same hour. Senators now average 15.9 committee and subcommittee assignments.[28]

Steps are being taken to ease this pressure and to streamline procedures. The Legislative Reorganization Act of 1970, by projecting a reduction in the size of a number of Senate committees, promises junior senators a greater opportunity to develop expertise and to hold leadership positions earlier in their careers. The tight schedules of representatives may have been relieved somewhat by the installation of electronic voting equipment. During 1970, the House consumed 238 hours for roll calls and quorum calls—about 28 per cent of the time the House was in session. Electronic voting has cut the half-hour votes to a 15-minute voting period. Another mechanical innovation is the amplification system now installed in the Senate.

The Legislative Reorganization Act of 1970 increased the number of professional staff members for each standing committee. It also strengthened staff assistance available to Congress from the General Accounting Office and the Congressional Research Service (formerly the Legislative Reference Service).

A number of other provisions in the Legislative Reorganization Act of 1970 have increased the visibility and accountability of legislative actions. However, increased staffing, along with better floor and committee procedures, will not overcome the unrepresentative composition of committees, with military types dominating the committees and subcommittees that authorize and appropriate funds for the Defense Department. Part of that ideological bias is, in fact, caused by liberals who concentrate their interests on such committees as Senate Foreign Relations, Senate Labor and Public Welfare, and House Education and Labor. Surely, a seat on Armed Services is important for urban constituencies, in terms of establishing a balance between military and domestic spending.

Other techniques are available for broadening congressional participation. In hearings held in 1969, the Senate Foreign Relations Committee conducted an intensive inquiry into the Safeguard ABM system, antisubmarine warfare, and MIRV's—items normally considered on the agenda of the Armed Services Committee. This form of encroachment was made possible when the Foreign Relations Committee scrutinized those weapons systems within the larger context of arms control and the Nonproliferation Treaty. From 1968 to 1972, the Joint Economic Committee held hearings on "Economics of Military Procurement," "The Military Budget and National Economic Priorities," and "The Acquisition of Weapons Systems." Those hearings contributed important insights into deficiencies within the executive branch. Extensive hearings in the area of government procurement, held by the House Committee on Government Operations in 1969, helped uncover additional defects in the management of defense contracts.

Still another technique for broader participation is the bicameral, bipartisan group known as Members of Congress for Peace Through Law. Its special subgroup on military spending has offered an independent analysis of weapons systems and force levels. The Democratic Study Group in the House has also prepared a separate analysis of the defense budget. Private groups, such as The Brookings Institution, publish studies on the range of options that are available for strategic nuclear forces and general-purpose forces.

Legislative reassertion is not in itself, of course, a foolproof antidote for future Vietnams and large defense budgets. Congress's past record of partnership with the military is plain enough. But neither is their hope in legislative acquiescence in a hypothetically all-wise, omnipotent, and beneficent President. When Presidential power is used in a furtive and dissembling manner, when executive expertise becomes another word for incompetence and deceit, and when Presidential policies have such calamitous effects on our citizens and on peoples in distant lands, then surely it is time for the constitutional pendulum to swing.

That is why Congress has begun to build an independent expertise to monitor and question foreign commitments, which all too often have been the personal undertakings of the President, supported by the bureaucracy, rather than commitments by Congress and the nation as a whole. To complement this new congressional expertise, there must be a new temperament and set of attitudes: a courage to resist being stampeded into granting power simply because the President waves the flag; an ability to distinguish between a need for speed and mere recklessness;

a strength and resolve to defer to no one in the exercise of independent judgment. Most important: a determination to treat "reassertion" not as a temporary phenomenon, needed to restore constitutional balance, but as a permanent, nondelegable legislative responsibility. Congress has demonstrated rather impressively that it can change its attitudes and procedures and contribute intelligently to foreign-policy–making. The larger question is whether it has the will and the staying power to contribute from one year to the next, in times of crisis as well as relative calm, without reverting to its former acquiescence in the President.

NOTES

[1] Arthur M. Schlesinger, Jr., and Alfred de Grazia, *Congress and the Presidency: Their Role in Modern Times* (Washington, D.C.: American Enterprise Institute, 1967), p. 28; Commager's testimony: *Changing American Attitudes Toward Foreign Policy,* hearings before the Senate Foreign Relations Committee, 90th Cong., 1st Sess., p. 21 (1967); March, 1969, Conference: "The Power of the Pentagon," *The Progressive* (June, 1969), and *American Militarism: 1970,* ed. Erwin Knoll and Judith Nies McFadden (New York: Viking Press, 1969); J. William Fulbright, "American Foreign Policy in the 20th Century Under an 18th-Century Constitution," 47 *Cornell Law Quarterly* 1, 2 (Fall, 1961).

[2] Holbert N. Carroll, *The House of Representatives and Foreign Affairs* (Boston: Little, Brown, 1966), p. 20; Dean Acheson, *A Citizen Looks at Congress* (New York: Harper & Bros., 1956), p. 83.

[3] *United States* v. *Curtiss-Wright,* 299 U.S. 304, 319–320.

[4] Joel Francis Paschal, *Mr. Justice Sutherland: A Man Against the State* (Princeton: Princeton University Press, 1951), p. 93; George Sutherland, *Constitutional Power and World Affairs* (New York: Columbia University Press, 1919).

[5] *Knauff* v. *Shaughnessy,* 338 U.S. 537, 551 (1950); *New York Times Co.* v. *United States,* 403 U.S. 713, 719 (1971).

[6] Arthur Maass, "In Accord With the Program of the President?" 4 *Public Policy* 77, 81 (1953); Samuel P. Huntington, "Strategic Planning and the Political Process," 38 *Foreign Affairs* 285, 291–92 (January, 1960).

[7] Richard M. Pfeffer, ed., *No More Vietnams?* (New York: Harper & Row, 1968), p. 11; *The Military Budget and National Economic Priorities* (Part 1), hearings before the Joint Economic Committee, 91st Cong., 1st Sess., p. 72 (1969).

[8] *Ibid.,* p. 54; 115 *Congressional Record* E2242 (daily ed., March 20, 1969); 115 *Congressional Record* E5466 (daily ed., July 1, 1969).

[9] *Government Procurement and Contracting* (Part 4), hearings before the

House Committee on Government Operations, 91st Cong., 1st Sess., pp. 1179–84 (1969).

[10] *The Military Budget and National Economic Priorities* (Part 2), p. 503; 115 *Congressional Record* S7089 (daily ed., June 25, 1969).

[11] *The Military Budget and National Economic Priorities*, p. 510; see also p. 504.

[12] *National Commitments*, Senate Report No. 129, 91st Cong., 1st Sess., p. 16 (1969).

[13] Jonathan B. Bingham, "Can Military Spending Be Controlled?" 48 *Foreign Affairs* 51, 59–60 (October, 1969).

[14] 115 *Congressional Record* S5253 (daily ed., May 16, 1969).

[15] For details, see Louis Fisher, *President and Congress: Power and Policy* (New York: Free Press, 1972), pp. 212–24.

[16] *United States Security Agreements and Commitments Abroad* (Part 1), hearings before the Senate Committee on Foreign Relations, 91st Cong., 1st Sess., pp. 6–7 (1969).

[17] *National Commitment*, Senate Report No. 129, 91st Cong., 1st Sess., p. 28 (April 16, 1969).

[18] *Public Papers of the Presidents, 1962*, p. 396 (May 15, 1962) and p. 485 (October 22, 1962).

[19] *Public Papers of the Presidents, 1963–1964*, II, p. 931 (August 5, 1964); 110 *Congressional Record* 18084, 18551 (August 5–7, 1964).

[20] *Public Papers of the Presidents, 1958*, p. 549 (July 15, 1958); *ibid., 1965*, II, p. 616 (June 1, 1965).

[21] *Weekly Compilation of Presidential Documents*, VI, no. 18, 597 (April 30, 1970).

[22] *New York Times*, February 9, 1971, 17:6.

[23] *Department of State Bulletin*, Vol. LXVIII, No. 1769, p. 652 (May 21, 1973).

[24] See Martin Lichterman, "To the Yalu and Back," Inter-University Case Program No. 92 (Indianapolis: Bobbs-Merrill, 1963).

[25] *Mitchell* v. *Laird*, 476 F.2d 533, 538 (1973).

[26] *National Commitments*, Senate Report No. 129, 91st Cong., 1st Sess., p. 26 (1969).

[27] James A. Robinson, *Congress and Foreign Policy Making*, rev. ed. (Homewood, Ill.: Dorsey Press, 1967), p. 176.

[28] Charles O. Jones, "Congressional Committees and the Two-Party System," a paper presented to the House Select Committee on Committees, p. 4 (June 1973).

5

Power in Foreign Relations

Adolf A. Berle

Should the President be controlled in his conduct of foreign relations—since he seems able to involve the country in war without its consent? If control is needed, then how much and how applied?

These are the questions, by no means new, presented by current politics resulting from Vietnam and the Middle East—as they were presented to President Truman when the cold war took shape in the late 1940's—and to President Franklin D. Roosevelt as the Fascist-Nazi threat developed in the 1930's—and, indeed, as World War I engrossed Woodrow Wilson's attention after 1914. The capacity of an American President to engage the country in armed operations has been a perennial issue since John Adams found himself in an undeclared war with France as early as 1798. James Madison was viciously attacked for allegedly having maneuvered the country from covert to overt war with England in 1812. With more justice, in 1848, President Polk was accused of baiting Mexico into attacking the United States and so creating a state of war he wanted, through the exercise of his Presidential power as commander in chief in disposition of the American army along the Mexican border. The classic case was that of America's entry into World War I, which was accomplished by a personal decision of President Wilson in 1917—though a buildup of circumstances had been proceeding for more than two years—and Wilson adhered to constitutional practice.

In two instances—the War of 1812 and the Mexican War of 1848—opposition to the President split the country with a bitterness surpassing the controversy of 1970; however, the precise accusations differed slightly from today's. At present, it is insisted that three Presidents—John F. Kennedy, Lyndon B. Johnson, and Richard M. Nixon—have strained, if they [have] not usurp[ed], powers granted to the President by the American Constitution. This goes beyond the charges leveled against Polk and Madison. They had scrupulously followed constitutional procedures; the Congress of the United States had duly "declared war." The thrust of the accusation against them was that, in both cases, the President had manipulated events to produce a condition of affairs in which the Congress had little alternative. In 1970,* of course, the charge is that the President has engaged in war without asking the authority of the Congress—and particularly so in his invasion of Cambodia in May, 1970. That operation exacerbated a contention put forward earlier—but now fanned to red heat—that the Presidential power, constitutional perhaps but in any case *de facto*, is completely out of control, must be curbed, constrained, and checked lest the United States find itself a virtual dictatorship in the field of international affairs generally and particularly in matters of war and peace.

I here present an entirely unpopular thesis. I maintain that the Presidential power in foreign affairs is not out of control by the Congress and by American public opinion—given the chaotic condition of foreign relations throughout the world. If measures are needed, they should be directed toward better and more accurate information for the American public, assuring that American public opinion will function more continuously and more responsibly as it deals with the day-to-day decisions a President must make, and the country should be aware of the significance of this fact. I am opposed to any other form of control. Attempts to impose limits have been made before; and

---

* Berle delivered this paper in 1970, before the so-called end of the Vietnam war. —*The Editors.*

they have led, in some cases, to ghastly results as history took (it frequently does [take]) wholly unforeseen turns.

One such attempt was made after World War I. Claims were made that merchant bankers (J. P. Morgan & Co.), working with merchants-of-death (Bethlehem Steel Co., *et al.*) to assure the victory of the Anglo-French-Russian Entente Powers, had influenced the United States to declare war on Germany. Before that declaration, they had "involved" the United States by floating Anglo-French war loans in the American financial market, and by causing the sale of munitions of war—on credit— to the Allied powers. In time, so-called neutrality legislation was passed requiring the President, when war broke out abroad, to proclaim U.S. neutrality and to limit, stringently, American shipments of munitions to any belligerent. This legislation was on the books in the decade of the 1930's. One of its early impacts was to constrict munitions shipments to Spain when France, with the support of Mussolini and Hitler, attacked and overset the Spanish Republican Government. Another effect was the hindrance of aid to the Western Allies as World War II broke out in 1939. In both instances, the attempted control of freedom of action worked exactly contrary to the intent of the legislation. The same result, I am sure, would occur if attempts were made to limit the freedom of action of the President. The reasons behind this are worth examining.

First, assumption is invariably made that the United States ought not to be involved in hostilities except by formal congressional action, or as a result of hostile attack. Factually, all degrees of involvement can occur before either stage is reached. This was what happened in 1915 and 1916, when submarine sinkings, climaxing with that of the *Lusitania*, increasingly killed Americans, though war did not legally exist—and similar involvement occurred again in 1940–41, when Germany proclaimed a blockade of Great Britain. It is by no means certain that noninvolvement will or can be procured by keeping American ships and American individuals off the seas, or that victory of the blockading power will contribute to the safety or well-being of the United States. Yet, it is precisely in dealing with such situations that the Presidential power is most determinative. Handling these incidents gives the President his opportunity—or imposes on him the duty—to lead international developments toward their next phase, be it peace or war; and it is by no means sure that avoidance of war necessarily produces peace.

Second, a stage in international law has been reached in which conventional legal relations are ill defined. Under the U.N. Charter, as under other documents and treaties, war has been renounced as an instrument of policy. Obviously, the renunciation is strictly theoretical—states of armed conflict exist in many parts of the world. What has been eliminated is the formal recognition by belligerents of the legal existence of a "state of war." (Parenthetically, I raise the question whether the world is better off as a result. Formal recognition of a state of war brings with it legal restrictions on the belligerents, and enforcement of these restrictions through the laws of neutrality—none of which exist today.) As illustrations: North Korea [versus] South Korea; North Vietnam versus South Vietnam; North Vietnam versus Cambodia; Soviet Union versus Czechoslovakia; the Arab-Negro civil war in the Sudan; and Egypt versus Israel.

Presidential power is at its height when the White House has to deal with these undeclared states of war. Presidential problems, it may be added, under such circumstances are most serious and most puzzling. Abrogation of the practice of declaring war absolves the President of practicing legal "neutrality," as he would have been required to do under the old rules. Instead, he must comply with the actions taken by the U.N. Security Council—if that body acts—or possibly by the Assembly of the United Nations when it acts under the "United for Peace" formula; but the United States itself has both a voice and a veto in the Security Council and has substantial influence in the Assembly. In all cases, the President can, and indeed must, issue instructions. Where action is involved—as in the Dominican situation in 1965 or the Cuban missile crisis in 1962—the decision to act or decline action (the latter no less causative than the former) is a direct Presidential responsibility. I can think of no limitations, set in advance, that, when the crisis crunch comes, are not likely to look as the neutrality legislation of mid-1930's looked in 1939–40. Predetermined rules of action are far less safe than, and cannot take the place of, statesmanship.

Protection against misuse of Presidential power, indeed, is

urged primarily by those who object to the use of American force in Southeast Asia. Some of these objections go to most extreme lengths. One of them, in an article syndicated for the *New York Times*, maintains that President Nixon and his advisers are "war criminals" and should be tried accordingly; that the United States should be forced "to admit and accept defeat in Southeast Asia"; and that work should be undertaken toward "Dissolution before Decay." Yet, his copartisans were simultaneously pumping anti-Semitism into the ghettos of Harlem and Chicago in aid of Arab warfare against Israel. Clearly, these people are not seeking peace, but rather success in war for belligerents whom they like (these do not include the United States).

Struggle nominally to protect against an overpowerful Presidency can mask a scarcely concealed design to cripple the United States itself, to achieve its defeat and its ultimate dissolution. Historically, as wars have impended, movements to control the Presidency have emerged. In most of these movements, there has been a large element of sincere and dedicated pacifism, endemic in America. But, unhappily, there have also been small but violently motivated elements in these movements whose real desire was victory for some other country, usually an enemy of the United States, whose representatives attempted to play American politics to their own advantage. At present, it is highly unpopular to make the preceding statement; so-called peace groups everywhere arise, shrieking that their motives are being attacked, that the late Senator Joseph McCarthy rides again, et cetera. So, I must recall a few fragments of history.

Let us begin with 1915 and the involvement of the German Imperial Government in the Presidential campaign leading to the re-election of President Wilson in 1916. Rightly, Kaiser Wilhelm's government judged Wilson's reactions unfavorable, and (perhaps wrongly) considered [its] interests would be better served—and the United States kept farther from intervening in World War I—by the election of Charles Evans Hughes. Through a group of propagandists, amply provided with German money, they financed various organizations dedicated toward maintaining U.S. peace and isolation from European wars. This did not make the many young men (I was one of them) who voted for Hughes into pacifists, still less pro-German; but it did make them into a pressure group directed against the White House.

Moreover, it is not easy to forget attempts to strip the American President of his powers as World War II took the center of the stage. Pacifist blocs inveighed, in 1939, against the wickedness of American compulsory military service. Hitler and his Propaganda Minister, Goebbels, stimulated some of this through Nazi organizations in America. They had substantial support from the Communist Party and its allied "front organizations"; for, at that time, the Hitler-Stalin pact was in full force. One of the standard contentions was that the President—then Roosevelt—could not be trusted, was not a "real American," was in the pocket of the British imperialists, and must be "controlled." The language was, almost *literatim*, the language used today in attacks on President Nixon and, before him, on President Johnson.

I am far from asserting that those now demanding measures to curb White House authority are propaganda agents for foreign powers. They are not. But I have lived at the White House during similar periods, and I cannot be so naïve as to think that the very able and extreme propaganda machinery for orthodox Marxism-Leninism maintained by the Soviet Union, and for the different interests of Communist China, have had no voice in this discussion. They have had. When their voices demand control over Presidential powers, as they have [demanded], it is because they have concluded (like the Kaiser, Hitler, and Stalin in their times) that the President is not likely to act as they would choose. President Kennedy reacted badly in the Cuban missile crisis of 1962, and again in 1963 in sending "advisers" to Vietnam—in both cases, in opposition to one or other of the Marxist-Leninist factions. President Johnson reacted in Santo Domingo in 1965 and later escalated the Vietnamese operation. President Nixon de-escalated in Vietnam, but somewhat added to the scope of the operation by his brief foray into Cambodia. Attack on these moves, in large measure, has come from pacifist motives. But a good deal of it has been stimulated by foreign governments that have not been happy when Presidents of the United States blocked or hindered their designs for conquest.

My candid, if unfashionable, conclusion differs from presently popular analysis. The rumpus kicked up was not because the Presidents in question misused their powers. It was because they used their powers legitimately to act and to achieve objectives that their critics did not want. These critics may have been right —but that is a different debate and a different issue.

All the same, the fact remains that the United States has become involved in a war that most of the country would like to end, and of which—rightly or wrongly—a substantial faction actively and rigorously disapproves. The involvement did come insidiously and became apparent only after many thousands of men were on battle duty. It grew to full-scale war proportions without any expression of the national will by the Congress, because the men thus engaged could not be abandoned and therefore had to be supported until disengagement could be worked out. Are we—is the United States—subject to major risks, military and political, at the sole decision of its chief executive? If we think (as I do) that no limitations on executive action can now be laid out, is there a method of assuring that such action will take place and the relevant decisions will be taken under the scrutiny of public opinion?

Support or opposition by public opinion is likely to be crucial. Not only may a President be defeated at the next election, he may be denied the money, the munitions, or the supplies to carry out initiatives he has taken or measures he has proposed. I am by no means sure that the measures taken by Presidents Kennedy and Johnson in Southeast Asia would have been condemned, as they later were, had they been openly and publicly announced, their implications exposed to public debate, and the objective—maintaining a balance of power in the Orient—fully discussed. I am clear that the decisions taken, if justifiable, lost a large measure of success potential because they were not opened to the analysis and discussion needed to develop the degree of public support capable of carrying them to a successful conclusion. And if not justifiable, the opportunity was lost to demonstrate their weaknesses and perhaps to guide the Southeast Asian operation into less perilous directions. The change I would like to see made lies not in the fact of Presidential powers but in the conduct of the President's dialogue as it is progressively exercised.

Specifically, I think the President should formally appoint a Presidential representative to speak for him (when he does not choose to speak in person) at periodic joint meetings of the House Committee on Foreign Affairs and the Senate Committee on Foreign Relations. At such meetings, the President or his representative should be expected to answer questions, much as the British Cabinet members respond to inquiries from the House of Commons. In the usual course of these meetings, it might be expected that the Secretary of State would represent the President; but it is not difficult to imagine situations where the Secretary of Defense or perhaps a White House assistant would be appropriate. I would hope these sessions could occur at regular intervals, say every two weeks—and oftener in time of crisis, less often when affairs were running quietly. The President —that is to say, his office—should be expected to provide a précis of the situation and its possibilities at each meeting, and to answer questions. The President should have the privilege of declining to reveal or discuss matters that he believes should be kept confidential, but his direction of policy ought to be a matter of general knowledge and of general debate.

Clearly enough, the result of such general debate might be congressional action limiting the President's power to act in any given problem. Such action might be highly salutary, or it might be extremely ill advised. In 1939, there was vigorous discussion of the position and possible involvement of the U.S. Army. The military establishment was kept in existence by a margin of only one vote. But this is of the nature of democracy. On the historical side, the American record stands up well by comparison with less popular forms of government. The risk of too much publicity is far less, in my judgment, than the risks resulting from secrecy. Maintenance of a continuous dialogue between the President— who ultimately has and exercises power—and the Congress, press, and public communication media offers the possibility of keeping the use of Presidential power close to the real desires of the United States.

Never, probably, has an American President held more absolute power than he does today. So the logic of things demands that the President talk about his power—what he is doing with it, the results he hopes to achieve, the risks he must run, and the obligations he considers controlling. Well handled, this dialogue might modify the course of foreign affairs, making its practice less mysterious, more down-to-earth, and closer to the people whose lives are affected.

6

Congress and the Making of American Foreign Policy

Arthur Schlesinger, Jr.

The problem of the control of foreign policy has been a perennial source of anguish for democracies. The idea of popular government hardly seems complete if it fails to embrace questions of war and peace. Yet, the effective conduct of foreign affairs appears to demand, as Tocqueville argued long ago, not the qualities peculiar to a democracy but "on the contrary, the perfect use of almost all those in which it is deficient." Steadfastness in a course, efficiency in the execution of policy, patience, secrecy—are not these more likely to proceed from executives than from legislatures? But, if foreign policy becomes the property of the executive, what happens to democratic control? In our own times, this issue has acquired special urgency, partly because of the Indochina war, with its aimless persistence and savagery, but more fundamentally, I think, because the invention of nuclear weapons has transformed the power to make war into the power to blow up the world. And, for the United States, the question of control of foreign policy is, at least in its constitutional aspect, the question of the distribution of powers between the Presidency and the Congress. . . .

The war power has historically involved a competition between the power of the Congress to authorize war and the power of the President as commander in chief. It is important to state the issue with precision. The issue is not the declaration of war in a strict sense. Long before Under Secretary Katzenbach startled the Senate Foreign Relations Committee, in 1967, by pronouncing the declaration of war "outmoded," Hamilton had written, in the 25th *Federalist*, "The ceremony of a formal denunciation of war has of late fallen into disuse." One study of European and American wars shows that, between 1700 and 1870, hostilities began in 107 cases without declaration of war; in only ten cases was there a declaration of war in advance of hostilities. Though the United States has engaged in a number of armed conflicts in the last two centuries, it has only made five formal declarations of war (of which four—all but the War of 1812— recognized the prior existence of states of war).

The real issue is congressional authorization—whether or not by declaration of war—of the commitment of American forces in circumstances that involve or invite hostilities against foreign states. One aspect of this issue emerged clearly during the undeclared naval war with France in 1798–1801. Mr. Katzenbach injudiciously testified that "President John Adams' use of troops in the Mediterranean" (by which he presumably meant Adams's use of the fleet in the Atlantic) was "criticized at the time as exceeding the power of the Executive acting without the support of a congressional vote." Others, before and since, have cited this conflict as an early precedent in the cause of Presidential warmaking. In fact, when trouble with France began, Adams called Congress to meet in special session "to consult and determine on such measure as in their wisdom shall be deemed meet for the safety and welfare of the said United States." In due course, Congress turned more belligerent than the President and, in the spring of 1798, passed some twenty laws to encourage Adams to wage the war. Adams's Attorney General described the conflict as a "maritime war *authorized* by both nations," and, in 1800, the Supreme Court, called up to define the conflict, drew a distinction between "perfect" and "imperfect" wars. As it concluded, in a unanimous decision, if war *be declared in form, it is called solemn, and is of the perfect kind. . . . But hostilities may subsist between two nations, more confined in its nature and extent; being limited as to places, persons, and things; and this is more properly termed imperfect war. . . . Still . . . it is a war between two nations, though all the members are not authorized to commit hostilities such as in a solemn war.*

Both sorts of war, whether solemn or nonsolemn, complete or limited, were deemed to require some mode of congressional authorization. When John Marshall assumed leadership of the Court in 1801, he reinforced the point in a second case arising out of the trouble with France. "The Congress," he ruled, "may authorize general hostilities . . . or partial war."

Jefferson similarly acknowledged the congressional right to license hostilities by means short of a declaration of war, while, at the same time, he affirmed the right of the executive to repel sudden attack. When an American naval schooner was fired on by a Tripolitania cruiser in the Mediterranean, it repulsed the attack with signal success; but, Jefferson instructed Congress, its commander was "unauthorized by the Constitution, without the sanction of Congress, to go beyond the line of defense," so the enemy vessel, having been "disabled from committing further hostilities, was liberated with its crew." Jefferson went on to ask Congress to consider "whether, by authorizing measures of offense also, they will place our force on an equal footing with that of its adversaries." Again, fearing incursions into Louisiana by the Spanish in Florida in 1805, he declined to broaden defense against sudden attack into defense against the threat of sudden attack and said in a special message: "Considering that Congress alone is constitutionally invested with the power of changing our condition from peace to war, I have thought it my duty to await their authority for using force. . . . The course to be pursued will require the command of means which it belongs to Congress exclusively to yield or to deny."

In this case, Congress chose to deny. But, half a dozen years later, a more belligerent Congress led a more reluctant President into war. In 1812, Madison, now that he was the executive and the War Hawks of the legislature were demanding hostilities with Britain, may well have reflected ruefully on his argument of 1798 about the supposed greater interest of the executive in war.

When the Seminole Indians were conducting raids into American territory in 1818, President Monroe chose not to consult Congress before ordering General Andrew Jackson to chase the raiding parties back into Spanish Florida, where Jackson was soon fighting Spaniards and hanging Englishmen. But tangling with foreigners was incidental to Jackson's ostensible objective, which was punishing Indians. We would now call the principle on which he and Monroe acted "hot pursuit." Where direct conflict with a foreign state was the issue, Monroe was more cautious. When he promulgated his famous Doctrine, he neither consulted with Congress nor sought its subsequent approval; but, when Colombia requested U.S. protection under the Monroe Doctrine, John Quincy Adams, Monroe's Secretary of State, carefully replied that the Constitution confided "the ultimate decision . . . to the Legislative Department."

Jackson himself, as President, meticulously respected this point. Though he enlarged the executive power with relish in other areas, on the question of the war-making power he followed not his own example of 1817 but Jefferson's of 1801. Thus, in 1831, after ordering an armed vessel to South America to protect American shipping against Argentine raiders, he said, "I submit the case to the consideration of Congress, to the end that they may clothe the Executive with such authority and means as they deem necessary for providing a force adequate to the complete protection of our fellow citizens fishing and trading in these seas." When France persisted in her refusal to pay long-outstanding claims for damage to American shipping during the Napoleonic wars, Jackson, instead of moving on his own, took care to ask Congress for a law "authorizing reprisals upon French property, in case provision shall not be made for the payment of the debt." (Albert Gallatin observed that this "proposed transfer by Congress of its constitutional powers to the Executive, in a case which necessarily embraces the question of war or no war," was "entirely inconsistent with the letter and spirit of our Constitution," and Congress turned Jackson down.) When Texas rebelled against

Mexico and sought U.S. recognition as an independent republic, Jackson referred the matter to Congress as a question "probably leading to war" and therefore a proper subject for "previous understanding with that body by whom war can alone be declared and by whom all the provisions for sustaining its perils must be furnished."

Still, the executive retained the ability, if he so desired, to contrive a situation that left Congress little choice but to give him a declaration of war. James K. Polk demonstrated this in 1846, when, without congressional authorization, he sent American forces into disputed land, where they were attacked by Mexican units who, not unreasonably, considered it Mexican territory. Polk quickly obtained a congressional declaration of war, but many members of Congress had the uneasy feeling that the President had put something over on them. Two years later, with the war still on, the House resolved by a narrow margin that it had been "unnecessarily and unconstitutionally begun by the President of the United States." Perhaps so; but, unlike some later Presidents, Polk did have behind him not just a congressional or U.N. resolution, but a formal declaration of war by the Congress. In any case, this was the situation that provoked Congressman Lincoln of Illinois into his celebrated attack on Presidential war-making:

> *Allow the President to invade a neighboring nation, whenever he shall deem it necessary to repel an invasion . . . and you allow him to make war at pleasure. Study to see if you can fix any limit to his power in this respect. . . . If, today, he should choose to say he thinks it necessary to invade Canada, to prevent the British from invading us, how could you stop him? You may say to him, "I see no probability of the British invading us," but he will say to you, "Be silent; I see it, if you don't."*

IV

The prevailing view in the early Republic, it has been suggested, was that congressional authorization was clearly required for the commitment of American forces overseas in circumstances that involved or invited hostilities against foreign states. But what if the hostilities contemplated were not against foreign governments but were in protection of American honor, law, lives, or property against Indians, slave traders, pirates, smugglers, frontier ruffians, or foreign disorder? Early Presidents evidently decided, as a practical matter, that forms of police action not directed against a sovereign nation did not rise to the dignity of formal congressional concern. These were mostly trivial episodes; and, when Senator Goldwater, with such fugitive engagements in mind, said, "We have only been in five declared wars out of over 150 that we fought," he was stretching the definition of war in a way that could comfort only those who rejoice in portraying the United States as incurably aggressive throughout its history.

Jackson in Florida was an early example; but the commitment of armed force without congressional authorization was by no means confined to North America or to the Western Hemisphere. American naval ships in these years took military action against pirates or refractory natives in place as remote as Sumatra (1832, 1838, 1839), the Fiji Islands (1840, 1855, 1858), and Africa (1820, 1843, 1845, 1850, 1854, 1858, 1859). As early as 1836, John Quincy Adams could write, "However startled we may be at the idea that the Executive Chief Magistrate has the power of involving the nation in war, even without consulting Congress, an experience of fifty years has proved that in numberless cases he has and must have exercised the power."

Adams, who in any case (at least till the Mexican War came along) regarded the power of declaring war as an "Executive act," mistakenly turned over by the Founding Fathers to the Congress, somewhat exaggerated. Still the spreading employment of force overseas by unilateral Presidential decision, even if not yet against sovereign governments, was a threat to the congressional monopoly of the war power. In the meantime, the demonstration by Monroe of the unilateral Presidential power to propound basic objectives in foreign policy, the demonstration by Polk of the unilateral Presidential capacity to confront Congress with *faits accomplis*, the demonstration by Pierce of the unilateral Presidential power to threaten sovereign states (as when he sent

Commodore Perry and a naval squadron to open up Japan in 1854)—all these further diminished the congressional voice in the conduct of foreign affairs. Congress continued to fight back, particularly on the question of the war power. It took, for example, special pleasure in rejecting half a dozen requests for the authorization of force from the punctilious Buchanan, who believed that "without the authority of Congress the President cannot fire a hostile gun in any case except to repel the attacks of an enemy."

Perhaps it was Buchanan's strict constructionism that led to the drastic expansion of Presidential initiative under his successor; for Lincoln may well have delayed the convocation of Congress till ten weeks after Fort Sumter lest rigid constitutionalists on the Hill try to stop him from doing what he deemed necessary to save the life of the nation. In this period of executive grace, he reinforced Sumter, assembled the militia, enlarged the army and navy beyond their authorized strength, called out volunteers for three years' service, disbursed unappropriated moneys, censored the mail, suspended habeas corpus, and blockaded the Confederacy—measures that, as he said, "whether strictly legal or not, were ventured upon under what appeared to be a popular demand and a public necessity; trusting then as now that Congress would readily ratify them." He added that it was with deepest regret he thus employed what he vaguely called the "war power"; however, "he could but perform this duty, or surrender the existence of the Government."

No President had ever undertaken such sweeping actions in the absence of congressional authorization. No President had ever confronted Congress with such a massive collection of *faits accomplis*. Benjamin R. Curtis, who had been one of the two dissenting justices in the Dred Scott case, wrote that Lincoln had established a "military despotism." But Congress gave retroactive consent to Lincoln's program; and, two years later, the Court, in the Prize cases, found constitutional substance (narrowly; the vote was 5–4) for his idea of the "war power" by attaching it to his authority as commander in chief and to his right to defend the nation against attack. Throughout the war, Lincoln coninued to exercise wide powers independently of

Congress. The Emancipation Proclamation, for example, was a unilateral executive act, pronounced under the war power without reference to Congress. But Lincoln's assertion of the war power took place, it should not be forgotten, in the context of a domestic rebellion and under the color of a most desperate national emergency. There is no suggestion that Lincoln supposed he could use this power in foreign wars without congressional consent.

v

The Presidential prerogative has not grown by steady accretion. Nearly every President who has extended the reach of the White House has provoked a reaction toward a more restricted theory of the Presidency, even if the reaction never quite cuts Presidential power back to its earlier level. When Lincoln expanded Presidential initiative, Congress took out its frustrations by harassing him through the Committee on the Conduct of the War, impeaching his successor, and eventually establishing a generation of congressional government. In this period of relative military quiescence (there were only 17 instances of American military action abroad in the twenty years after the Civil War as compared to 38 in the twenty years before the war), the locus of conflict shifted from the war power to the treaty power. The Senate's constitutional right to consent to treaties—even though it had long since lost to George Washington its claim for a voice in negotiations and to his successors its power to confirm the appointment of negotiators—turned out to be more solidly embedded in the structure of government than the constitutional right of the Congress to declare war.

In the years after the Civil War, the Senate freely exercised its power to rewrite, amend, and reject treaties negotiated by the President. Indeed, it ratified no important treaty between 1871 and 1898. Writing in 1885, Woodrow Wilson observed that the President was made to approach the Senate "as a servant conferring with a master. . . . It is almost as distinctly dealing with a foreign power as were the negotiations preceding the proposed treaty. It must predispose the Senate to the temper of an overseer." Wilson grimly noted that the treaty-making power had become the "treaty-*marring* power"; and, a dozen years later, John Hay told Henry Adams that he did not believe "another important treaty would ever pass the Senate."

Secretaries of State regarded the assertion of senatorial prerogative as the mindless expression of institutional jealousy. As Secretary of State Richard Olney observed in one case, "The Treaty, in getting itself made by the sole act of the executive, without leave of the Senate first had and obtained, had committed the unpardonable sin. It must be either altogether defeated or so altered as to bear an unmistakable Senate stamp . . . and thus be the means both of humiliating the executive and of showing to the world the greatness of the Senate." Hay regarded the one-third veto as the "original," the "irreparable" mistake of the Constitution, now grown to "monstrous shape," and wrote, "The attitude of the Senate toward public affairs makes all serious negotiations impossible."

Ways had to be found to evade the veto. One was the use of the joint resolution, which required only a majority of the Congress as against two-thirds of the Senate; by such means Texas was annexed in 1845 and Hawaii in 1898. Another was the use of agreements entered into directly by the President with foreign states. The "executive agreement" had the legal force of a treaty; and, though largely confined, in the nineteenth century, to technical matters, it could be the vehicle of large purposes. It was, for example, the means by which Britain and the United States agreed, in the Rush-Bagot accord of 1817, to disarm the Great Lakes and by which the United States, in 1898–99, developed the policy of the Open Door in China.

Still, Congress remained in the saddle. As Henry Adams put it in a famous complaint:

> *The Secretary of State exists only to recognize the existence of a world which Congress would rather ignore; of obligations which Congress repudiates whenever it can; of bargains which Congress distrusts and tries to turn to its advantage or to reject. Since the first day the Senate existed, it has always intrigued against the Secretary of State whenever the*

*Secretary has been obliged to extend his functions beyond
the appointment of Consuls in Senators' service.*

But, just as executive domination had produced a shift in power
over foreign policy toward Congress after the Civil War, so
congressional domination was beginning to produce a shift back
to the Presidency. And, in clamoring for war with Spain, Congress became its own executioner. Writing in 1900, Wilson elo-
quently portrayed the impact of that war upon the lodgment
and exercise of power within the federal system. When foreign
affairs dominate the policy of a nation, he said, "its Executive
must of necessity be its guide: must utter every initial judgment,
take every first step of action, supply the information upon which
it is to act, suggest and in large measure control its conduct. The
President of the United States is now . . . at the front of affairs,
as no president, except Lincoln, has been since the first quarter
of the nineteenth century."

VI

Oddly, Congress, in its salad years, had not asserted itself on
the question of the war power, perhaps because it so generally
agreed with the use the executive made on his own motion of
American forces abroad. Victory over Spain now made the
United States a world power; and, in 1900, President McKinley
set the tone for the new century by sending 5,000 American
troops to China. The pretext was the protection of American
lives and property; in fact, the Americans joined an international force, besieged Peking, and helped put down the Boxer
Rebellion. This was done without reference to Congress and
without serious objection from it. The intervention in China,
resulting, among other things, in the exaction of an indemnity
from the Chinese Government, marked the start of a crucial shift
in the use of the armed forces overseas. Where, in the nineteenth
century, military force committed without congressional authorization had been typically used in police actions against private
groups, now it was beginning to be used against sovereign states.
In the next years, Theodore Roosevelt and Taft sent American

forces into Caribbean countries and, in some cases, even installed provisional governments—all without prior congressional sanction.

In 1912, in an effort to meet the constitutional problem, J. Reuben Clark, the Solicitor of the State Department, offered a distinction between "interposition" and "intervention." Interposition meant simply the insertion of troops to protect lives and property; it implied neutrality toward the government or toward contesting forces within the country; and, since it was a normal exercise of international law, it did not, Clark argued, require congressional approval. Intervention, on the other hand, meant interference in sovereign affairs; it implied an act of war and required congressional authorization.

Whatever merit this distinction might have had in the nineteenth century when the United States was a small power, by the twentieth century a great power could hardly interpose anywhere without intervening in sovereign affairs. On the other hand, it could be argued that the superior force of the United States was now so great, relative to the Caribbean states, that intrusion, whether interposition or intervention, did not invite the risk of war and therefore did not require congressional consent. Still, whatever the nuances of arguments, limitations were evaporating. The executive was becoming habituated to the unconstrained deployment of American forces around the world, and Congress chose not to say him nay. Though Wilson received retroactive congressional approval for an incursion into Mexico in 1914 and the approval of the Senate for another in 1916, he did not seek congressional authorization when he sent troops to Siberia after World War I. Congressional resolutions of protest perished in committee.

The revival of Presidential initiative under Theodore Roosevelt and Wilson provoked the predictable reaction. The Senate, reasserting its prerogative, rejected the Versailles Treaty (though, when the elder Henry Cabot Lodge claimed, in his second reservation, that Congress had the "sole power" to "authorize the employment of the military or naval forces," his fellow isolationist, William E. Borah, called it a "recital which is not true"). By the 1930's, the Congress, regarding World War I as

the malign consequence of Presidential discretion in foreign
affairs, imposed a rigid neutrality program on the executive and
remained generally indifferent when Germany and Japan set
out on courses of aggression. The reassertion of the Presidential
prerogative in the years since must be understood, in part, as a
criticism of what happened when Congress tried to seize the
reins of foreign policy in the years 1919–39.

The outbreak of war, in 1939, found the President restrained
both by the neutrality laws and by the balance of power in Congress from doing what he deemed necessary to save the life of
the nation. Roosevelt responded, as Lincoln had eighty years before, by pressing to the utmost limits of Presidential power. But,
though doubtless encouraged by Justice Sutherland and the
Curtiss-Wright decision, he did this without grandiose claims of
executive authority. When he exchanged American destroyers
for British bases in an executive agreement [in] 1940—Senators
Fulbright and Church have both said that Roosevelt "usurped
the treaty power of the Senate"—he did not found his action on
novel authority claimed as commander in chief nor as inherent
powers of the Presidency, but on the construction of laws passed
by Congress in 1917 and 1935. Nor did the transaction involve
promises of future performance, and Roosevelt's circle of prior
consultation included even the Republican candidate for President.

When, in 1941, he sent American troops to Greenland and later
to Iceland, this was done in agreement with the Danish Government in the first case and the government of Iceland in the
second; moreover, the defense of Greenland and, less plausibly,
Iceland could be considered as part of hemisphere security.
Senator Robert A. Taft declared that Roosevelt had "no legal or
constitutional right to send American troops to Iceland" without
authority fnom Congress. Few of his colleagues echoed this protest. The Selective Service Act of 1940 had contained a provision
that draftees could not be used outside the Western Hemisphere
(except in American possessions); but the younger Lodge, who
sponsored this provision, evidently doubted its force and called
it a "pious hope."

In instituting a convoy system and issuing the "shoot at sight" order to the navy in the North Atlantic, Roosevelt was bringing the nation, without congressional authorization, into undeclared naval war with Germany. Senator Fulbright has latterly charged that he "circumvented the war powers of the Congress." But the poignant character of Roosevelt's dilemma was made clear when, in August, 1941, the House of Representatives renewed the Selective Service Act by a single vote. If Congress came that close to disbanding the army at home, how could Roosevelt have reasonably expected congressional support for his forward policy in the North Atlantic? His choice was to go to Congress and risk the fall of Britain to Hitler or to proceed on his own with measures that, "whether strictly legal or not, were ventured upon under what appeared to be a popular demand and a public necessity; trusting then as now that Congress would readily ratify them."

Roosevelt did not, like later Presidents, seek to strip Congress of powers in the name of the inherent authority of the commander in chief. The most extraordinary prewar decision—Lend-Lease—was authorized by Congress following intensive and exacting debate. After America entered the war, Roosevelt asked Congress for authority to send military missions to friendly nations. Both Roosevelt and Hull, remembering the fate of Wilson, made elaborate efforts to bring members of Congress from both parties into the discussion of postwar policy through the Advisory Committee on Postwar Foreign Policy and through congressional representation at Bretton Woods, San Francisco, and in the delegations to the United Nations. The United Nations Participation Act of 1945 took express care to protect the war powers of Congress.

VII

The towering figure of Franklin Roosevelt, the generally accepted wisdom of his measures of 1940–41, his undisputed powers as commander in chief after Pearl Harbor, the thundering international agreements pronounced at wartime summits of the Big Two or the Big Three—all these factors, combined with the memory of the deplorable congressional performance in foreign affairs during the years between the wars, gave Americans, in the postwar years, an exalted conception of Presidential power. Moreover, Roosevelt's successor, a man much read in American history and of doughty temperament, regarded his office, in the words of his last Secretary of State, as a "sacred and temporary trust, which he was determined to pass on unimpaired by the slightest loss of power or prestige." Dean Acheson himself, though an eminent lawyer, was impatient with what he saw as constitutional hair-splitting and encouraged the President in his stout defense of high prerogative. Nor were they alone. As early as 1945, Senator Vandenberg was asserting that the "President must not be limited in the use of force" in the execution of treaties; and, when Vandenberg asked the retired Chief Justice, Charles Evans Hughes, whether the President could commit troops without congressional approval, Hughes replied, "Our Presidents have used our armed forces repeatedly without authorization by Congress, when they thought the interests of the country required it." It must be added that American historians and political scientists, this writer among them, labored to give the expansive theory of the Presidency due historical sanction.

Above all, the uncertainty and danger of the early cold war, with the chronic threat of unanticipated emergency always held to require immediate response, with, above all, the overhanging possibility of nuclear catastrophe, seemed to argue all the more strongly for the centralization of the control over foreign policy, including the use of armed forces, in the Presidency. And the availability of great standing armies and navies notably enlarged Presidential power; before World War II, Presidents (Lincoln excepted) could call on only such limited force as was already in existence. Where Truman required congressional consent either because of the need for appropriations (the Marshall Plan) or for treaty ratification (NATO), he rallied that support effectively. But he decided not to seek formal congressional approval for the commitment of American forces to hostilities in Korea (though he consulted congressional leaders informally before American troops went into action) lest he diminish the Presidential prerogative. This was followed by his decision, also proposed without reference to Congress, to send four divisions to reinforce the American army in Europe. These initiatives greatly alarmed conservative members of Congress. On January 3, 1951, Congressman Frederic Coudert of New York introduced a resolution declaring it the sense of the Congress that no "additional military forces" could be sent abroad "without the prior authorization of the Congress in each instance." Two days later, in a full-dress speech before the Senate, Taft returned to the argument he had made against Roosevelt ten years earlier. "The President," he said,

> *simply usurped authority, in violation of the laws and the Constitution, when he sent troops to Korea to carry out the resolution of the United Nations in an undeclared war. . . . I do not believe the President has the power without congressional approval to send troops to one country to defend it against a possible or probable attack by another country.*

Tom Connally, the Chairman of the Senate Foreign Relations Committee, responded with a stirring assertion of high prerogative. "The authority of the President as Commander in Chief to send the Armed Forces to any place required by the security interests of the United States," he said, "has often been questioned, but never denied by authoritative opinion." Secretary of State Acheson went even further:

> *Not only has the President the authority to use the Armed Forces in carrying out the broad foreign policy of the United States and implementing treaties, but it is equally clear that this authority may not be interfered with by the Congress in the exercise of powers which it has under the Constitution.*

Acheson added irritably: "We are in a position in the world today where the argument as to who has the power to do this, that, or the other thing, is not exactly what is called for from America in this very critical hour."

The debate also divided scholars. Henry Steele Commager wrote, "Whatever may be said of the expediency of the Taft-

Coudert program, this at least can be said of the principles involved—that they have no support in law or in history." The
present writer, with a flourish of historical documentation and,
alas, hyperbole, called Taft's statements "demonstrably irresponsible." In reply, Professor Corwin, who had studied the constitutional position of the Presidency for many years with sardonic
concern, pronounced Commager and Schlesinger (with some justice) "high-flying prerogative men" who ascribed to the President a "truly royal prerogative in the field of foreign relations
. . . without indicating any correlative legal or constitutional
control to which he is answerable."

The Great Debate of 1951 ended inconclusively in the passage
of a "sense of the Senate" resolution in which the Senate approved the sending of Truman's four divisions but asserted that
no additional ground troops should be sent to Western Europe
"without further congressional approval." The Administration
opposed this ceiling; Senator Nixon of California was among
those who voted for it. Where Acheson noted that the resolution
was "without force of law" and "had in it a present for everybody," Taft applauded it as a "clear statement by the Senate that
it has the right to pass on any question of sending troops to Europe to implement the Atlantic Pact." Both were right; and since
no subsequent President has tried to increase the American army
in Europe, the resolution has never been tested.

In areas more clearly dependent on the appropriations power,
notably in foreign aid, Congress neither then nor later hesitated
to tie up executive programs with all manner of hortatory pre-
scriptions, rigid stipulations, and detailed specifications, often
against executive desire. In 1948, it forced an additional $400
million in aid to China; in 1950, over strong executive objection,
it imposed a mandatory loan to Spain. Nor did it hesitate, in
1951–52, to go beyond the Administration in using economic aid
to encourage not only economic cooperation but political integration in Western Europe. This congressional effort to shape foreign policy through appropriations did not relent in subsequent
years; and the greatest dependency of foreign policy on appropriations has meant that, in this sector at least, the Presidency
has lost power to Congress. When Monroe issued the Monroe
Doctrine, he did not seek congressional assent, but when Ken-

nedy called for the Alliance for Progress, he was at the mercy of Congress every step along the way.

The postwar argument between the Congress and the Presidency spilled over to the treaty power as well. Members of Congress feared that the executive agreement, which had started out (with notable exceptions like Rush-Bagot) as a vehicle on minor matters, was now threatening to supersede the treaty as the means of major commitment. In December, 1950, when Prime Minister Attlee came to Washington, a resolution sponsored by, among others, Senator Nixon declared it the sense of the Senate that the President not only report in full to the Senate on his discussions but refrain from entering into any understandings or agreements. The Secretary of State dismissed this (as President Nixon would today) as "plainly . . . an infringement of the constitutional prerogative of the President to conduct negotiations." Still, the resolution received thirty votes. Concern over the abuses of the executive agreement, already set off by hysteria among conservatives about the Yalta records, soon flowed into the movement for the Bricker Amendment.

This Amendment went through a succession of orchestrations; but the pervading theme was that treaties and executive agreements should become effective as internal law only through legislation valid in the absence of a treaty. This would mean not only that a treaty could not authorize what the Constitution forbids but that action by the House of Representatives and, in some cases, by state legislatures might be necessary to give it full effect. One version specifically empowered Congress "to regulate all executive and other agreements with any foreign power or international organization." When moderate conservatives joined with liberals to resist the Amendment, Senator Knowland plucked out the section on executive agreements and offered a bill requiring that all such agreements be transmitted to the Senate within sixty days of their execution. Though the Senate passed this bill, in July, 1956, the House failed to act. In 1972, when Senator Case of New Jersey, a liberal Republican, revived the Knowland idea, the Senate, with liberals in the lead, passed it almost unanimously, and a liberal Democrat, Senator Pell of Rhode Island, recently remarked that the Bricker Amendment, "if put up today, would be voted overwhelmingly by all of us."

VIII

The congressional prottst susbsided, in part because the election of a Republican President, in 1952, seemed to promise a period of executive restraint and congressional influence, and in part because Congress, no less than the executive, accepted the presuppositions of the cold war. Moreover, as so often, the acquisition of power altered perspectives. Secretary of State Dulles opposed the Bricker Amendment as strongly as any Democrat; and, while the Eisenhower Administration was active in seeking joint resolutions at times of supposed vital decision in foreign affairs, it did so not because it thought Congress had any authority in the premises but because the resolution process, by involving Congress in the takeoff, would incriminate it in a crash-landing (this valuable aerial metaphor had been invented by Harold Stassen in 1946. The resolution process now became a curious ceremony of propitiation in which Presidents yielded no claims and Congress asserted few, but which provided an amiable illusion of partnership; it was in domestic terms what someone had said of the Briand-Kellogg Pact—"an international kiss."

Sometimes, even members of Congress considered such resolutions superfluous. When President Eisenhower, recalling Truman's omission in 1950, asked, in 1955, for a resolution to cover possible American military activity around Formosa, Sam Rayburn, Speaker of the House and presumably an incarnation of the congressional prerogative, said, "If the President had done what is proposed here without consulting the Congress, he would have had no criticism from me." The Formosa Resolution at least contained language by which the President was "authorized to employ the Armed Forces," however lightly the executive regarded that language, but Congress loosened even that pretense of control by adding that he could use these forces "as he deems necessary" in the defense of Formosa and the Pescadores. When Eisenhower sought a Middle East Resolution in 1957, the Senate Foreign Relations Committee this time deleted the idea of congressional authorization. Senator Fulbright even expressed the fear that any resolution might limit the President's power as commander in chief to defend the "vital interests" of the nation.

And when Eisenhower, in what in retrospect seems a mysterious and, indeed, hazardous mission, sent 14,000 troops to Lebanon the next year, he cited as authority for this action, not at all his own resolution but the now capacious Presidential prerogative.

On the other hand, Eisenhower had acknowledged the practical importance of congressional support when, in 1954, he yielded to congressional (as well as British) opposition and declined to commit American force to the relief of Dien Bien Phu. At the same time, however, he reduced the significance of the troop-commitment issue by confiding an increasing share of American foreign operations to an agency presumed beyond the reach of Congress, the Central Intelligence Agency. In the Eisenhower years, the CIA became the primary instrument of American intervention overseas, helping to overthrow governments in Iran (1953) and Guatemala (1954), failing to do so in Indonesia (1958), helping to install governments in Egypt (1954) and Laos (1959), organizing an expedition of Cuban refugees against the Castro regime (1960). Congress had no oversight over the CIA. It even lacked regular means of finding out what it was up to. There was a joint congressional committee on atomic energy but none (none to this day) on secret intelligence operations.

The cold war created both a critical environment and an uncritical consensus; and these enabled even a relatively passive President, a "Whig" like Eisenhower, to enlarge the unilateral authority of the executive. Nor did either the President or the Congress see this as a question of usurpation. During the 1950's, and much of the 1960's, most of Congress, mesmerized by the supposed need for instant response to constant crisis, overawed by what the Senate Foreign Relations Committee later called the "cult of executive expertise," accepted the "high-flying" theories of the Presidential prerogative. In early 1960, Senator John F. Kennedy observed that, however large the congressional role in the formulation of domestic programs, "it is the President alone who must make the major decisions of our foreign policy." As late as 1961, Senator Fulbright contended that "for the existing requirements of American foreign policy we have hobbled the President by too niggardly a grant of power." While he found it "distasteful and dangerous to vest the executive with powers unchecked and unbalanced," the question, he concluded, was "whether we have any choice but to do so." Republicans were no less devoted to the crisis of executive supremacy. "It is a rather interesting thing," Senator Dirksen, then Republican leader, told the Senate in 1967, "—I have run down many legal cases before the Supreme Court—that I have found as yet no delimitation on the power of the Commander in Chief under the Constitution." "I am convinced," said Senator Goldwater, "there is no question that the President can take military action at any time he feels danger for the country or, stretching a point, for its position in the world."

In this state of political and intellectual intimidation, Congress forgot even the claim for consultation and was grateful when the executive bothered to say what it planned to do. ("The distinction between solicitation of advice in advance of a decision and the provision of information in the wake of a decision would seem to be a significant one," the Senate Foreign Relations Committee finally commented in 1969. Pointing out that, in the cases of the Cuban missile crisis and the Dominican intervention, congressional leaders were informed what was to be done only a few hours before the decisions were carried out, the Committee added dryly, "Such acts of courtesy are always to be welcomed; the Constitution, however, envisages something more.") In this mood, too, Congress acquiesced in national commitment through executive agreement—as, for example, in the case of Spain, where the original bases agreement of 1953 was steadily escalated by official pronouncement through the years until the Foreign Relations Committee could conclude, in 1969, that the sum of executive declarations was a virtual commitment on the part of the United States to come to the aid of Spain. Senator Fulbright recently remarked a little bitterly, "We get many treaties dealing with postal affairs and so on. Recently, we had an extraordinary treaty dealing with the protection of stolen art objects. These are treaties. But when we put troops and take on commitments in Spain, it is an executive agreement."

The case of Thailand is equally astonishing. In 1962, Secretary of State Rusk and the Thai Foreign Minister expressed, in a joint declaration, "the firm intention of the United States to aid

Thailand . . . in resisting Communist aggression and subversion." While this statement may have been no more than a specification of SEATO obligations, the executive branch thereafter secretly built and used bases and consolidated the Thai commitment in ways that would still be unknown to Congress and the electorate had it not been for the indomitable curiosity of Senator Symington and his Subcommittee on Security Arrangements and Commitments Abroad. The Subcommittee also uncovered interesting transactions involving the executive branch with Ethiopia (1960), Laos (1963), and South Korea (1966). The case of Israel is even more singular. Here a succession of executive declarations through five Administrations have produced a virtual commitment without the pretense of a treaty or even an executive agreement.

In this mood, also, Congress accepted the Americanization of the Vietnam war in 1965. "If this decision was not for Congress under the Constitution," Professor Bickel has well said, "then no decision of any consequence in matters of war and peace is left to Congress." As for the Tonkin Gulf Resolution, though President Johnson liked to flourish it as proof that Congress had indeed make a decision, he himself really did not think, as he later put it, that the "resolution was necessary to do what we did and what we're doing." As he unfolded his view of Presidential power in 1966: "There are many, many, who can recommend, advise and sometimes a few of them consent. But there is only one that has been chosen by the American people to decide."

Listing twenty-four statutes facilitating the fighting in Vietnam, Senator Goldwater said, in 1971, "Congress is and has been involved up to its ears with the war in Southeast Asia." The argument that Congress thereby "authorized" the war, especially by voting appropriations, has a certain practical strength up to the point as Judge Frank Coffin put it in a 1971 decision of the First Circuit Court) where Congress asserts a conflicting claim of authority, which it has not done. But, also as a practical matter, it is rare indeed for parliaments to deny supplies to fighting men, and too much cannot be inferred from the refusal to punish the troops for the sins of those who sent them into the line. It is true that members of the British Parliament voted against supply bills during the American Revolution, but this was before

104 *Arthur Schlesinger, Jr.*

the Reform Acts had created constituencies broad enough to include large numbers of relatives of men in combat. At the height of his opposition to the Mexican War, Congressman Lincoln said, "I have always intended, and still intend, to vote supplies." Still, though Congress has placed restrictions on troop deployment, it had not, by the middle of 1972, interposed a decisive obstacle to Presidential escalation of the war.

IX

If President Johnson construed the high prerogative more in the eighteenth-century style of the British King than of the executive envisaged by the Constitution, his successor carried the inflation of Presidential authority even further. In asserting that his power as the commander in chief authorized him to use American ground troops to invade Cambodia—and to do so without reference to, or even the knowledge of, Congress—President Nixon indulged in Presidential war-making beyond a point that even his boldest predecessors could have dreamed of. Those who had stretched the executive war power in the past had done so in the face of visible and dire threat to national survival: Lincoln confronted by rebellion, Roosevelt by the Third Reich. Each, moreover, had done what he felt he had to do without claiming constitutional sanction for every item of Presidential action.

But, in justifying the commitment of American troops to war in a remote and neutral country, Nixon cited no emergency that denied time for congressional action, expressed no doubt about the total legality of his own initiative, and showed no desire even for retroactive congressional ratification. All he was doing, he told the Senate Republican leader in June, 1970, was fulfilling the "Constitutional duty of the Commander in Chief to take actions necessary to protect the lives of United States forces." This was no more, he implied, than the routine employment of Presidential power; it required no special congressional assent, not even the fig-leaf, shortly repealed and abandoned, of the Tonkin Gulf Resolution. William Rehnquist of the Department of Justice, himself soon escalated by the President to the Supreme Court, called it a "valid exercise of his constitutional authority as Commander-in-Chief to secure the safety of American forces"—a proposition that might not have deeply moved the Nixon Administration had it been advanced by the Presidium to explain why the Red Army was justified in invading a neutral country to secure the safety of Russian forces. "The President's authority to do what he did, in my view," Rehnquist concluded, "must be conceded by even those who read Executive authority narrowly." It was, in fact, challenged by even those who read executive authority broadly.

The government thus committed armed forces to hostilities, first in Cambodia, then in Laos and North Vietnam (for the air force remains a part of the armed forces), on the basis of a theory of defensive war so elastic that a President could freely and on his own initiative order armed intervention in any country housing any troops that might in any conceivable circumstance be used in an attack on American troops. If this seemed an extraordinary invasion of the congressional war power, there seemed a comparable invasion of the appropriations power when Henry Kissinger informed Hanoi, in secret negotiation, that the United States "could give and undertake, a voluntary contribution by the President, that there would be a massive reconstruction program for all of Indochina, in which North Vietnam could share to the extent of several billion dollars."

Congress appeared increasingly impotent in the face of the size and momentum of the postwar institutions of American foreign policy—an institutional array spearheaded by an aggressive Presidency and supported by a military and intelligence establishment virtually beyond congressional reach. Indeed, large sections of the electorate were coming to feel that foreign policy had escaped from democratic control, and that the institutions would have their way however the voters might vote.

Excess, as usual, invites reaction; and the Senate, with due timidity, reacted. What Versailles had done to the congressional prerogative, Vietnam now did to the Presidential prerogative. But Congress did not react by frontal attack on the means by which the President continued the war, though various members of Congress urged this course on their colleagues. The Senate reacted rather by passing, in June, 1969, by 70 to 16, the

National Commitments Resolution, described by the Senate Foreign Relations Committee as an "invitation to the executive to reconsider its excesses, and to the legislature to reconsider its omissions in the making of foreign policy." Neither invitation was accepted.

The Senate also reacted, in April, 1972, by passing a War Powers bill, from the workings of which Vietnam was specifically exempted. This bill, conceived and bravely promoted by Senator Javits, has, from some views, substantial defects. Had it been on the statute books in past years, it would surely have prevented Roosevelt from responding to Hitler in the North Atlantic in 1941 and would surely not have prevented Johnson from escalating the war in Vietnam (for Johnson would have received—indeed, did receive—overwhelming congressional support for escalation at every point till the middle of 1968). If passed by the Congress, the bill might be more likely to become a means of inducing formal congressional approval of warlike Presidential acts than of preventing such acts. Moreover, the principle on which the bill is based—that the President must carry out the policy directives of Congress in the initiation and prosecution of military hostilities—might itself have bellicose consequences the next time War Hawks dominate the legislative branch. Still, the Senate's passage of the bill—especially by the impressive margin of 68 to 16—might have been expected to have some cautionary influence in reminding the President that Congress, in its pathetic way, thought it had some voice in the determination of peace and war. It had no such effect. A fortnight after its passage, President Nixon, again without reference to Congress, threw the American air force into devastating attacks on North Vietnam.

If there is an imbalance of powers, if Congress has lost authority clearly conferred on it by the Constitution, it can only be said that Congress has done little to correct the situation. Its complaints have been eloquent; its practical action has been slight. Its problem has been less lack of power than lack of will to use the powers it has—the power of appropriation; the power to regulate the size of the armed forces; the power, through joint resolutions, to shape foreign policy; the power to inform, investigate, and censure. As late as the summer of 1972, the Senate, in declining Senator Cooper's amendment to the aid bill, which proposed to cut off funds for American troops and bombing in four months, relinquished, in the words of the *Washington Post,* the "only opportunity it has ever dared afford itself to make an independent and conclusive judgment of the war."

In the present as in the past, Congress has preferred to renounce responsibility—which is why the Presidency has retained power. "We may say that power to legislate for emergencies belongs in the hands of Congress," said Justice Jackson in the Steel Seizure case, "but only Congress itself can prevent power from slipping through its fingers." The situation today, for all the wails of congressional self-pity, is much the one that Lincoln feared in 1848: "Allow the President to invade a neighboring nation [or, today, a nation on the other side of the world], whenever *he* shall deem it necessary to repel an invasion . . . and you allow him to make war at pleasure. Study to see if you can fix *any limit* to his power in this respect."

x

The Abraham Lincoln who had thus challenged the Presidential prerogative of Polk was the same Abraham Lincoln who, a dozen years later, gave the Presidency greater powers over war and peace than ever before, as the Andrew Jackson who showed such deference to Congress in the 1830's was the same Andrew Jackson who, a dozen years earlier, had charged without congressional authority into Spanish Florida. This is a critical point in understanding the nature of the issue. For nothing has been more characteristic of the perennial debate than the way in which the same people, in different circumstances and at different points in their lives, have argued both sides of the issue.

Richard M. Nixon had one set of views in 1951 on the question of whether Congress could control troop commitments and executive agreements. By 1971, he had an opposite set of views. Senator Fulbright, moving in the reverse direction, has long since repented his belief that the President needs more control over foreign policy. Professor Corwin's "high-flying prerogative men" of twenty years ago have zoomed downward on this question in recent times. Professor Commager has, in effect, accepted the Taft-Coudert case in his testimony in favor of the War Powers bill; and this writer, while remaining skeptical about the War Powers bill, would freely concede that Senator Taft had a much more substantial point than he supposed twenty years ago. But, to make that point, Senator Taft had to explain away the views of *his* father, the Chief Justice, who had written, in 1916, that the President as commander in chief "can order the Army and Navy anywhere he will, if the appropriations furnish the means of transportation." And, while the younger Senator Taft has followed his father rather than his grandfather, such heirs of Taft as Goldwater and Rehnquist are today very high-flying prerogative men. For that matter, Professor Corwin's own record was not all that immaculate. While he defended the congressional prerogative in 1951, in 1940 he had raised the question "whether the President may, without authorization by Congress, take measures which are technically acts of war in protection of American rights and interests abroad," and replied: "The answer returned both by practice and by judicial doctrine is yes." Even as late as 1949, Corwin described the power "to employ without congressional authorization the armed forces in protection of American rights and interests abroad wherever necessary" as "almost unchallenged from the first and occasionally sanctified judicially."

There are several reasons for this chronicle of vacillation. For one thing, the issues involved are ones of genuine intellectual difficulty, about which reasonable men may well find themselves changing their minds. For another, power usually looks more responsible from inside than from outside. For another, general questions often assume different shapes in different lights. It is agreeable to claim constitutionality for policies one supports and agreeable, too, to stigmatize policies one opposes as unconstitutional. All these reasons tend toward a single conclusion: that the problem we face is not primarily constitutional. It is primarily political. History offers the lawyer or scholar almost any precedent he needs to sustain what he may consider, in a concrete setting, to be wise policy. There is simply no absolute solution to the constitutional issue. This is no doubt why the Supreme Court has been so skittish about pronouncing on the problem. In our long and voluble judicial history, the decisions bearing even marginally on the question can be numbered on the fingers of one hand, and the illumination they provide is, at best, flickering if not dim.

If this is so, we must restrain our national propensity to cast political questions in constitutional terms. Just as in other years we went too far in devising theories of spacious Presidential power because we agreed with the way one set of Presidents wanted to use this power, now we are likely to go too far in limiting Presidential power because we disagree with the projects of another set of Presidents. We must take care not to convert a passing historical phase into ultimate constitutional truth. Professor Bickel has even suggested that "Congress should prescribe the mission of our troops in the field, in accordance with a foreign and war policy of the United States which it is for Congress to set when it chooses to do so. And Congress should equally review and settle upon an appropriate foreign policy elsewhere than in Vietnam, and reorder the deployment of our forces accordingly." There is no great gain in replacing high-flying Presidential men by high-flying congressional men, nor is James Buchanan necessarily the model President.

As the guerrilla war between the Presidency and the Congress for control over foreign policy has dragged along through our history, the issue is sometimes put as if one or the other were the safer depository of authority. Congressional judgment, Adolf Berle once argued, "tends to lag behind the facts in an international case to which the President must address himself. . . . Defense means seeing trouble in advance and moving to prevent it. The President's estimates of what will happen have usually been better than those of men who do not live with the problems." Senator Goldwater opposed the War Powers bill because, as he said, "I would put more faith in the judgment of the Office of President in the matter of warmaking at this time than I would of Congress." But Senator Fulbright, who in 1961 feared the "localism and parochialism" of Congress, now believes the "collective judgment of the Congress, with all its faults, could be superior to that of one man who makes the final decision, in the executive."

History does not support any general assignment of superior

virtue to either branch. In spite of Madison, the Congress is not always a force for restraint (as he himself discovered in 1812) nor the executive always a force for bellicosity. One need go back no further than the Cuban missile crisis to recall, as Robert Kennedy has told us, that the congressional leaders, including Senators Russell and Fulbright, "felt that the President should take more forceful action, a military attack or invasion, and that the blockade was far too weak a response." Those of us who hate the Indochina war may see more hope today in the Congress than in the Presidency; just as those who grew up in the days when Congress rejected Versailles and promulgated the neutrality acts saw more hope in the executive. But it would be folly to regard either Presidential or congressional wisdom as a permanent condition. Neither branch is infallible, and each needs the other— which is, I guess, the point the Founding Fathers were trying to make.

There is no worse fallacy than to build final answers on transient situations. The questions of the war power and the treaty power are, and must remain, political questions. This is not a zone of clear-cut constitutional prescription. It is rather what Justice Jackson, in his brilliant opinion in the Steel Seizure case, described as

> *a zone of twilight in which [the President] and Congress may have concurrent authority, or in which its distribution is uncertain. Therefore, congressional inertia, indifference or quiescence may sometimes, at least as a practical matter, enable, if not invite, measures on independent presidential responsibility. In this area, any actual test of power is likely to depend on the imperatives of events and contemporary imponderables rather than on abstract theroies of law.*

While the Constitution sets outer limits on both Presidential and congressional action, it leaves a wide area of "joint possession." Common sense, therefore, argues for congressional participation as well as for Presidential responsibility in the great decisions of peace and war.

To restore the constitutional balance, it is necessary in this period to rebuke Presidential pretensions, as it has been necessary in other periods to rebuke congressional pretensions. Perhaps Tocqueville was not so profound after all (for once) in his theory of the antagonism between democracy and foreign policy. Perhaps Bryce (for once) was more to the point when he argued that the broad masses are capable of assessing national interests and of sustaining consistent policies. So far as judging the ends of policy is concerned, Bryce said, "History shows that [the people] do this at least as wisely as monarchs or oligarchies, or the small groups to whom, in democratic countries, the conduct of foreign relations has been left, and that they have evinced more respect for moral principles."

We are still told about the supposed structural advantages of the executive as portrayed in the *Federalist*—unity, secrecy, superior sources of information, decision, dispatch. These advantages seem less impressive today than they must have been 180 years ago. Our sprawling executive branch is often disunited and is chronically incapable of secrecy. Its information is no longer manifestly superior and is often manifestly defective. The need for decision and dispatch has been greatly exaggerated; apart from Korea and the Cuban missile crisis, no postwar emergency has demanded instant response. Moreover, there was far more reason for unilateral executive action in times when difficulties of transport and communication could delay the convening of Congress for weeks than there is in our age of the telephone and the jet aircraft. What remains to the President is his command of the institutions of war and his undeniable ability to create situations that will make it hard for Congress to reject his request. Here, it might be well to recall the warning of the *Federalist:* "How easy would it be to fabricate pretences of approaching danger."

But, in demythologizing the Presidency, we must take care not to remythologize the Congress. If it is extreme to say that the President can send troops anywhere he pleases without congressional authorization, it is equally extreme to say he cannot do so short of war without congressional authorization (even Senator Taft proposed no limitations on Presidential deployment of the navy and air force). In this area, John Norton Moore and

Quincy Wright have proposed a test worth careful consideration: that the President must obtain prior congressional authorization in all cases where regular combat units are committed to
what may be sustained hostilities, or where military intervention
will require congressional action, as by appropriations, before
it is completed. This would leave the President with independent authority to deploy forces short of war (and, of course, to
repel attack), while it would assure congressional authority to
limit or prohibit Presidential commitment when war impends.
But this provision, however attractive, would not have stopped
escalation in Vietnam, where President Johnson would have had
no difficulty in getting the necessary authorization. The War
Powers bill, though excessively rigid in its definition of situations
where the President is authorized to act and unconvincing in its
reliance on a thirty-day deadline, contains valuable provisions
for Presidential reporting to the Congress once hostilities begin.
Congressman Jonathan Bingham has proposed a simpler approach, which would avoid the rigidities of the War Powers bill
but retain its affirmation of congressional control of undeclared
hostilities. Citing the Executive Reorganization Act as a precedent, he would give either house of Congress power to terminate
such hostilities by resolution. Some declaration of congressional
power in this area would serve as a useful check on Presidents.

As for the treaty power, Senator Case's efforts to bring executive agreements within congressional purview and to induce the
executive to submit major agreements in the form of treaties are
long overdue. But the notion that executive agreements must be
rigorously confined to minor matters, and that all important international undertakings must be subject to senatorial veto,
would bring us back to the frustrations of Olney and Hay. Does
anyone seriously suggest that every time a President meets another chief of state their understandings can be extinguished by
one-third of the Senate? Would even high-flying congressional
men contend that the Monroe Doctrine, the Emancipation Proclamation, the Fourteen Points, and the Atlantic Charter were
cases of Presidential usurpation? And in the period ahead, with
the bipolar simplicities of the cold war giving way to the shifting complexities of a multipolar world, the executive simply
cannot operate just on the leading strings of Congress. There has

to be a middle ground between making the American President a czar and making him a puppet.

Senator Fulbright once distinguished between two kinds of power involved in the shaping of foreign policy—that pertaining to its direction, purpose, and philosophy; and that pertaining to the day-to-day conduct of foreign affairs. The former, he suggested, belonged peculiarly to Congress, the latter to the executive. The trouble was that Congress was reversing the order of responsibility. "We have tended to snoop and pry in matters of detail, interfering in the handling of specific problems in specific places which we happen to chance upon. . . . At the same time we have resigned from our responsibility in the shaping of policy and the defining of its purposes, giving away things that are not ours to give: the war power of the Congress, the treaty power of the Senate and the broader advice and consent power." Perhaps it would be well to recall the hope expressed by Senator Vandenberg in 1948 that the habit of senatorial intervention in foreign affairs would not become "too contagious because . . . only in those instances in which the Senate can be sure of a complete command of all the essential information prerequisite to an intelligent decision should it take the terrific chance of muddying the international waters by some sort of premature and ill-advised expression of its advice to the Executive."

XI

Vandenberg was everlastingly right in his emphasis on information; for a flow of information to Congress is indispensable to a wise use of both the war and the treaty powers. And in no regard has Congress, until very recently, been more negligent than in acquiescing in executive denial of information. As Woodrow Wilson said long ago,

> *Unless Congress have and use every means of acquainting itself with the acts and the disposition of the administrative agents of the government, the country must be helpless to learn how it is being served; and unless Congress both scrutinize these things and sift them by every form of discussion, the country must remain in embarrassing, crippling*

ignorance of the very affairs which it is most important that it should understand and direct.

In Wilson's judgment, "The informing function of Congress should be preferred even to its legislative function." The executive has devised no more effective obstacle to the democratic control of foreign policy than the secrecy system that has grown to such appalling proportions since World War II.

It is time for Congress to reject the "if you only knew what we knew" pose by which the executive deepens the congressional inferiority complex. Members of Congress, at least those who read the *New York Times,* know more than they think and, in general, would not receive blinding illumination if they read Top Secret documents, too. While the executive, through its diplomatic, military, and intelligence operatives, has an abundance of short-run information not easily available to Congress, experience shows that this information is seldom essential to long-run judgments. Nor is executive information all that infallible; one has only to recall the theory prevailing in the executive bureaucracy a few years back that Hanoi and the Vietcong were the spearhead of a system of Chinese expansion in Southeast Asia. If the executive "had been subjected more quickly and more closely to the scrutiny of informed public and congressional opinion," Senator McGovern has said, ". . . it may not have fallen prey to its own delusions and fantasies."

And, as former government officials readily concede, there is no reason, in most cases, why Congress should be denied classified information. Thus George Ball: "I think there is very little information that Congress should ever be denied"; McGeorge Bundy: "I do not believe most of what is highly classified . . . should be kept from responsible members of the Congress at all. Indeed I believe the opposite." Nor should members of Congress be denied the opportunity to interrogate public officials presently shielded from them by the promiscuous invocation of executive privilege. Ball, calling executive privilege a "myth, for I find no constitutional basis for it," contends it should be invoked only when the President makes the decision himself and communicates that decision to Congress. George Reedy would even take the position "that the President has no executive privilege whatever in any public question." This is going a little far. The executive branch must retain the capacity to protect its internal processes of decision, and the President must, on occasion, assert a power to resist the disclosure of information against what he seriously believes to be the public interest. But Senator Fulbright's bill to restrain the flagrant abuse of executive privilege surely deserves enactment.

If Congress really wants to reclaim lost authority, it can do little more effective than to assure itself a steady and disinterested flow of information about foreign affairs. More than ever, information is the key to power. That is why the MacArthur hearings were so valuable in 1951; why the hearings conducted in recent years by the Senate Foreign Relations Committee under Senator Fulbright's leadership have done more to turn opinion against the Vietnam war than other, more tangible weapons in the congressional arsenal. Perhaps the flow of information could be usefully institutionalized—as in Benjamin V. Cohen's proposal for the establishment by Congress of a commission of eight: two from the House, two from the Senate, four from the executive branch, empowered to exchange information and views on critical questions of foreign affairs.

XII

Structural change can effect only limited improvements. The greater hope, perhaps, lies in increasing sensitivity to the problem of "joint possession" of constitutional powers. Greater awareness of the problem, to which so many for so long were oblivious, has recently led serious men into serious consideration of the issues of constitutional balance. In the future, such awareness may both restrain conscientious Presidents and reinvigorate responsible Congresses.

Nor can structural change save us from the exasperations of choice. We must recognize both that our government must operate within constitutional bounds and that, within this spacious area, questions involved in the control of foreign policy are political rather than constitutional. If we do this, we will perhaps stop turning passing necessities, or supposed necessities, into constitutional absolutes. For a self-styled strict constructionist, President Nixon has gone very far, indeed, in anointing manifest excesses with the lotion of constitutional sanctity.

In this regard, he compares unfavorably with such Presidents as Jefferson, Lincoln, and Franklin Roosevelt. Faced with infinitely more genuine emergencies, they had considerably more excuse for expansion of the Presidential prerogative. But they did not claim that they were doing nothing more than applying routine Presidential authority. Lincoln, particularly, in his troubled justification for the suspension of habeas corpus, said, "Would not the official oath be broken if the government should be overthrown, when it was believed that disregarding the single law would tend to preserve it?" Jefferson put the case more generally:

> *To lose our country by a scrupulous adherence to written law, would be to lose the law itself, with life, liberty, property and all those who are enjoying them with us; thus absurdly sacrificing the end to the means. . . . The line of discrimination between cases may be difficult; but the good officer is bound to draw it at his own peril, and throw himself on the justice of his country and the rectitude of his motives.*

A conscientious President must distinguish between the exception and the rule. Emergency may compel him to abandon the rule in favor of the exception; but he must not pretend—as Jefferson, Lincoln, and Roosevelt declined to pretend and as Johnson and Nixon have pretended—that the exception *is* the rule. Rather, like Lincoln in 1860, the executive may, at his own peril, undertake measures about whose strict legality he may be in doubt, and do so not under an illusion of constitutional righteousness but in terms of a popular demand and a public necessity. In the end, he must rest such acts on the assent of Congress, the justice of his country, and the rectitude of his motives. Only Presidents who distinguish emergency from normality can both meet emergency and preserve the constitutional order. As Justice Jackson said in the Korematsu case, "The chief restraint upon those who command the physical forces of the country, in the future as in the past, must be their responsibility to the political judgments of their contemporaries and to the moral judgments of history."

III

The Presidential Condition

7

On the Isolation of Presidents

George E. Reedy

Throughout most of our history, the Presidency has served satisfactorily as the major unifying force in our national life. The possibility which I, personally, regard as a certainty that it is rapidly losing its capacity to sustain and foster a democratic consensus raises some disturbing questions. This development is so recent that, for the time being, discussions of practical solutions must, of necessity, be largely speculative. The purpose of this essay is to suggest some tentative steps for immediate consideration and to propose some objectives for scholarly inquiry.

THE PROBLEM

In order to keep the discussion within manageable bounds, it is essential to restate my thesis on the isolation of the Presidency. This development rests upon factors that were built into the office by the Constitution, but which did not assume their present serious proportions until the advent of a truly mass society, with its overriding requirement for a decision center that can react quickly to emergencies containing the possibility of catastrophe. In a simpler age, the aloofness of the chief executive was probably a positive virtue. It served as an offset to the intransigent sectional passions that, in the highly individualistic atmosphere that persisted even after the closing of the frontier, were quite capable of tearing the nation to pieces, unless checked. Furthermore, until quite recently, the isolation of the office from popular pressures was not truly langerous. The United States could survive four—or even eight—years of bad leadership; the President did not have at his command instruments of social control that would make possible the institution of genuine dictatorship; and the time interval between a decision and the effectuation of a decision was sufficiently great to permit the operation of the checks and balances built into our system.

The social and economic interdependence that characterizes modern life has changed the factors upon which the conclusions in the previous paragraph are based. The exact point at which the change took place cannot be stated with any degree of certainty. But it is useful to consider, as an important milestone, the advent of the New Deal, with its successful assertion of the principle that it is legitimate to use federal power as an engineering instrument to enhance the public welfare. That principle is now accepted by all except the extreme right or the extreme left, and any argument over it is moot, even though it has become apparent that the "public welfare" is rather difficult to define. Nevertheless, the practice of the concept involves consequences with which we must deal, and they have not been considered sufficiently.

The first consequence is that enhancing the public welfare necessarily requires the surrender of a degree of individuality and an increasing degree of interdependence. It also means a higher degree of social vulnerability to individual action and, consequently, a sharper reaction from more stable elements in society to nonconformists who threaten, or appear to threaten, economic and social stability. This has brought about a type of polarization we have not had before. On the one hand, young people who have no memories of the economic horrors of the Depression and minorities who have not shared in the economic gains of the past forty years find the conformity that goes with interdependence to be oppressive. On the other hand, those who have participated in the advance regard dissidence as the opening wedge for a return to the dark days of economic in-security. Under these circumstances, the problem of sustaining national unity takes on new dimensions. It is not resolved merely by maintaining national symbols. Instead, a very subtle form of political brokerage—the art by which leaders assure highly diverse elements in the population that they are getting a fair hearing—is needed. It is an art that can be practiced successfully only by sensitive politicians.

In the second place, social engineering requires social controls and the application of mass information techniques that tend to treat people as roughly comparable units rather than indi-vidual human beings. Even so humane an act as the establish-ment of a social security system calls for the registration of citizens in the mass. Furthermore, the conscious change of institu-tions necessitates the use of forms of coercion ranging all the way from incentives to outright policing. The necessity for such devices increases directly with the degree of interdependence in a society, and it is rather obvious that we can look forward to an era of ever increasing controls unless we fall into social disintegration. In addition to these factors, the international tensions of the past twenty-five years have brought about the maintainance of permanent military forces so large and so well organized that the concept of an armed citizenry capable of resisting an oppressive government is obsolete. Thus, we have a situation in which previously unforeseen instruments of power have been placed in the hands of a chief executive at the same time that events are forcing him to make basic decisions with less time for reflection and under circumstances that force him to focus his attention up on masses of statistics rather than indi-vidual human beings.

In the third place, the checks-and-balances system, although it still exists, has been vitiated to a large degree. This is largely a function of the necessity for quick reaction time—a necessity that enhances the power of the initiative inherent in the Presidency and permits the chief executive to commit irrevocable acts before his decision processes can be subjected to outside scrutiny. At all times, he has sufficient money available to carry out military operations to a point where competing branches of government must rally to his support. Legal interpretations of the interstate commerce and public welfare clauses of the Constitution have become sufficiently broad that he can exercise federal police powers even to the extent of coercing industry into observing his pricing policies in fields where no specific law governs. Nearly four decades of experience have produced a rough form of parallelism between the executive and the judiciary, and court decisions in modern times are more likely to sustain than overturn national policy. The ultimate power of impeachment is far too clumsy and far too divisive in and of itself to be used except in extreme circumstances, where the nation is probably lost anyway. None of this is to argue that Presidential powers have been abused or that, in a world where reaction time to an atomic attack is about 15 minutes, grants of considerable power are unnecessary. To the contrary, it appears to me that recent Presidents have exercised their authority with remarkable restraint, so far as repression of dissent is concerned. The more compelling question is what has happened to the environment in which the executive lives and works, and how this environment affects his judgment.

Past studies of the Presidency have focused generally on the question of what the man has done to, or with, the job. The point raised here is the direct opposite—what the job does to the man and the consequences for our society. There is a personal quality to political leadership that ultimately overrides all other considerations, and, whatever may be the components that enter into a man's individual psychology, his relationship to other human beings is a determining factor in what he will do. In this respect, the basic factor in the President's position is that he can shape his immediate environment to his liking to a degree denied to any other citizen of the United States. His immediate environment is the executive branch of the government, with over 2.5 million civilian employees and a like number of men and women in uniform, and annual budgets inching up toward $300 billion despite stern efforts to hold them down.

Naturally, there are limitations to his power, and there would be limitations even should the President bring the nation into what is generally described as an absolute dictatorship. But, with the passage of time, these limitations appear more and more as frustrations rather than vector forces that must be taken into account in resolving political problems. The congressional power has been reduced to that of harassment exercised only when the legislators sense executive weakness, and, even so, it has been demonstrated that the President need not sustain legislative majorities in order to rule. Components of the executive branch can sabotage his programs, and individual Presidents have complained about their inability to "get things done." But, in practice, the sabotage can exist only as long as the President ignores it. Anything to which he gives his personal attention will be done. And, while popular approval can destroy his effectiveness as a national leader, it cannot dislodge him from office and substitute someone else until his term has been concluded.

These circumstances surround a man with an atmosphere of adulation, composed of both sycophancy and genuine respect for the office, which can find parallels only in divine-right monarchies. This is not a trivial matter. Every man has a tendency to interpret the universe in terms of his immediate environment, and everything surrounding a President is designed to please him. Personal, adversary relationships in which he must come to terms with others on a day-to-day basis are absent, and virtually all the information he receives is presented by people who desire to retain his favor. This is a situation that has two deleterious effects. First, the information that reaches the White House has gone through a filtering process that may not alter facts (although even this is possible), but which has stripped those facts of the unpleasant nuances and the controversial passions that are essential to valid political judgments. Second, the atmosphere of the White House itself is one that tends to dull the sensitivities of the politician to the emotions of other people. These are both situations that tend to isolate a man from the realities of democratic politics, which basically consist of resolving differences between contentious people and persuading them to work together, in some kind of harmony, toward national goals.

Isolation from reality is inseparable from the exercise of power. It is inherent in the positions of industrial leaders, labor leaders, intellectual leaders, or any persons who can bid others to do their will. But there is always a question of degree. Only the President achieves an ultimate of power in our society (or at least an approximation to an ultimate). All other leaders have peers who can speak to them on a one-to-one basis without any sense of awe or subordination. This is the one office that has been almost totally isolated from the necessity most human beings face of accommodating themselves to the desires of others.

This does not mean that a President is shielded completely from unpleasant comment or attack. Senators and representatives can make blistering speeches from the floors of their respective chambers. Unfortunately, these rarely coincide with the tone of what they say within the executive mansion, and thus the chief executive is frequently left with the impression that he is the victim of duplicity. Newspaper editorials and television commentaries can be bitter. But these enter the White House as mechanical contrivances, which can be cut off, and there is a very human tendency to ascribe such criticism to a conspiracy rather than to genuine feeling. The ultimate cushioning, however, is the realization that the Presidency is the summit of political ambition, and that there is nowhere else to go. Under such circumstances, a man who does not expect to serve in public office again can easily persuade himself that he will be vindicated by the verdict of history, and that his detractors will look very small in the long view.

It is too much to expect a man to make sensitive judgments on the enduring will and tolerance levels of the people whom he has been commissioned to lead under such circumstances. He has available to him the methods of modern, scientific polling, which have been brought to a relatively high degree of accuracy. But, at best, they reflect only a crude majority, which can be broken up very easily, and, in addition, they reflect only *where* that majority stands—not *why* it stands, and what must be done to lead people instead of just going along with them. Government by poll can be a stagnant proposition, indeed.

The effects of this situation on our national life are readily apparent. Without entering into an argument on the substantive merits of Southeast Asian policy, it is quite clear that overoptimistic reports on the balance of forces in Vietnam and over-optimistic assessments of the reaction of the American people to the war led us into a bitter divisiveness with few precedents in our history. And it is equally clear that the Nixon Administration failed totally to open up some channels of communication with dissident elements in our population that may be in a minority, but which are quite capable of tearing our nation apart or—more likely—provoking repression that can put an end to democracy.

It is quite apparent that we have neither the programs nor the resources (or, at least, the will to dedicate the resources) for the early resolution of the substantive problems that have brought about our current turmoil. We need time—considerable time—to make a real dent in urban decay, economic opportunity, and the deep disaffection of the student population. In some instances, we need considerable time just to gain some understanding of the components of the problem. But time is one commodity that is in short supply. The words "now" and "nonnegotiable demand" are becoming increasingly popular even in instances where they are arrant nonsense. And it is unlikely that the so-called silent majority will permit this situation to continue.

Too many elements in our population are unwilling to concede the need for time, because the people involved have lost confidence in our national leadership. This is an inevitable result of Administrations that seek either to ride roughshod over popular feeling or to confine their expressions to voicing the will of the majority. The fine art of political brokerage at the highest level appears to be fading, and people will not grant time to a system that they feel is closed to them. As the Presidency grows remote, the system takes on more and more a "closed" appearance. Probably the fundamental problem of the present day is to restore that confidence, and this is not an easy matter.

POSSIBLE COURSES

For the immediate present, the only corrective factor of significance is widespread awareness of the problem. This is a difficult concept to accept in an age of change, where we have been conditioned to embrace sweeping solutions. Nor should it be accepted without immediate steps to work out long-range plans that ultimately will supply us with some reasonably satisfactory answers.

It is quite unrealistic, however, to look for drastic change, such as a basic rewriting of our Constitution in the foreseeable future. A lengthy period of education is essential to acquaint the American people with the fundamental issues. Although the remoteness of Washington from the "grass roots" has become something of a byword, it is doubtful whether very many Americans understand the specific causes. After living with the Presidency for 180 years, it is difficult to conceive of alternative forms of government. And it is dangerous to attempt fundamental revision without a popular base of support and comprehension.

Furthermore, the preconditions for sweeping change do not exist. Historically, basic charters of government have been drafted only in the wake of revolution (as in the United States and the Soviet Union), national catastrophe (as in Louis Napoleon's France or Kaiser Wilhelm's Germany), or release from colonial status (as in India or Ghana). Despite the very evident disintegration in our national unity, we do not qualify under any of these categories; nor is there any deep-seated desire to become qualified.

The odds against rewriting our Constitution, however, do not preclude the possibility of some important changes that, over a period of time, could become fundamental. The principle is simply to determine goals, identify existing trends that can evolve toward those goals, and then seek, by pragmatic means, to accelerate those trends as rapidly as possible. At the time I finished my book *The Twilight of the Presidency*, I had just about reached the conclusion that the American system had lost its flexibility, and such a process would not work. Events since then have led me to conclude that my pessimism was unjustified, and that there is still room for maneuver within the existing framework.

In this respect, the evolution of the British Government from an absolute monarchy to a modern democracy provides some instructive examples. I would not suggest an effort on our part to duplicate the British structure, as I would consider any such proposal to be idle. I am interested, however, in the method by which the shift was made without any "grand design" and largely by allowing normal political forces to have free play. The transition took place over a period of several centuries, thus permitting us to look with a reasonable degree of confidence at what happened.

There were many factors, but it seems reasonable to conclude that the development of British democracy centered around the struggle between the King and Parliament for control of the ministers who operated the government. It was not a simple, straight-line progression. The tide shifted back and forth between the contestants, and a series of balances were struck, each one of which probably seemed permanent to the politicians of the time, but which was eventually succeeded by another. Despite the zigzags, the over-all picture began with Kings who had full political power and called Parliament into session at their own convenience and evolved into Parliaments with full political power who regarded Kings as the symbol of continuity and legitimacy.

Throughout the eight centuries that this process took place, the major parliamentary weapon was control over the Kingdom's finances—not through any specific grant of authority, but because the Commons represented the wealth-producing classes. The men who framed the American Constitution took note of this factor and wrote the "power of the purse" principle into the Constitution as the principal legislative check against abuse of executive authority. They devised other curbs as well. In addition, however, they separated the legislative and executive functions and thus set limits on the type of struggle that was taking place in Great Britain, and which, at that time, had not swung decisively to the parliamentary side.

It was a wise decision, in my judgment. I have not had the opportunity to study the conditions under which it was made, and I would not presume to speak authoritatively on the reasoning that went into it. But I have had an opportunity to observe the workings of the modern American Government as an active participant in both the legislative and the executive branches. The British system, as it has been described to me, would weaken our executive leadership below the point of effectiveness. I suspect that it works in England only because of a type of party discipline that is inconceivable in our Senate House of Representatives.

But we need not question the wisdom of the basic separation in order to conclude that the balance of power has swung too heavily toward the executive branch. The legislative curbs are exercised today only in instances where a President's position has so deteriorated that he can be defied with impunity (as was Lyndon Johnson in his last year in office), or where a President has exercised exceedingly poor political judgment (as in the instance of the Haynesworth and Carswell nominations by Richard Nixon). There is a personal quality to both situations that makes it difficult to regard them as assertions of congressional prestige. They do not compel the *office* of the Presidency to give the kind of continuing consideration to the legislative branch that I believe is needed.

That Congress is in a mood for vigorous assertion of legislative prestige is apparent from recent foreign-policy and defense debates. The basic weakness of various amendments offered thus far, which would limit the President's war powers, is that they bring Congress dangerously close to an exercise of what should be executive authority over the deployment of military forces. Congress is not equipped to exercise such authority, and the political sense of most of the members warns them that an effort to do so is dangerous to their fortunes. It would afford the President an excellent vehicle for shifting the blame for foreign-policy failures to the legislative branch of the government—and it is unrealistic to assume that the vehicle would be unused or ineffective.

A more promising avenue for channeling legislative unrest into constructive action lies in the power of Congress to demand information as a basis for legislative action. This approach has been tried in the past and abandoned on the plea that it would "hamstring" executive authority, and because legislative committee chairmen believed it would infringe upon power they already had. But it is quite possible that the present mood of the nation and the present mood of Congress itself make this a possibility worth exploring.

At present, the congressional authority to demand information is exercised through standing committees, which have specific legislative functions. In theory, both the Appropriations Committee and the Government Operations Committee are "catchalls." But, in practice, the first divides itself into rigid subcommittees, and the latter is concerned with malfeasance, misfeasance, and nonfeasance. There is no overview of governmental policies, except on an occasional, *ad hoc* basis, when two groups meet jointly, or in the field of economics.

The need for an overview is particularly glaring in the field of foreign policy. In the modern world, our relations with other nations involve every aspect of organized human activity—diplomacy, military force, economic power, human resources, natural resources, law, and even the postal service. The President can —and does—take all these categories into account upon arriving at decisions. But congressional reaction to such decisions assumes that they can be broken down into components that can be considered in isolation from each other. This is the reason that public hearings before the foreign relations committees of either house are shot through with a tone of unreality. The members of the committee have neither the mandate nor the expertise to delve into all relevant factors and are therefore at a disadvantage vis-à-vis the representatives of the executive branch.

This may well be a propitious time to propose the creation of an over-all congressional committee, with members drawn from all the standing committees of the Congress, and with full power to require regular reports on the international situation and on the executive branch's plans to cope with it. Such a group would not—and should not—be granted legislative authority. But its access to information should be limited only by practical considerations of time and manageability, as will be outlined subsequently. There should be no limitations based upon security considerations.

The major value of this proposal is that it would compel the

President to consider the problems of doing a "selling job" on Congress in advance of major moves. This is a reasonably close approximation of political justification to the American people —theoretically a cornerstone of democracy. He would be confronted with political consequences *in advance* of action, and, although he could still go ahead, he would have ample warning of the repercussions.

This is a somewhat more potent instrument than it may appear upon first examination. Presidents are usually political creatures whose senses have been dulled by an environment that permits apocalyptic descisions to be carried out before they have encountered the opposition of other strong-minded men. An advance discussion of such events as the Bay of Pigs, the escalation in Vietnam, or the invasion of Cambodia might have been the needed "shock therapy" that would have averted the type of disunity we have in our nation today.

Obviously, there will always be situations in which no advance consultation is possible. If the official explanations can be taken at their face value (and, within limits, I believe they can), the sending of troops to the Dominican Republic and the retaliatory bombing of oil storage in North Vietnam were in that category. But such instances are relatively rare and can easily be exempted from any special reporting requirements. The major policy moves that have thrown this nation into turmoil were all subject to months of preliminary planning.

The proposal would, of course, encounter strong opposition. It would be argued that the President would be circumscribed in his ability to lay careful plans that could be unveiled at the last minute to the "confusion" of the "enemies" of the United States. There would be repetitions of the assertion that diplomacy could not be practiced in a "goldfish bowl," and that it would hand an incalculable advantage to Communism, with its capacity to observe the utmost in secrecy. Such arguments do not bother me. In light of the history of the Bay of Pigs, the Vietnam escalation, and the Cambodian invasion, I am not very impressed. The most easily observable fact about "secret diplomacy" is that it has not worked very well.

Naturally, this would mean a considerable amount of turmoil

in Congress. Even though the committee were to observe a high degree of circumspection in handling the information it had received, the "word" would spread rapidly. This would have an inhibiting effect on executive action—which is precisely what I conceive to be the objective. The President could not avoid giving due consideration to the human resources he must mobilize in order to lead the nation to effective goals. And this is far more important in determining national policy than his capacity to spring "surprises" upon an assumed adversary.

Basically, however, I believe that this is a step that, at this time, is feasible. It would involve issues that are comprehensible to the American people as a whole, and which could be debated upon their merits. An atmosphere has been created in which there is a healthy skepticism of leaving decisions to men who have more information than is presumably available to the public. Finally, it would institutionalize congressional investigating authority, so that it would continue after temporary, exacerbating situations had vanished. The President could never relieve himself of the feeling that he is accountable to someone else.

In this essay, I am attempting to give no details of the mandate for the committee. This requires more study. Legal experts would have to determine how far the charter could be extended without running afoul of the Constitution. Safeguards would have to be written in to insure that the group were not smothered in meaningless information about inconsequential activities. These are all solvable problems, but they can be solved only with the application of expert knowledge. At the moment, I am interested only in a principle—that there be an institutionalized recognition of the right of Congress to be informed, in advance, of executive moves that might alter the balance of world power and the consensus within our country.

In view of the magnitude of the problem, this might seem too modest a proposal. It is not for anyone who believes that the development of government is an evolutionary process, in which there are no final developments short of a complete collapse. The executive has been encroaching on the legislative by a series of steps no one of which can be resisted *per se*. It is time for the legislative to reverse the process and start nibbling away at executive authority. This suggestion could be the first nibble.

8

Public Opinion and the President

John E. Mueller

Writers on the Presidency usually include, somewhere in their catalogues of powers, checks, balances, influences, and hats, the relation of the President to public opinion. It has some power over him, they are quite sure, and he some power over it, but the mechanism of the relationship is usually seen to be amorphous and its workings mysterious.

The purpose of this essay is not so much to render the mysterious intelligible, a vulgar and unsportsmanlike activity even if it were possible, but, rather, to dissect the relationship to examine some of its component parts. Specifically, through the use of data from public-opinion polls, efforts will be made to separate out and label the sorts of people who, for varying reasons, are inclined to support the President on an issue. Some suggestions about how they got there and how long they are likely to last will also be made. Since most of my research in this area has been concerned with popular attitudes toward Presidential policies in the wars in Korea and Vietnam, most of the examples will come from this background. But it is hoped that the points made will be more broadly relevant to Presidential power.

Because of the way polls are usually constructed (it has no

doubt been noted somewhere that they are imperfect instruments), much of this analysis will sort the population into a series of fairly standard social and economic categories (social class, income, sex, race, party, et cetera) to see how these relate to support for Presidential policies. Often, however, efforts will be made to suggest popular inclinations of a more psychological nature, for which the standard categories can sometimes be taken to be cloudy but fairly sincere reflections.

It would probably be wise to stress that it is the opinions of the general public that are being discussed in this paper, not those of the large, articulate elite, whose vocal protests and clamor are often taken by politicians to be the functional equivalent of public opinion. For many purposes, the politicians may be wise to make this substitution, for the attitudes of this elite can be more significant politically than those of the masses. But that is a different matter.

PARTISANS

It will come as no great news that, no matter what the subject of the policy—war, peace, welfare, education, crime, nudity, drugs, inflation—the President can count on a fair amount of support from people who identify with his own party, as well as a fair amount of opposition from those who identify with the other party. Those who call themselves independents almost invariably fit neatly between. In terms simply of his own popularity, for example, the President has been approved, on the average, by 75 per cent of friendly partisans and only by 39 per cent of unfriendly ones, while independents approve at an average rate of about 55 per cent. Partisans of all shades will tend to rally to his support whenever there is an international crisis of reasonable magnitude, but the good will of unfriendly partisans, in these cases, fades about 50 per cent faster than that of supporters of the President's party and about 30 per cent faster than that of independents.

What happens is that many people use their party identification as a short-cut method for arriving at a position on an issue. Rather than sort through the intricacies of argument on the issue, they prefer to take as cue the word of the leadership of their party—a process that, for many, is quite sensible.

Party polarization on an issue, therefore, depends on the degree to which the positions of the leaders of the parties differ. Where there is little visible difference, little partisan cleavage will be noted in the population. Where the President has a policy and the opposition is unclear in its position, there will be moderate polarization as Presidential partisans are attracted disproportionately to support him on the issue. Where leadership divergence is clear, polarization in popular opinion will be quite intense.

Examples can be gathered from poll questions on policy during the Korean war. When the public was asked its preferences for hypothetical war policies of an escalatory or de-escalatory nature on which the parties did not differ, little differences among the party partisans were found. When the question involved approval of a particular Presidential policy—again, whether of an escalatory or de-escalatory nature—on which the Republicans had not taken a clearly different position, Democrats were found to be notably more approving than Republicans. And when the parties clearly differed on the issue, as when President Truman decided to fire General MacArthur, partisan polarization was quite pronounced.

Curiously, partisan polarization is likely to be more intense among well-informed people than among poorly informed ones. This seems to be partly due to the fact that the well informed are more likely to know what their party's position is on an issue. Thus, the well informed seem to be quite willing to take party cues as a short-cut to policy thinking, and they seem generally to prefer this method of thinking to the application of personal, ideological perspectives. It is usually easier to predict a well-informed person's position on a question of war policy by assuming he will adopt his party's position as his own than it is by assuming he will apply his own predilections toward, say, isolationism or internationalism or toward war or peace.

It is often possible to see the importance of information and party referents in a simpler way—by artificially informing the respondent about the position of the leadership and seeing how this alters response patterns. One then finds opinion on "policy

X" to be barely polarized, opinion on the "President's policy X" to be quite polarized. As can be seen, the ability of the poll question writer to manipulate in order to generate interesting newspaper copy is considerable.

If conditions change, polarity can be reversed as readily in politics as in physics. This seems to have happened with the Vietnam issue. During the Johnson Administration, Democrats were persistently more inclined to deny that "we" made a mistake in getting into the fighting there. By October, 1969, however, Republicans had become more supportive of the war than Democrats on this measure. In a fairly important sense, then, by the time the new Administration was a year old, Johnson's war had begun to become Nixon's war. Part of this change was due, of course, to the increasingly single-minded opposition to the war from prominent Democratic spokesmen, including some who had been active in the Johnson Administration.

One final item is worthy of note in this connection. Perhaps as a way to rationalize their policy position, supporters of the President's own party are more likely to anticipate that his programs will be successful than adherents of the opposition. Thus, during the Truman and Johnson Administrations, Democrats were less likely than Republicans to be pessimistic about the progress being made in the wars and in the peace talks. This is also a topic on which polarities can be reversed: Of the partisan groups, Republicans were more pessimistic that the war in Vietnam would be ended in 1967, but Democrats were more pessimistic that it would end in 1969.

BELIEVERS

Regardless of the position of party leadership, there are cases in which cues found in the issue itself will suggest most adequately a group's response.

The most obvious case is that of ideology. Some people do have a fairly well-worked-out perspective on political choices and can be expected to opt for, say, the liberal or conservative position on any given issue. If the President is pursuing a course of action in harmony with their ideological perspective, they will support him; if not, they will oppose him on the issue.

Although a great deal of philosophical speculation about ideological perspectives has been generated, it is important to note that most empirical analysis of public response finds that, even under quite generous definitions, ideologues constitute only a very small minority of the population. In fact, on a large number of seemingly important political issues, many people appear to have no meaningful opinion whatever. This is seen in various ways in the polls. The most straightforward is to ask the respondent, in a nonpatronizing way, whether he happens to have an opinion on the issue; often, many will volunteer that they don't. Another is to ask the respondent the same question on successive interviews and to tally the many who are inconsistent. One can also ask questions on a single survey that are logically related and assess the degree of illogic in the population.

And it is also possible to ask comparable populations the same question worded in slightly different ways, to see how easily manipulable opinion on the issue is; it was once learned that 46 per cent of the American public thought the United States should "forbid" public speeches against democracy, while fully 62 per cent felt the government should "not allow" such speeches. It should be stressed, however, that such instability is very much related to knowledge and intensity on the issue. An experiment with question wording in 1941, on the policies of Adolf Hitler, found opinion entirely uninfluenced by wording changes.

Much of the absence and instability of opinion derives from a truly monumental ignorance on many issues by many people. To give one example: As late as 1968, 24 per cent of the population did not know whether most of China had a Communist government. Actually, this is something of an improvement; in 1964, the figure stood at 28 per cent. Under these circumstances, the willingness of many of follow policy cues promulgated by trusted party leaders is certainly far preferable to a reliance on their own knowledge and reasoning ability.

Nevertheless, though small in number, ideologues do exist. Their behavior is difficult to analyze over time, because no sound measure of ideological position has been devised and consistently administered in the polls. The closest one can come is to look at the responses of Jews as a sort of imperfect surrogate for the liberal position on most issues. In war policy, one can see a notable shift here. Jews strongly supported the Korean war but tended from the beginning to oppose the war in Vietnam, although both wars were developed under Democratic Administrations. It is likely that this reflects the liberal position on the wars. In fact, Jews seem to be the only subgroup of all those usually sorted out by poll questions whose position on the two wars differs.

When one relaxes a bit from the search for the more or less pure ideologue and takes each issue separately, it is often possible to find subgroups inclined to support or oppose the Presidential position for reasons related to personal beliefs or perspectives. Self-interest is one such motivating force, as farmers are inclined to favor price supports and workers to oppose wage controls. There are also influencing factors deriving from group background and experiences, as white Southerners favor segregation and blacks oppose police actions against antiwar demonstrators.

Curiously, in the area of war policy, self-interest does not seem to be related to a person's sentiments. Although data are fragmentary, polls conducted during World War II, the Korean war, and the war in Vietnam find that neither men likely to be inducted nor their close relatives are particularly inclined to be dovish (or hawkish) on war policy.

Related to these considerations, but somewhat more ephemeral, are psychological predispositions associated with certain social characteristics. Sex, for example, proves to be a fairly good predictor of the respondent's position on war policy. No matter what the party leadership suggests, no matter what present policy is, women are persistently less willing to sanction the application of force or the increased application of force to solve problems. Compared to men, they oppose wars, escalation, bombing raids, and "strong measures," and they favor peace, peace talks, de-escalation, bombing halts, and withdrawal from warlike situations.

These positions derive presumably from sex roles in the society in which men are expected to be firm and aggressive, women quiet and demure. The sexual difference also shows up rather repeatedly in bargaining experiments, in which it is found that women prove to be notably bad bargainers because they are likely to seek ways to avoid the bargaining conflict itself, thereby reducing joint and individual profits.

Some fortuitous evidence from a 1953 survey suggests that an effect of women's liberation could be to diminish this sexual difference on war policy, although the inference is a bit oblique. That survey contained a question about a proposed use of atomic artillery shells in the Korean war. The respondents were also asked what was the fastest speed they had ever driven a car. The intriguing result, when these two questions were cross-tabulated, was that fast drivers were more likely to favor the use of nuclear weapons than slow drivers. Suspecting a con-taminating effect from sex in this relation, since men are both fast drivers and favorable to strong measures in wars, the relation was looked at separately for the two sexes. When this was done, it was found that driving speed was entirely unrelated to war-policy preferences among men, but that fast women drivers were strikingly more likely to favor the use of nuclear weapons than slow ones.

More to the point, perhaps, was another question, which asked whether the then current Kinsey report should be discussed so widely and openly. Those favorable were more inclined to favor the use of the atomic weapons in Korea. Again, sex was controlled for, since men tended to approve both Kinsey and the weapons; again, for men, the Kinsey question proved to be a poor predictor; and, again, presumably liberated women—those favorable to the Kinsey discussion—were distinctly more like men on the atomic weapon issue than their unliberated peers.

Another social variable that relates rather persistently to war policy is race. It is rather common to note that blacks opposed the war in Vietnam to a notably greater degree than whites, and that they were inclined to favor withdrawal and to oppose escalation. It is often suggested that this phenomenon was related to the racial upheaval taking place in the country at the same time as the war. The problem with the explanation, however, is that poll data show blacks to have had the same relative posi-tion on the Korean war and on World War II. And the relation-ship remains reasonably firm when social class is controlled for.

This response pattern, apparently rather deeply based on the black experience and psychology, clearly deserves further study.

FOLLOWERS

Thus far, considerations have been of opinion types in the population whose existence contributes rather little to a President's power over public opinion. To be sure, a President, by making an issue a partisan one, can generate extra support from friendly partisans who now have a firm cue to follow; but, at the same time, he is likely to drive from his support partisans whose natural instinct is to side with the opposition. Furthermore, the power of making an issue a partisan one rests almost as much with the opposition leadership as with the President.

Believers, pretty much by definition, are relatively unmanipulable. Since they already know what they are inclined to want, the President cannot lead them like friendly partisans. One Presidential strategy to maximize support in this area would be to find out what kinds of believers are most numerous on an issue and then to modify his position accordingly, so that he now appears in their vanguard. Another approach, adopted with varying degrees of success by different Presidents, is to muddy the issue, so that he appears to agree with believers on all sides of a given issue. Thus, we find history filled with Presidents who were liberal conservatives or conservative liberals, hawkish doves or dovish hawks, adopting firm but flexible postures on highly imprecise issues. (We also find many Presidents accused of hypocrisy and a lack of credibility.) These procedures are often wise politics, but few would consider them exercises of power in any meaningful sense.

The real opportunity for Presidential leadership, however, concerns those in the population who can be labeled "followers." Particularly in the area of foreign affairs, these are citizens who, whatever their partisan or ideological predilections, are inclined to rally to the support of the President no matter what he does.

The President's strength in this area seems to derive from the majesty of the office and from his singular position as head of state. Followers seem to identify with the country and with its leadership, and seem to be susceptible to social and political influences in this direction. They swim in the mainstream, to apply the jargon of yesteryear. For them, the President *is* the country, for many purposes, and there is therefore a certain popular loyalty to the man that comes with the office, which tends to place him above politics. Few Americans want their son to become a politician, but many would like to see him become President. Whatever his party, the President invariably comes out at or near the top on Gallup's yearly most-admired-man sweepstakes. In 1968, eight of the ten most admired men were present or past Presidents, or were prime contenders for the office.

The existence of followers means that the President, particularly in the short run, has more flexibility in foreign policy than might at first appear to be the case—a proposition rarely noted by journalists or politicians, but often by public-opinion analysts. Followers tend to reject proposals for forceful or accommodating policies in the abstract if such policies imply an alteration of "our" present course; but, once the President has adopted the new policy, many in the group will follow his lead. Thus, followers cannot be classified in terms familiar from the discussion of believers: If the Administration is using force, followers will respond like hawks; if it is seeking peace, they will respond like doves.

Sometimes, the propensities of the follower group can be activated in an extraordinarily simple manner on polls. One can simply frame a hypothetical question: "Suppose policy x *were* the President's policy, would you then go along with it?" When asked about policies seemingly unpopular at the time, like the recognition of Communist China or withdrawal from Vietnam, such questions stimulate considerable changes in public response.

This phenomenon helps explain major shifts in public opinion after policy changes. The Harris Poll, for example, reports that support for bombing the Hanoi-Haiphong area increased among those Americans with opinions from 50 to 80 per cent after the bombing of military targets there was begun in 1966. Similarly, Gallup found, in March of 1968, that 51 per cent of the public opposed a halt of the bombing of North Vietnam. After President

Johnson had partially halted the bombing, and before Hanoi had responded by agreeing to preliminary peace talks, this proportion had dropped in a Harris Poll to 24 per cent.

Followers are found disproportionately among the more affluent, the better educated, and the young. When the attitudes of people with these characteristics are assessed on issues of foreign and defense policy, they usually are found to be at least somewhat more favorable to whatever happens to be the Presidential policy than are the poor, the poorly educated, and the old. Although much of the attitude of the members of the follower groups probably stems from their closer identification with the country and its leadership, it should be noted that they are also more likely to know at any given point what the Presidential policy *is;* whereas the poor, the poorly educated, and the old are more likely to respond randomly to the survey stimulus as well as to select the "no opinion" response more frequently.

It should be emphasized that these observations very much held for attitudes toward American policy in Vietnam. Thus, those who argued that opposition to the war tended to come from the "youthful, well-educated, affluent" segments of the public were simply flatly wrong. For the most part, the people listed are precisely the ones who were the most likely to support the war, to find it "morally justified," and to agree with American tactics there.

Vocal opposition to the war in Vietnam seemed to come so disproportionately from the young that innumerable commentators, regardless of the poll findings, concluded that "youth" was in revolt over the war. But young people are the most obvious element of almost any political movement presumably because of their physical energy and their lack of occupational and familial obligations—in 1964, it may be recalled, journalistic pundits professed to see an attraction of young people to the Goldwater movement. The poll data argue that, while *some* young people may have been deeply opposed to the war, "youth" as a whole was generally more supportive of the war than were older people.

Studies indicate quite clearly that the young people who opposed the war, as well as their well-educated older colleagues, were very disproportionately associated with the "better" schools in the country. In cross-sectional polls, however, their attitudes were overwhelmed by the legions among the young and the educated who enjoyed no such association. It is of interest to consider why these associations should have led to opposition to the war and the President's policy there.

One element in the explanation concerns the relatively liberal and left-liberal atmosphere at the better universities. Studies from both the Vietnam and the McCarthy periods demonstrate that these schools are quite distinctive in this regard. Since, as noted above, political liberals were inclined to oppose the Vietnam war, it is not surprising to find that opposition to the war in Vietnam centered at places where liberals were concentrated —the better universities.

But, in part, this begs the question. What must be discussed is why the better universities are relatively liberal places. It could be that the more intelligent a person is, the more likely he is to adopt the liberal philosophy. However comforting this thought may be to liberals, it is of questionable validity, since, in decades past, the better universities were often bastions of conservatism. Or, it may be that pliable student minds are being bent to the left by a band of liberal professors. But this explanation fits poorly with studies that find student values and attitudes unaffected in any such gross way by the college experience. A better explanation might draw on an observation made earlier about the liberalism of Jews. Outside of a few sections in a few cities, the only easily identifiable places that Jews are found in striking disproportion are the colleges and universities of the land—and very particularly in the better ones. Thus, the liberalism of those associated with the better universities may not derive from anything endemic in the university situation. Rather, it may stem from the influence of a major subpopulation in the university community inclined toward liberalism and war opposition regardless of its association with the college.

It has been observed, in the discussions of partisans and followers, that many people, in reaching an opinion on a policy, do not attempt to separate the issue from the personality embracing it. With respect to the followers in the population, this phenomenon, as noted, gives the President a major advantage. For when he associates himself with an issue, particularly one in the foreign-policy area, there is a tendency for the office and its symbolic identification with the country also to become associated with the issue. Thus, as opponents of Presidential policy know well, opposition to a Presidential policy can seem an unpatriotic position to many people. This problem of the association of personality with issues was the most damaging to the Vietnam antiwar movement. Not only were the flag and patriotic righteousness associated with the President and his policies, but the opposition, for its part, came to be associated with rioting, disruption, and bomb throwing, and war protesters, as a group, enjoyed negative popularity ratings to an almost unparalleled degree. In fact, it is conceivable that, because the antiwar cause was associated with an extraordinarily unpopular reference group, the war in Vietnam would have had somewhat *less* support in the general population if there had been no vocal opposition.

One final comment should be appended to this discussion about the follower mentality. Whereas the President has considerable scope for leadership with the followers, particularly in the short run, other members of the respected political elite, particularly if they can avoid associations with unpopular groups, can sometimes divert some of this potential support from the President. Followers can be led, and their preferred leader is the President; but, when there is a clear split in the political elite, many will be diverted to follow partisan or ideological leaders. During the Korean war, for example, the well educated were noticeably willing to support the idea that the Communists should be driven from south Korea—an issue on which the political elite was united; but they were noticeably split over the idea of bombing China—an issue on which the political elite was clearly divided. For his own interests, then, the President may find himself trying to head off elite opposition —perhaps by appealing to the ideal of patriotism and the great consensus. And, should opposition develop, he may find it appealing to try to discredit the argument by discrediting the person making it—perhaps by questioning the opponent's intelligence, mental stability, patriotism, virility, or associations.

To conclude this discourse, three issues regarding polls, popular attitudes, and Presidents suggest themselves: (1) the absolute number problem, (2) the case of dynamics in public opinion, and (3) the issue of elections.

1. News releases from the polling agencies commonly deal with simple, absolute numbers: 60 per cent said to approve of bombing North Vietnam, 30 per cent of birth control, 80 per cent of universal military training. It can be inferred from some of the earlier discussion, and it will be directly declared now, that *such numbers have very little meaning by themselves.* This is mainly because opinion on so many issues is highly susceptible to changes in question wording. During the Korean war, for example, it was found that measured popular support for the war could be increased some 10 or 15 percentage points if questions were worded so that the respondent in order to oppose the war was required to admit the United States had made a mistake in entering the war, and support was raised another 15 or 20 points if he had, in addition, to seem to oppose the halting of the Communists. With such data, it is no task at all to demonstrate that a silent majority favored—or opposed—the war.

This is not to say, of course, that polls can tell us nothing about popular attitudes. It is simply to argue that such analysis must be done carefully, in context, and often with considerable tedium. One can compare the reactions of different population subgroups to the same question. One can assess popular reactions to the same question posed at different points in time. And one can make explicit use of the question-wording problem by examining varying reactions to differently worded questions on the same topic, in a effort to assess the most important components of the attitude response. In all cases, however, the exercise involves a *comparison* of response, not elaborate exegeses on a single dangling number.

2. The analysis has stressed static opinion relationships more than dynamic ones: at any point in time, it has been observed, the President will garner support disproportionately from friendly

partisans, congenial believers, and all sorts of followers. But, even when the President does not alter his position, he may experience, over time, declining or increasing support on an issue. Support for the wars in Korea and Vietnam, for example, declined according to the same logarithmic pattern as a function of the number of American casualties. Except for President Eisenhower, each President, since polls were invented, has experienced declining popularity as the public grew accustomed to his face. And the gain in popularity that Presidents experience when the country undergoes an international crisis tends to fade as time goes by.

There are a number of mechanisms that seem to cause such changes. One of these is a dramatic event that changes the meaning of the issue. The Chinese entry into the Korean war, for example, radically altered the scope and meaning of the American venture there. A riot in a black ghetto can affect white attitudes toward integration.

But most changes seem related to maneuverings within the political elite in the manner suggested earlier. As noted, when the President dramatically changes his policy, many followers will cheerfully go along. And, as prominent politicians become active on an issue and diverge publicly from the Presidential position, partisans are likely to find their instincts aroused, believers to discover something new to grasp, and followers to be led astray. Thus, notable drops in support for the Vietnam war seem to have accompanied the Fulbright hearings of 1966 and the Republican convention of 1968, where the respectable left, then the respectable right, denounced the war for varying reasons. And, in the aftermath of a rally-round-the-flag crisis, politicians who had previously been silent in the interests of national unity begin openly to discuss, to question, and to demur.

It is remarkable how stable public opinion is on most issues when there is little change of position by leadership groups. There are, of course, fluctuations from time to time, and some of them may be quite erratic. But, in general, the American public is quite likely to respond today to an issue—internationalism, say, or civil liberties, or farm-price supports—with much the same degree of enthusiasm as it did six months ago or three years ago. In fact, it is this phenomenon that accounts, in part, for the frustrating unwillingness of polling agencies to ask the same question repeatedly. Trend lines that do not fluctuate, they know, make poor newspaper copy.

3. While the considerations in this essay are expected, in general, to hold at all times, it should be noted that things are somewhat different during election campaigns, when public opinion becomes a most vital consideration. The opposition party becomes less amorphous as a public commentator. It nominates a champion and proceeds flagrantly to politicize every issue on which it can find advantage. In response, the President must descend somewhat from his throne to enter the battle. Thus, partisans are likely to find things comfortably black and white, while followers become confused.

Political campaigns rarely sharpen issues, however. Rather, they personalize them even more than normally, and ideologically oriented believers are likely to become even more confused than those who would ordinarily be Presidential followers. The believers are often heard to complain that they are unable to discern a policy difference between the two candidates.

Not only do issues become increasingly politicized and personalized, but contenders make efforts to alter their importance to the public. Specifically, parties try to raise the importance of an issue on which they feel they have a natural advantage. Thus, poll data document the success of the Republicans in increasing the importance, as issues, of the Korean war in 1952 and of law and order in 1968.

It is this election campaign problem, especially as it affects the followers, that is most likely to lead to timidity when the President considers exercising his power to lead public opinion. For, while many will follow his lead in the short run, their continued loyalty in the campaign situation, with debate raging and alternative personalities—and occasionally alternative policies—proposed, can by no means be guaranteed.

9

The President and the Press

Daniel P. Moynihan

As his years in Washington came to an end, one President wrote a friend:

> *I really look with commiseration over the great body of my fellow citizens, who, reading newspapers, live and die in the belief that they have known something of what has been passing in the world in their time.*

A familiar Presidential plaint, sounded often in the early years of the Republic and rarely unheard thereafter. Of late, however, a change has developed in the perception of what is at issue. In the past, what was thought to be involved was the reputation of a particular President. In the present, what is seen to be at stake, and by the Presidents themselves, is the reputation of government—especially, of course, Presidential government. These are different matters and summon a different order of concern.

There are two points anyone would wish to make at the outset of an effort to explore this problem. First, it is to be acknowledged that, in most essential encounters between the Presidency and the press, the advantage is with the former. The President has a near limitless capacity to "make" news that must be reported, if only by reason of competition between one journal, or one medium, and another. If anything, radio and television news is more readily subject to such dominance. Their format permits of many fewer "stories." The President-in-action almost always takes precedence. The President also has considerable capacity to reward friends and punish enemies in the press corps, whether they be individual journalists or the papers, television networks, news weeklies, or whatever these individuals work for. And, for quite a long while, finally, a President who wishes can carry off formidable deceptions. (One need only recall the barefaced lying that went with the formal opinion of Roosevelt's Attorney General that the destroyer–naval-base deal of 1940 was legal.)

With more than sufficient reason, then, publishers and reporters alike have sustained, over the generations, a lively sense of their vulnerability to governmental coercion or control. For the most part, their worries have been exaggerated. But, like certain virtues, there are some worries that are best carried to excess.

The second point is that American journalism is almost certainly the best in the world. This judgment will be disputed by some. There are good newspapers in other countries. The *best* European journalists are more intellectual than their American counterparts, and some will think this a decisive consideration. But there is no enterprise anywhere the like of the *New York Times*. Few capitals are covered with the insight and access of the *Washington Post* or the *Washington Evening Star*. As with so many American institutions, American newspapers tend to be older and more stable than their counterparts abroad. The *Hartford Courant* was born in 1764, twenty one years before the *Times* of London. The *New York Post* began publication in 1801, twenty years before the *Guardian* of Manchester. What, in most other countries, is known as the "provincial" press—that is to say, journals published elsewhere than in the capital—in America is made up of a wealth of comprehensive and dependable daily newspapers of unusually high quality.

The journalists are in some ways more important than their journals—at least to anyone who has lived much in government. A relationship grows up with the reporters covering one's particular sector that has no counterpart in other professions or activities. The relationship is one of simultaneous trust and distrust, friendship and enmity, dependence and independence. But it is the men of government, especially in Washington, who are the more dependent. The journalists are their benefactors, their conscience, at times almost their reason for being. For the journalists are, above all others, their audience, again especially in Washington, which has neither an intellectual community nor an electorate, and where there is no force outside government able to judge events, much less to help shape them, save the press.

That there is something wondrous and terrible in the intensities of this relationship between the press and the government is perhaps best seen at the annual theatricals put on by such groups of journalists as the Legislative Correspondents Association in Albany or the Gridiron in Washington. To my knowledge, nothing comparable takes place anywhere else in the world. These gatherings are a kind of ritual truth telling, of which the closest psychological approximation would be the Calabrian insult ritual described by Roger Vailland in his novel *The Law,* or possibly the group-therapy practices of more recent origin. The politicians come as guests of the journalists. The occasion is, first of all, a feast: the best of everything. Then, as dinner progresses, the songs begin. The quality varies, of course, but, at moments, startling levels of deadly accurate commentary of great cruelty are achieved. The politicians sit and smile and applaud. Then, some of them speak. Each one wins or loses to the degree that he can respond in kind; stay funny and be brutal. (At the Gridiron, John F. Kennedy was a master of the style, but the piano duet performed by Nixon and Agnew in 1970 was thought by many to have surpassed anything yet done.) A few lyrics appear in the next day's papers, but what the newspapermen really said to the politicians remains privileged—as does so much of what the politicians say to them. The relationship is special.

How is it, then, that this relationship has lately grown so troubled? The immediate answer is, of course, the war in Vietnam. An undeclared war, unwanted, misunderstood, or not understood at all, it entailed a massive deception of the American people by their government. Surely a large area of the experience of the 1960's is best evoked in the story of the man who says, "They told me that if I voted for Goldwater there would be 500,000 troops in Vietnam within a year. I voted for him, and, by God, they were right." The story has many versions. If he voted for Goldwater, we would be defoliating the countryside of Vietnam; the army would be sending spies to the 1968 party conventions; Dr. Spock would be indicted on conspiracy charges; and so on. By 1968, Richard Rovere described the capital as "awash" with lies.

The essential fact was that of deceit. How else to carry out a full-scale war that became steadily more unpopular with none of the legally sanctioned constraints on the free flow of information that even the most democratic societies find necessary in such circumstances? This situation did not spring full-blown from the involvement in Southeast Asia. It was endemic to the cold war. At the close of World War II, official press censorship was removed, but the kinds of circumstance[s] in which any responsible government might feel that events have to be concealed from the public did not go away. The result was a contradiction impossible to resolve. The public interest was at once served and dis-served by secrecy; at once dis-served and served by openness. Whatever the case, distrust of government grew. At the outset of the U-2 affair in 1960, the U.S. Government asserted that a weather plane on a routine mission had been shot down. The *New York Times* (May 6, 1960) reported just that. *Not* that the U.S. Government *claimed* it was a weather plane, but simply that it was. Well, it wasn't. Things have been the same since.

But there are problems between the Presidency and the press that have little to do with the cold war or with Vietnam, and which—if this analysis is correct—will persist or even intensify should those conditions recede, or even dissolve, as a prime source of public concern. The problems flow from five basic circumstances that together have been working to reverse the old balance of power between the Presidency and the press. It is the thesis here that, if this balance should tip too far in the direction of the press, our capacity for effective democratic government will be seriously and dangerously weakened.

I

The first of these circumstances has to do with the tradition of "muckraking"—the exposure of corruption in government or the collusion of government with private interests—which the Amer-

ican press has seen as a primary mission since the period 1880–
1914. It is, in Irving Kristol's words, a "journalistic phenomenon
that is indigenous to democracy, with its instinctive suspicion and
distrust of all authority in general, and of concentrated political
and economic power especially." Few would want to be without
the tradition, and it is a young journalist of poor spirit who does
not set out to uncover the machinations of some malefactor of
great wealth and his political collaborators. Yet, there is a cost, as
Roger Starr suggests in his wistful wish that Lincoln Steffens's
The Shame of the Cities might be placed on the restricted shelves
of the schools of journalism. Steffens has indeed, as Starr declares,
continued "to haunt the city rooms of the country's major newspapers." The question to be asked is whether, in the aftermath
of Steffens, the cities were better or merely more ashamed of
themselves. Looking back, one is impressed by the energy and
capacity for governance of some of the old city machines. Whatever else, it was popular government, of and by men of the
people. One wonders: Did the middle- and upper-class reformers
destroy the capacity of working-class urban government without
replacing it with anything better, so that half a century later
each and all bewail the cities as ungovernable? One next wonders
whether something not dissimilar will occur now that the focus
of press attention has shifted from City Hall to the White House.
(And, yet, a miracle of American national government is the
almost complete absence of monetary corruption at all levels,
and most especially at the top.)

The muckraking tradition is well established. Newer, and
likely to have far more serious consequences, is the advent of
what Lionel Trilling has called the "adversary culture" as a con-
spicuous element in journalistic practice. The appearance, in
large numbers, of journalists shaped by the attitudes of this
culture is the result of a process whereby the profession thought
to improve itself by recruiting more and more persons from
middle- and upper-class backgrounds and trained at the universities associated with such groups. This is a change but little
noted as yet. The stereotype of American newspapers is that of
publishers ranging from conservative to reactionary in their
political views, balanced by reporters ranging from liberal to

radical in theirs. One is not certain how accurate the stereotype ever was. One's impression is that, twenty years and more ago, the preponderance of the "working press" (as it liked to call itself) was surprisingly close in origins and attitudes to working people generally. They were not Ivy Leaguers. They now are or soon will be. Journalism has become, if not an elite profession, a profession attractive to elites. This is noticeably so in Washington, where the upper reaches of journalism constitute one of the most important and eduring *social* elites of the city, with all the accoutrements one associates with a leisured class. (The Washington press corps is not leisured at all, but the style is that of men and women who *choose* to work.)

The political consequence of the rising social status of journalism is that the press grows more and more influenced by attitudes genuinely hostile to American society and American government. This trend seems bound to continue into the future. On the record of what they have been writing while in college, the young people now leaving the Harvard *Crimson* and the Columbia *Spectator* for journalistic jobs in Washington will resort to the Steffens style at ever escalating levels of moral implication. They bring with them the moral absolutism of George Wald's vastly popular address, "A Generation in Search of a Future," that describes the Vietnam war as the "most shameful episode in the whole American history." Not tragic, not heartbreaking, not vastly misconceived, but *shameful*. From the shame of the cities to the shame of the nation. But nobody ever called Boss Croker any name equivalent in condemnatory weight to the epithet "war criminal."

II

An ironical accompaniment of the onset of the muckraking style directed toward the Presidency has been the rise of a notion of the near omnipotency of the office itself. This notion Thomas E. Cronin describes as the "textbook President," Cronin persuasively argues that, in the aftermath of Franklin Roosevelt, a view of the Presidency, specifically incorporated in the textbooks of recent decades, was developed that presented seriously "inflated and unrealistic interpretations of Presidential competence and beneficence," and which grievously "overemphasized the policy change and policy accomplishment capabilities" of the office. Cronin cites Anthony Howard, a watchful British commentator:

> *For what the nation has been beguiled into believing ever since 1960 is surely the politics of evangelism: the faith that individual men are cast to be messiahs, the conviction that Presidential incantations can be substituted for concrete programs, the belief that what matters is not so much the state of the nation as the inspiration-quotient of its people.*

In his own researches among advisers of Kennedy and Johnson, Cronin finds the majority to hold "tempered assessments of Presidential determination of 'public policy.'" Indeed, only 10 per cent would describe the President as having "very great impact" over such matters.

Working in the White House is a chastening experience. But it is the experience of very few persons. Watching the White House, on the other hand, is a mass occupation, concentrated especially among the better-educated, better-off groups. For many, the experience is one of infatuation followed much too promptly by disillusion. First, the honeymoon—in Cronin's terms, the "predictable ritual of euphoric inflation." But then the "Camelot of the first few hundred days of all Presidencies fades away. . . . Predictably, by the second year, reports are spread that the President has become isolated from criticism." If this is so, he has only himself to blame when things go wrong. And things do go wrong.

If the muckraking tradition implies a distrust of government, it is nonetheless curiously validated by the overtrusting tradition of the "textbook Presidency," which recurrently sets up situations in which the Presidency will be judged as having somehow broken faith. This is not just the experience of a Johnson or a Nixon. Anyone who was in the Kennedy Administration in the summer and fall of 1963 would, or ought to, report a pervasive sense that our initiative had been lost, that we would have to get re-elected to get going again.

Here, too, there is a curious link between the Presidency and the press. The two most important *Presidential* newspapers are the *New York Times* and the *Washington Post* (though the *Star* would be judged by many to have the best reporting). Both papers reflect a tradition of liberalism that has latterly been shaped and reinforced by the very special type of person who *buys* the paper. (It is well to keep in mind that newspapers are capitalist enterprises that survive by persuading people to buy them.) Theirs is a "disproportionately" well-educated and economically prosperous audience. The geographical areas in which the two papers circulate almost certainly have higher per capita incomes and higher levels of education than any of comparable size in the nation or the world. More of the buyers of these two papers are likely to come from "liberal" Protestant or Jewish backgrounds than would be turned up by a random sample of the population; they comprise, in fact, what James Q. Wilson calls the "Liberal Audience." Both the working-class Democrats and the conservative Republicans, with exceptions, obviously, have been pretty much driven from office among the constituencies where the *Times* and the *Post* flourish. It would be wrong to ascribe this to the influence of the papers. Causality almost certainly moves both ways. Max Frankel of the *Times,* who may have peers but certainly no betters as a working journalist, argues that a newspaper is surely as much influenced by those who read it as vice versa.

The readers of the *New York Times* and the *Washington Post,* then, are a special type of citizen: not only more affluent and more liberal than the rest of the nation, but inclined, also, to impose heavy expectations on the Presidency, and not to be amused when those expectations fail to be met. Attached by their own internal traditions to the "textbook Presidency," papers like the *Times* and the *Post are* reinforced in this attachment by the temperamental predilections of the readership whose character they inevitably reflect. Thus, they help to set a tone of pervasive dissatisfaction with the performance of the national government, whoever the Presidential incumbent may be and whatever the substance of his policies.

III

A third circumstance working to upset the old balance of power between the Presidency and the press is the fact that Washington reporters depend heavily on more or less clandestine information from federal bureaucracies, which are frequently, and in some cases routinely, antagonistic to Presidential interests.

There is a view of the career civil service as a more or less passive executor of policies made on high. This is quite mistaken. A very great portion of policy ideas "bubble up" from the bureaucracy, and, just as importantly, a very considerable portion of the "policy decisions" that go down never come to anything, either because the bureaucrats cannot or will not follow through. (The instances of simple inability are probably much greater than those of outright hostility.) Few modern Presidents have made any impact on the federal bureaucracies, save by creating new ones. The bureaucracies are unfamiliar and inaccessible. They are quasi-independent, maintaining, among other things, fairly open relationships with the congressional committees that enact their statutes and provide their funds. They are usually willing to work with the President, but rarely to the point where their perceived interests are threatened. Typically, these are rather simple territorial interests: not to lose any jurisdiction, and, if possible, to gain some. But, recurrently, issues of genuine political substance are also involved.

At the point where they perceive a threat to those interests, the bureaucracies just as recurrently go to the press. They know the press; the press knows them. Both stay in town as Presidential governments come and go. Both cooperate in bringing to bear the most powerful weapon the bureaucracies wield in their own defense, that of revealing Presidential plans in advance of their execution. Presidents and their plans are helpless against this technique. I have seen a senior aide to a President, sitting over an early morning cup of coffee, rise and literally punch the front page of the *New York Times*. A major initiative was being carefully mounted. Success depended, to a considerable degree, on surprise. Someone in one of the agencies whose policies were to be reversed got hold of the relevant document and passed it on to the *Times*. Now everyone would know. The mission was aborted. There was *nothing* for the Presidential government to do. No possibility of finding, much less of disciplining, the bureaucrat responsible. For a time, or rather from time to time, President Johnson tried the technique of not going ahead with any policy or appointment that was leaked in advance to the press. Soon, however, his aides began to suspect that this was giving the bureaucracy the most powerful weapon of all, namely, the power to veto a Presidential decision by learning of it early enough and rushing to the *Times* or the *Post*. (Or, if the issue could be described in thirty seconds, any of the major television networks.)

What we have here is disloyalty to the Presidency. Much of the time what is involved is no more than the self-regard of lower-echelon bureaucrats who are simply flattered into letting the reporter know how much *they* know, or who are just trying to look after their agency. But just as often, to repeat, serious issues of principle are involved. Senator Joseph McCarthy made contact with what he termed the "loyal American underground" —State Department officials, and other such, who reputedly passed on information to him about Communist infiltration of the nation's foreign-policy and security systems. President Johnson made it clear that he did not trust the Department of State to maintain "security" in foreign policy. Under President Nixon, the phenomenon has been most evident in domestic areas, as OEO warriors struggle among themselves to be the first to disclose the imminent demise of VISTA, or HEW functionaries reluctantly interpret a move to close some fever hospital built to accommodate an eighteenth-century seaport as the first step in a master plan to dismantle public medicine and decimate the ranks of the elderly and disadvantaged.

It is difficult to say whether the absolute level of such disloyalty to the Presidency is rising. One has the impression that it is. No one knows much about the process of "leaking" except in those instances where he himself has been involved. (*Everyone* is sooner or later involved. That should be understood.) The process has not been studied, and little is known of it. But few would argue that the amount of clandestine disclosure is decreasing. Such disclosure is now part of the way we run our affairs. It means, among other things, that the press is fairly continuously involved in an activity that is something less than honorable. Repeatedly, it benefits from the self-serving acts of government officials who are essentially hostile to the Presidency. This does the Presidency no good, and, if an outsider may comment, it does the press no good, either. Too much do they traffic in stolen goods, and they know it.

This point must be emphasized. The leaks that appear in the *Post* and the *Times*—other papers get them, but, if one wants to influence decisions in Washington, these are clearly thought to be the most effective channels—are ostensibly published in the interest of adding to public knowledge of what is going on. This budget is to be cut; that man is to be fired; this bill is to be proposed. However, in the nature of the transaction, the press can publish only half the story—that is to say, the information that the "leaker" wants to become "public knowledge." What the press *never* does is say who the leaker is and why he wants the story leaked. Yet, more often than not, this is the more important story: that is to say, what policy wins if the one being disclosed loses, what individual, what bureau, and so on.

There really are ethical questions involved here that have not been examined. There are also serious practical questions. It would be my impression that the distress occasioned by leaks has used up too much Presidential energy, at least from the time of Roosevelt. (Old-time brain-trusters would assure the Johnson staff that nothing could compare with FDR's distractions on the subject.) The primary fault lies within government itself, and one is at a loss to think of anything that might be done about it. But it is a problem for journalism as well, and an unattended one.

IV

The fourth of the five conditions making for an altered relation between the Presidency and the press is the concept of objectivity with respect to the reporting of events and, especially, the state-

ments of public figures. Almost the first canon of the great newspapers, and by extension of the television news networks that,
by and large, have taken as their standards those of the best
newspapers, is that the "news" will be reported whether or not
the reporter or the editor or the publisher likes the news. There
is nothing finer in the American newspaper tradition. There is,
however, a rub, and it comes when a decision has to be made as
to whether an event really is news or simply a happening, a non-
event staged for the purpose of getting into the papers or onto
the screen.

The record of our best papers is not reassuring here, as a
glance at the experience of the Korean and the Vietnam wars
will suggest. Beginning a bit before the Korean hostilities broke
out, but in the general political period we associate with that
war, there was a rise of right-wing extremism, a conspiracy-
oriented politics symbolized by the name of Senator Joseph
McCarthy, and directed primarily at the institution of the Presidency. There was, to be sure, a populist streak to this movement:
Yale and Harvard and the "striped-pants boys" in the State Department were targets, too. But to the question "Who promoted
Peress?" there was only one constitutional or—for all practical
purposes—political answer, namely, that the President did.
McCarthy went on asking such questions, or rather making such
charges, and the national press, which detested and disbelieved
him throughout, went on printing them. The American style of
objective journalism made McCarthy. He would not, I think,
have gotten anywhere in Great Britain, where, because it would
have been judged he was lying, the stories would simply not have
been printed.

Something not dissimilar has occurred in the course of the
Vietnam war, only this time the extremist, conspiracy-oriented
politics of protest has been putatively left-wing. Actually, both
movements are utterly confusing if one depends on European
analogues. McCarthy was nominally searching out Communists,
but his preferred targets were Eastern patricians, while his supporters were, to an alarming degree, members of the Catholic
working class. The Students for a Democratic Society, if that
organization may be used as an exemplar, was (at least in its
later stages) nominally revolutionist, dedicated to the overthrow

of the capitalist-imperialist-fascist regime of the United States. Yet, as Seymour Martin Lipset, Nathan Glazer, and others have shown, its leadership, and perhaps also its constituency, were disproportionately made up of upper-class Jewish and Protestant youth. By report of Steven Kelman, who lived as a contemporary among them at Harvard, the SDS radicals were "undemocratic, manipulative, and self-righteous to the point of snobbery and elitism." Peter Berger, a sociologist active in the peace movement, has demonstrated quite persuasively—what others, particularly persons of European origin like himself have frequently seemed to sense—that, despite the leftist ring of the slogans of SDS and kindred groups, their ethos and tactics are classically fascist: the cult of youth, the mystique of the street, the contempt for liberal democracy, and the "totalization of friend and foe [with] the concomitant dehumanization of the latter," as in the Nazi use of *"Saujuden"* ("Jewish pigs".)

In any case, the accusations that have filled the American air during the period of Vietnam have been no more credible or responsible than those of McCarthy during the Korean period, and the tactics of provocation and physical intimidation have, if anything, been more disconcerting. Yet, the national press and, especially, television have assumed a neutral posture, even at times a sympathetic one, enabling the neofascists of the Left to occupy center stage throughout the latter half of the 1960's, with consequences to American politics that have by no means yet worked themselves out. . . .

If the press is to deserve our good opinion, it must do better in such matters. And it should keep in mind that the motivation of editors and reporters is not always simply and purely shaped by a devotion to objectivity. In the course of the McCarthy era, James Reston recalled the ancient adage that, translated from the Erse, proposes that, "If you want an audience, start a fight." This is true of anyone who would find an audience for his views or simply for himself. It is true also for anyone who would find customers for the late city edition. T. S. Matthews, sometime editor of *Time,* retired to England to ponder the meaning of it all. In the end, all he could conclude was that the function of journalism was entertainment. If it is to be more—and that,

surely, is what the Rosenthals and Bradlees and Grunwalds and
Elliotts want—it will have to be willing, on occasion, to forgo
the entertainment value of a fascinating but untruthful charge.
It will, in short, have to help limit the rewards that attend
this posture in American politics.

v

The final, and by far the most important, circumstance of
American journalism relevant to this discussion is the absence of
a professional tradition of self-correction. The mark of any developed profession is the practice of correcting mistakes, by
whomsoever they are made. This practice is, of course, the great
invention of Western science. Ideally, it requires an epistemology
that is shared by all respected members of the profession, so that,
when a mistake is discovered, it can be established as a mistake to
the satisfaction of the entire professional community. Ideally,
also, no discredit is involved: To the contrary, honest mistakes
are integral to the process of advancing the field. Journalism
will never attain to any such condition. Nevertheless, there is a
range of subject matter about which reasonable men can and
will agree, and within this range American journalism, even of
the higher order, is often seriously wide of the mark. Again
Irving Kristol:

> *It is a staple of conversation among those who have ever been
> involved in a public activity that when they read the* Times
> *the next morning, they will discover that it has almost never
> got the story quite right and has only too frequently got it
> quite wrong.*

Similar testimony has come from an editor of the *New York
Times* itself. In an article published some years ago in the
Sunday *Times Magazine,* A. H. Raskin had this to say:

> *No week passes without someone prominent in politics,
> industry, labor or civic affairs complaining to me, always in
> virtually identical terms: "Whenever I read a story about*

*something in which I really know what is going on, I'm
astonished at how little of what is important gets into the
papers—and how often even that little is wrong." The most
upsetting thing about these complaints is the frequency with
which they come from scientists, economists and other
academicians temporarily involved in government policy
but without any proprietary concern about who runs the
White House or City Hall.*

This is so, and, in part, is unavoidable. Too much happens
too quickly: That the *Times,* or the *Post* or the *Star* should
appear once a day is a miracle. (Actually, they appear three or
four times a day in different editions.) But, surely, when mistakes are made, they ought to be corrected. Sometimes they are,
but not nearly enough. It is in this respect that Kristol is right
in calling journalism the "underdeveloped profession." . . .

In the wake of so lengthy an analysis, what is there to prescribe? Little. Indeed, to prescribe much would be to miss the
intent of the analysis. I have been hoping to make two points—
the first explicitly, the second largely by implication. The first is
that a convergence of journalistic tradition with evolving cultural
patterns has placed the national government at a kind of operating disadvantage. It is hard for government to succeed: This
theme echoes from every capital of the democratic world. In
the United States, it is hard for government to succeed and just
as hard for government to appear to have succeeded when, indeed, it has done so. This situation can be said to have begun
in the muckraking era with respect to urban government; it is
now very much the case with respect to national government, as
reflected in the "national press," which primarily includes the
New York Times, the *Washington Post, Time, Newsweek,* and
a number of other journals.

There is nothing the matter with investigative reporting; there
ought to be more. The press can be maddeningly complacent
about real social problems for which actual countermeasures, even
solutions, exist. (I spent a decade, 1955–65, trying to obtain some
press coverage of the problem of motor-vehicle design, utterly

without avail. The press, from the most prestigious journals on down, would print nothing but the pap handed out by the automobile companies and wholly owned subsidaries, such as the National Safety Council.) The issue is not one of serious inquiry but of an almost feckless hostility to power.

The second point is that this may not be good for us. American government will only rarely and intermittently be run by persons drawn from the circles of those who own and edit and write for the national press; no government will ever have this circle as its political base. Hence, the conditions are present for a protracted conflict in which the national government keeps losing. This might once have been a matter of little consequence or interest. It is, I believe, no longer such, for it now takes place within the context of what Nathan Glazer has so recently described as an "assault on the reputation of America . . . which has already succeeded in reducing this country, in the eyes of many American intellectuals, to outlaw status." In other words, it is no longer a matter of this or that administration; it is becoming a matter of national morale, of a "loss of confidence and nerve," some of whose possible consequences, as Glazer indicates, are not pleasant to contemplate.

Some will argue that, in the absence of a parliamentary question-time, only the press can keep the Presidency honest. Here, we get much talk about Presidential press conferences and such. This is a serious point, but I would argue that the analogy does not hold. Questions are put in Parliament primarily by members of an opposition party, hoping to replace the one in office. Incompetent questions damage those chances; irresponsible questions damage the office. Indeed, British politicians have been known to compare the press lords to ladies of the street, seeking "power without responsibility." It would, of course, be better all around if Congress were more alert. Thus, the *Times* has reported that the GNP estimate in the 1971 Budget Message was not that of the Council of Economic Advisors but, rather, a higher figure dictated by the White House for political purposes. This is a profoundly serious charge. Someone has a lot to explain. It could be the Administration; it could be the *Times*. Congress should find out.

Obviously, the press of a free country is never going to be, and never should be, celebratory. Obviously, government at all levels needs, and will continue to get, criticism, and some of it will inevitably be harsh or destructive, often enough justifiably so. Obviously, we will get more bad news than good. Indeed, the content of the newspapers is far and away the best quick test of the political structure of a society. Take a morning plane from Delhi to Karachi. One leaves with a sheaf of poorly printed Indian papers filled with bad news; one arrives to find a small number of nicely printed Pakistani papers filled with good news. One has left a democracy and has entered a country that is something less than a democracy.

Nonetheless, there remains the question of balance. Does not an imbalance arise when the press becomes a too willing outlet for mindless paranoia of the Joseph McCarthy or New Left variety? Does it not arise when the press becomes too self-satisfied to report its own mistakes with as much enterprise as it reports the mistakes of others?

Norman E. Isaacs, a working journalist, has written thoughtfully about the possibility of establishing a "national press council." This, in effect, was proposed by Robert M. Hutchins's Commission on Freedom of the Press in 1947: "A new and independent agency to appraise and report annually upon the performance of the press." There are press councils in other democratic countries, which hear complaints, hand down verdicts, and even, as in Sweden, impose symbolic fines. There is a case to be made here, but I would argue that to set up such a council in this country at this time would be just the wrong thing to do. There is a statist quality about many of the press councils abroad: Often as not, they appear to have been set up to ward off direct government regulation. Freedom of the press is a constitutional guarantee in the United States: How that freedom is exercised should remain a matter for the professional standards of those who exercise it. Here, however, there really is room for improvement. First, in the simple matter of competence. The very responsibility of the national press in seeking to deal with complex issues produces a kind of irresponsibility. The reporters aren't up to it. They get it wrong. It would be astonishing were it otherwise.

Further, there needs to be much more awareness of the quite narrow social and intellectual perspective within which the national press so often moves. There are no absolutes here; hardly any facts. But there *is* a condition that grows more, not less, pronounced. The national press is hardly a "value-free" institution. It very much reflects the judgment of owners and editors and reporters as to what is good and bad about the country and what can be done to make things better. It might be hoped that such persons would give more thought to just how much elitist criticism is good for a democracy. Is this a shocking idea? I think not. I would imagine that anyone who has read Peter Gay or Walter Laqueur on the history of the Weimar Republic would agree that there are dangers to democracy in an excess of elitist attack. A variant of the Jacksonian principle of democratic government is involved here. Whether or not ordinary men are capable of carrying out any governmental task whatsoever, ordinary men are going to be given such tasks. That is what it means to be a democracy. We had best not get our expectations too far out of line with what is likely to happen, and we had best not fall into the habit of measuring all performance by the often quite special tastes, preferences, and interests of a particular intellectual and social elite. (Perhaps most importantly, we must be supersensitive to the idea that, if things are not working out well, it is because this particular elite is not in charge. Consider the course of events that led to the war in Indochina.)

As to the press itself, one thing seems clear. It should become much more open about acknowledging mistakes. . . . Doubtless the bane of any editor is the howling of politicians and other public figures claiming to have been misquoted. But often they *are* misquoted. At the very least, should not more space be allotted to rebuttals and exchanges in which the issue at hand is how the press performed?

Another possibility is for each newspaper to keep a critical eye on itself. In the article previously cited that he did for the Sunday *Times Magazine*, A. H. Raskin called for a "Department of Internal Criticism" in every paper "to put all its standards under re-examination and to serve as a public protection in its day-to-day operations." The *Times* itself has yet to establish such a department, but the *Washington Post* has recently set a welcome example here by inaugurating a regular editorial-page feature by Richard Harwood entitled "The News Business." Harwood's business is to check up on what his paper runs, and he is finding a good deal to check up on. (To all editors: *Please* understand there is nothing wrong with this. It is a routine experience of even the most advanced sciences. Perhaps especially of such.) Harwood has made a useful distinction between mistakes of detail—the ordinary garbles and slips of a fast-moving enterprise—and mistakes of judgment about the nature of events:

> *The mistakes that are more difficult to fix are those that arise out of our selection and definition of the news. Often we are unaware of error until much time has passed and much damage has been done.*
>
> *In retrospect, it seems obvious that the destructive phenomenon called "McCarthyism"—the search in the 1950's for witches, scapegoats, traitors—was a product of this kind of error. Joseph McCarthy, an obscure and mediocre senator from Wisconsin, was transformed into the Grand Inquisitor by publicity. And there was no way later for the newspapers of America to repair that damage, to say on the morning after: "We regret the error."*

Which will turn out, "in retrospect," to seem the obvious errors of the 1960's? There were many, but they are past. The question now is what might be the errors of the 1970's, and whether some can be avoided. One Richard Harwood does not a professional upheaval make, but he marks a profoundly important beginning. All major journals should have such a man in a senior post, and very likely he should have a staff of reporters to help him cover the "news business."

As for government itself, there is not much to be done, but there is something. It is perfectly clear that the press will not be intimidated. Specific efforts like President Kennedy's to get David Halberstam removed as a *Times* correspondent in Vietnam almost always fail, as they deserve to do. Nonspecific charges, such as those leveled by Vice President Agnew, get nowhere, either.

They come down to an avowal of dislike, which is returned in more than ample measure, with the added charge that, in criticizing the press, the government may be trying to intimidate it, which is unconstitutional.

What government can do and should do is respond in specific terms to what it believes to be misstatements or mistaken emphases; it should address these responses to specific stories in specific papers, and it should expect that these will be printed (with whatever retort the journal concerned wishes to make). Misrepresentations of government performance must never be allowed to go unchallenged. The notion of a "one-day story," and the consoling idea that yesterday's papers are used to wrap fish, are pernicious and wrong. Misinformation gets into the bloodstream and has consequences. . . .

In the end, however, the issue is one not of politics but of culture. The culture of disparagement that has been so much in evidence of late, that has attained such an astonishing grip on the children of the rich and the mighty, and that has exerted an increasing influence on the tone of the national press in its dealings with the national government, is bad news for democracy. Some while ago, the late Richard Hofstadter foresaw what has been happening:

> *Perhaps we are really confronted with two cultures (not Snow's), whose spheres are increasingly independent and more likely to be conflicting than to be benignly convergent: a massive adversary culture on the one side, and the realm of socially responsible criticism on the other.*

But, given what has been happening to the press in recent years and what is likely to go on being the case if current trends should continue on their present path, where is such "socially responsible criticism" to come from? Or, rather, where is it to appear in a manner that will inform and influence the course of public decision-making?

10

The Presidency Public Relations Script

Thomas E. Cronin *

One of the more disturbing elements in the growth of the Presidential establishment is the development and the recent enlargement of a huge public-relations apparatus. More than a hundred Presidential aides are now engaged in various forms of Presidential press-agentry or public relations—busily selling and packaging the President and his image. The consequences are many. This activity is devoted to the particular occupant of the White House, but, inevitably, it affects the Presidency itself, by projecting or reinforcing personalized images of the Presidency that are almost imperial in their suggestions of omnipotence and omniscience. Thus, the public-relations apparatus not only has directly enlarged the Presidential work force but has expanded public-relations expectations about the Presidency at the same time. More disquieting is the fact that, by its very nature, this type of press-agentry feeds on itself, and the resulting distortions encourage an ever increasing subordination of substance to style.

No President, to be very sure, wants to look unconcerned or weak. And, conditioned by a modern publicity imperative that

* This essay derives from a larger investigation of the state of the modern Presidency, and I am indebted to the Brookings Institution for support of studies of which this is a partial product.

dictates that public leadership actions must parallel show business theatrics, Presidential staff in larger and larger numbers are employed to show that the President really cares, and that he is doing more than he is. The much publicized flexing of Presidency muscles, continual stream of messages to the Congress, and the impressive "to-ing" and "fro-ing" about the globe are occasioned, in part, because the public expects boldness and leadership "shows." Soon, a President is pedaling faster to stay in the same place and needs yet more speech writers, directors of communications, overseers of public-information programs throughout the government, an increasingly activist Office of Telecommunications Policy, and, some fear, even a Domestic Voice of America.

Yet, if Presidents are listened to—and speak—as nothing more than shrewd public-relations men, the very integrity of the institution will be drastically undermined. Still, this is what all too often is happening. The temptation for Presidents to give the appearance of accomplishing more than they actually are characterizes all too well the past three Presidencies. These perceived Presidential publicity imperatives promote a script of means for carrying out Presidential activities, so that the appearance of "looking Presidential" becomes a paramount consideration quite apart from substantive commitments or what is right. These sensitivities and the evolution of what might best be called an "acting President" and a "theatrical Presidency" are understandably tempting precisely because they often do serve the short-term personal and political survival goals of a President.

Presidential aides—press secretaries, speech writers, media specialists, communications counselors, advertising executives, advance men, and so on—continually debate alternative means of carrying out Presidential tasks. Their "stock market" indicators are the Gallup Poll, favorable editorial opinion, "fat cat" donations to Presidential re-election treasuries, and, more broadly, their President's reputation. Concern for a President's popularity, survival and re-election frequently become elevated to ends quite apart from the purposes for which Presidential powers were granted.

Many of the image-tending, public-relations strategies involved here are almost universally associated with public leadership. Indeed, Machiavelli's *Prince* includes a key chapter on "How a Prince Must Act in Order to Gain Reputation." Other contemporary practices are more peculiar to an age of television, swift technological change, nuclear weapons, and experiments in large-scale democracy.

The script outlined below is offered here not necessarily to describe how any particular Presidency has operated but to suggest general patterns and practices upon which several recent Presidents and their lieutenants have relied. There is, to be sure, always a persisting tension between the functions of education and public relations. Indeed, it is often difficult to detect just where education ends and propaganda begins. Effective education surely includes promotion and persuasion. The one requires the other, and the two are exceedingly difficult to separate out from each other. Still, it is abundantly clear, or so I hope to persuade you, that much of what is produced at the White House is largely self-serving, cosmetic "acting" instead of the particularly much needed, educational, and chief-executive leadership so vital to produce change in desired directions.

DON'T JUST STAND THERE—DO SOMETHING!

Indecisiveness, more than anything else, can hurt a President's popularity. For many people, nothing is more reassuring than a President who gives the impression of knowing what to do and is willing to act, especially when others are confused. The accepted technique is to be positive, seize the initiative, have plans (even "secret plans," if necessary), announce new programs, fly here and there, make new appointments. Above all, do not convey the impression that you are sitting on your hands, or, worse yet, that you are asleep. In short, the best defense is an in-motion offense.

A President is generally esteemed if he takes some action, even a wrong one. Declaring oneself is always more popular than remaining neutral, especially in the face of a threat to the *status quo*. President Kennedy should have suffered a great loss of popularity after the incredibly embarrassing Cuban Bay of Pigs setback. But he did not; it actually soared up seven to ten points. George Gallup explains this phenomenon as follows:

> *People tend to judge a man by his goals, by what he is trying to do, and not necessarily by what he accomplishes or by how well he succeeds. People used to tell us over and over again about all the things that [Franklin] Roosevelt did wrong and then they would say, "I'm all for him, though, because his heart is in the right place; he is trying." That is the most important thing in the world!* [1]

During the 1960's, the political incentives seemed to propel energies away from rigorous policy experimentation and planning. *Pass now, plan later!* Presidents and congressional leaders were eager for quick results; they felt they were elected not to study policies but to make them and put them into operation! As one Kennedy-Johnson counselor later recalled:

> *People were always wanting to turn pilot projects into full-scale programs all over the place before they knew the result or before they tested whether things would work. Often we would argue this brief before the President. But again and again between the presidential message and later when it was enmeshed in congressional committees, the departmental and lobbying interests had worked on it in such a way that the program idea would get expanded and markedly changed in scope. Political advisors would always say that to line up the right number of votes you had to spread the program around. So before you had a chance to debug a program, it was being launched nation-wide! The Budget Bureau lost any influence it might have had on many programs because they were set up so rapidly and thrown into the political processes too quickly—everybody wanted results right away. This was also in the character of President Johnson. He was impatient about problem resolving programs; he wanted to do things right away and as fast as he could on a large scale.*

Bend Over Backwards: Disprove Your Stereotypes!

A President must behave in such a way as to counteract or disprove the most egregiously negative stereotypes people have of him. The public feared that General Eisenhower might be easily swayed by his military advisers, and that yet another war might result. Eisenhower not only disproved such fears but gave us one of the few modern peacetime Administrations. Eisenhower made tremendous cuts in the military budgets, and his military policies won little praise from the generals in the Pentagon; indeed, once elected, he may have been the least popular modern President in the military establishment. John F. Kennedy constantly behaved as if to counteract the stereotyped image that he was young, inexperienced, and not tough enough to deal with world leaders. As a result, he overcompensated, as in the humiliating Bay of Pigs debacle, in the perilous, if successful, handling of the Russian missile crisis in Cuba, and in the tragic involvement in Vietnam. And to still the people's fear of a Catholic President, Kennedy became so cautious about any commitments to the Church that his policies and practices have been characterized as perhaps the most anti-Catholic since those of President Millard Fillmore.

Lyndon Johnson had different stereotypes to counteract. Many thought of him as a parochial Southerner who would be soft on civil rights. Johnson himself recalled that he had voted against six major civil-rights bills when he was in Congress. He thought that such legislation was written more to humiliate the South than to help the black people. He also felt that his seat would be in danger if he were to vote otherwise. "I represented a conservative constituency. One heroic stand and I'd be back home, defeated, unable to do any good for anyone, much less the blacks and underprivileged," Johnson has said.[2] But he has also said that, as his national responsibilities (and ambitions) grew, and as he improved his ability to get things done, he became more aware of the need for change. In 1957 and 1960, he voted for moderate civil-rights acts. By 1963, he was seeking to demonstrate that a Southerner could rise above regional attitudes in these matters. In 1964 and 1965, it was as though Johnson wanted to prove once and for all that he should not be identified solely as a Southerner and a wheeler-dealer type of compromiser who would weasel his way out of the controversy over civil rights. He later recalled, in his memoirs, how he tried to outdo the Kennedy commitment:

> *When I sat in the Oval Office after President Kennedy died and reflected on civil rights, there was no question in my mind as to what I would do. I knew that, as President and as a man, I would use every ounce of strength I possessed to gain justice for the black American. My strength as President was then tenuous—I had no strong mandate from the people. I had not been elected to that office. . . . Even the strongest supporters of President Kennedy's civil rights bill in 1963 expected parts of it to be watered down in order to avert a Senate filibuster. . . . I had seen this "moderating" process at work for many years. I had seen it happen in 1957. I had seen it happen in 1960. I did not want to see it happen again. . . . I made my position unmistakably clear: We were not prepared to compromise in any way. . . . I wanted absolutely no room for bargaining. And I wanted everyone to know this, from the lowliest bureaucrat to the members of my Cabinet, from the poorest black man in the slums to the richest white man in the suburbs, from the staunchest Baptist in the South to the most devout Catholic in the North.[3]*

BE RESOLUTE AND FIRM: APPEAR DOMINANT— AT ALL COSTS, AVOID SEEMING "SOFT"!

To have taken decisive and resolute action of one sort or another is to win the admiration of a great following. Know the value of showmanship. Said Machiavelli: "Nothing causes a prince to be so much esteemed as great enterprises and giving proof of prowess." Let him keep his subjects' minds uncertain and astonished and occupied in watching their result. "And above all a prince must endeavor in every action to obtain fame for being great and excellent." [4]

Proclaim every new action as the "first order of business," as the nation's top priority, as a must for government and a right for the citizen. And confront all opponents with stern dichotomies: Love the country or leave it; prudent fiscal policy or budget-wrecking actions; peace with honor or peace with dishonor; and so on. Such simplicity insures good headlines, weakens the opposition, and inhibits serious dialogue.

Since the critical and important problems are not necessarily those that people want to hear about, place critical problems in an unreal light and pose illusory ones as if they were critical. When challenged for doing so, label your challengers as radicals, Nervous Nellies, or ivory-towered intellectuals, or all three.

Whatever the content of your programs and direction of your commitments, claim to be a "reform leader" dedicated to "innovations" and "responsible change." Condemn critics as obstructionists, on the one hand, or as mindless romanticists, on the other.

Know the value of a dangling secret and know, too, the delicate requirements of timing: There is a time for expeditious action, and there is a time for shrewd postponement. The urgency for a quick action is illustrated in John F. Kennedy's anxious response to the Russian propaganda triumph with the first manned orbital flight in 1961: "Is there any place where we can catch them? What can we do? Can we go around the moon before them? Can we put a man on the moon before them? If somebody can just tell me how to catch up. Let's find somebody —anybody. I don't care if it's the janitor over there, if he knows. . . . There is nothing more important." [5]

White House aides, especially those who work in domestic-policy matters, have often noted the need to move on new Presidential initiatives as early as possible. A counselor to three Presidents summed up his view on the vital importance of capitalizing on the opportunities of the first few months of an Administration:

Everything depends on what you do in program formulation during the first six or seven months. I have watched three presidencies and I am increasingly convinced of that. Times goes by so fast. During the first six months or so the White House staff is not hated by the Cabinet, there is a period of friendship and cooperation and excitement. There is some animal energy going for you in those first six to eight months, especially if people perceive things in the same light. If that exists and so long as that exists you can get a lot done. You only have a year at the most for new initiatives, a time when you can establish some programs as your own in contrast to what has gone on before. After that, after priorities are set, and after a president finds he doesn't have time to talk with Cabinet members, that's when the problems set in, and the White House aides close off access to Cabinet members and others.

Another—more speculative—example of timing in this case (in the direction of delay) is the claim that John Kennedy believed he should wait until after the election of 1964 before withdrawing troops from Vietnam. According to Kenneth O'Donnell, a key Kennedy aide, and confirmed by Senator Mike Mansfield, President Kennedy privately said, during the spring of 1963, that a complete withdrawal from Vietnam was needed. "But I can't do it until 1965—after I'm reelected. In 1965, I'll be damned everywhere as a Communist appeaser. But I don't care. If I tried to pull out completely now, we would have another Joe McCarthy red scare on our hands, but I can do it after I'm reelected." [6]

CLAIM TO BE A CONSENSUS LEADER WHEN THE POLLS ARE FAVORABLE AND A "PROFILE IN COURAGE" LEADER WHEN THEY ARE NOT

Prolong the Presidential honeymoon as long as possible. A President must replace partisan politics with consensus politics, be the leader for the whole country, and unite all factions. Honeymoons never last, however, and a President must seek other validation or verifications of his leadership. And nothing is more important for a President than to prove regularly his democratic credentials.

Hence, when the popularity ratings drop, emphasize that, though you are the President of all the people, there is a special responsibility to represent the underrepresented or the badly represented. This is a convenient strategy particularly when faced by a majority opposition against part of the Presidential legislative program. Say now that you are representing the "silent majority," or the next generation, or the minorities, or the young, or the ill fed; be portrayed thus as a moral leader. You are a "profile in courage leader, "doing what is right" rather than what is "popular."

The prerogative of claiming moral considerations in an unpopular decision is a well-established Presidential tradition. Consider President Nixon's explanation of why he sent U.S. troops to Cambodia in spring, 1970:

> *I have noted, for example, that a Republican Senator has said that this action I have taken means that my party has lost all chances of winning the November elections, and others are saying that this move against enemy sanctuaries will make me a one-term President. . . .*
>
> *I would rather be a one-term President and do what I believe was right than to be a two-term President at the cost of seeing America become a second-rate power and to see this nation accept the first defeat in its proud 190-year history.*[7]

In the early years of his Administration, Lyndon Johnson proudly walked around with assorted favorable polls stuffed in his pocket, the results of which were ever mentioned in his conversations as he pointed out the virtues of his consensus strategy. On one occasion, Johnson told reporters, with obvious delight, "This paper has the latest Gallup figures and I now rate higher than John Kennedy *ever* did." [8] As time wore on, public support and consensus politics measurably diminished, and so also, understandably, did Johnson's high value on the polls. Later in his Presidency, Johnson took the tack that he was doing what was right, even if, as with his civil-rights and Vietnam commitments, he was hurt significantly in the polls: "In this job a man must set a standard to which he's working. In my case, it is what my grandchildren think when I'm buried out there under the tree on the ranch. I think they will be proud of two things. What I did for the Negro and seeing it through in Vietnam for all of Asia. The Negro cost me 15 points in the polls and Vietnam cost me 20." [9]

TRAVEL WIDELY, BE A STATESMAN, RUN FOR A NOBEL PEACE PRIZE—AND BE YOUR OWN SECRETARY OF STATE

Consensus is easier to achieve on national defense and international peace aims than on the more divisive problems affecting the nation internally. Every President since Theodore Roosevelt has been mindful that, having achieved celebrity-number-one status at home, no prize is more cherished than a Nobel Peace Prize. TR won his in 1906, for his vigorous efforts in arranging the peace agreement between the Russians and Japanese a year or two earlier.

It is abundantly clear that the American people crave for statesmanship, and that, to make history's list of "great" Presidents, one must (1) make the world safe for democracy and (2) make the American dollar safe for the world. Hence, to appear to be an architect for a lasting peace is an image that takes over; it becomes an obsession.

Know the value of international travel, of person-to-person diplomacy, and the imperative of being your own Secretary of State. One can concentrate on foreign affairs with trips, summits, treaties, negotiations, and plans for generations of peace and still seem like an effective, or at least an adequate, President.

DO NOT LET THE VICE PRESIDENT OR ANY OTHER MEMBER OF THE CABINET OR WHITE HOUSE STAFF UPSTAGE OR OUTSHINE YOU

Avoid party responsibilities and fund-raising activities: Delegate those to your Vice President or Attorney General or to party officials. Highly partisan and divisive activities may routinely be assigned the Vice President (1) to keep him busy, (2) to insure

his popularity does not outstrip the President's, and (3) to demonstrate, by contrast, that the President is "above politics."

Accentuate the role of President as symbolic leader: Satisfy the
American passion for a benevolent father-image, for a superhero.
Ceremonial activities, close association with entertainment and
professional superstars and "winners," and Billy Graham–cloak-
tailing are top priorities. Charisma, in part, can be manufactured,
borrowed, and staged. But keep attractive politicians out of your
Cabinet, off your staff. Unretired politicians make questionable
cheerleaders.

CLAIM CREDIT WHEN THINGS GO RIGHT AND DECENTRALIZE BLAME; BE VERY SELECTIVE IN CHOOSING PROBLEMS FOR THEIR POTENTIAL CREDIT VALUE

President Kennedy knew the value of expropriating credit
when policies worked and decentralizing it when they did not.
At the conclusion of some White House discussions for handling
one complex foreign-policy problem, Kennedy cheerfully told
some of the participants: "I hope this plan works. If it does, it
will be another White House success. If it doesn't, it will be
another State Department failure." [10]

Presidents like to be loved, not excoriated—especially with the
floodlights of public attention constantly beaming down on them.
Precisely because their job can be so brutal, counselors to a
President are always under orders: "If we can't solve this problem, let's find problems we can solve." Or, at least, appear to
solve. Concentrate on those programs you can get passed. Concentrate on what you can do well. Concentrate on those matters
for which credit is obtainable.

PROCLAIM AN "OPEN PRESIDENCY" AND AN "OPEN ADMINISTRATION," BUT PRACTICE PRESIDENCY-BY-SECRECY, MANAGE THE NEWS, AND CIRCUMVENT THE WHITE HOUSE PRESS CORPS

Hold numerous news conferences during your honeymoon; but,
afterwards, appeal directly to the people by addresses over the

heads of the Washington press (when too many unkept promises can make news conferences embarrassing). Know well the convenience of secrecy: Secrecy helps to conceal limitations, mistakes, and arbitrariness.

Proclaim that the "news" is what the White House says it is. Generously, say that press conferences will be held when it serves the public interest—but do not explain that the appropriate time for a press conference is always to be decided backstage by the White House public-relations executives.

Know, too, that the best policy toward the White House press corps is that of "making them comfortable and leaving them ignorant." Keep them busy trekking to and from Camp David and various other Presidential retreats. Remember that Presidents who were the most honest, accessible, and candid—for example, Harry Truman—also had the lowest popularity ratings.

As one political scientist sums it up:

Like the movie star [the political star] is known primarily through pictures on screens and billboards, voices from loudspeakers, anecdotes in newspapers and magazines. These are appearances, and, as such, they are subject to certain kinds of manipulation. Like the movie star, the politician has the possibility of becoming a mythical character. In both cases, also, the myth can be a managed one.[11]

HISTORY AND HISTORIANS REWARD HIM WHO SEEMS TO PROTECT AND STRENGTHEN THE POWERS OF THE PRESIDENCY

Appear to expand the executive powers and leave the executive office a larger, more capable institution. Even if controversial in the short term, such ostensible enlargements will be praised almost always by posterity.

Criticize congressional measures to lessen Presidential discretion. Decry such efforts as reactionary and contrary to the spirit of strict construction of the Constitution. Remember, too, that the Supreme Court has invariably been more friendly to the Presidency than to Congress.

IF ALL ELSE FAILS, WAGE WAR ON THE PRESS, IMPUGN ITS
OBJECTIVITY, UNDERMINE CONFIDENCE IN ITS FAIRNESS AND
INTEGRITY; DENATIONALIZE NETWORKS, PACIFY PUBLIC
BROADCASTING, INVESTIGATE REPORTERS, AND INTIMIDATE
PUBLIC-AFFAIRS VIDEO JOURNALISM

Being President means never having to say you're sorry—or
wrong. Hence, when the public begins to question a President's
performance, he is, of course, tempted to blame his problems on
the press. Any credibility problem becomes theirs, not his.

Of particular concern today is the fact that television has
become *the* Presidential medium. When his popularity sags, and
when he is hedged in by Congress or by the Court, he turns to
television as an obvious platform from which to proclaim bold
initiatives and to dress up old platitudes in new slogans. Presidential announcements staged cleverly, and deceptively, can
nearly always resuscitate or reclaim former support by a dramatic
new video performance. Hence, a President elected for reasons
often unrelated to his leadership capabilities can engineer a
public reputation quite inconsistent with his substantive leadership performance. The selling of the Presidency can be as devious
as the original selling of the Presidential candidate.

The deceit lies in the subordination of policy substance to
Presidential style. In a world of rosy releases and enormously
expanded Presidential manipulation of data to accentuate the
positive, there is a compelling need for institutions or ombuds-
men who would decry as well as investigate the behavior of any
President who succumbs to that intoxicating elixir of publicity
flimflam.

In one sense, we have grown callously accustomed to officials
who fail to honor the doctrine of self-restraint implicit in the
First Amendment. We are uncomfortably close to witnessing an
institutionalized editor-in-chief component within the federal
government. The verdict, in part, is also that we are a nation
in search of heroes and of drama. For a President to admit confusion or uncertainty is, for him, to betray the public demand.
We continue to think of a President's decision as a lonely act of
will capable of being made with lightening-bolt speed. A Presi-

dent must be dramatic and exciting to maintain a public following, to live up to the public confidence, and to compete for news coverage, since he is merely one more form of entertainment in this increasingly wired nation. If a President is not traveling to a summit meeting, presiding over a crisis, or announcing some bold new domestic-policy war, he risks being relegated to the back pages and to little or no TV coverage. The incentives are strong to adopt this script and avoid boring the American public: Be dramatic, be novel, be international, be secret, be center stage, be decisive!

But a popular government without honest reports from the leaders is a contradiction. A democratic society can be achieved only if Presidents and the public alike are prepared to speak directly and candidly to each other and are equally prepared to criticize and correct the errors made against each other. Basic to these aims in contemporary America is a Presidency that listens and speaks—and can be listened and spoken to—as something substantially more than a cosmetic-laden, public-relations agency.

Sunlight they say is one of the best of disinfectants—but it must be coupled in this instance by at least three concrete remedies that would help open up the Presidency and make it more publicly answerable. First, by letting the salutary light of public attention shine more brightly on the Presidency, there should be an immediate upgrading of the coverage of the White House and the Presidential Establishment by the serious journals and news media of the nation. For too long, publishers and editors have believed that covering the Presidency means assigning one reporter to the White House press corps. Unfortunately, however, those who follow a President around on his travels are rarely in a position to do investigative reporting on what is going on inside the Presidential establishment and to unmask the complicated public-relations strategies that have now become so commonplace there. Covering the executive office of the President requires more than a mere President-watcher; it needs specialists who understand the arcane language and highly complicated, bureaucratic politics and practices that have developed in the Presidential Establishment.

Second, every reasonable effort should be made, by the press and the public alike, to insist on regularly held Presidential news conferences. It has often been said that Presidents easily dominate these affairs and use them for their own purposes. Sometimes, this is the case; sometimes, however, Presidents wish that this practice had never come about. For the regularly scheduled news conference offers the press a much-needed opportunity to ask embarrassing questions, to probe about arbitrary or devious Presidential activities, and to hold a President answerable. To be sure, these conferences are an imperfect device. But, held regularly and conducted properly, these sessions can be one of the most useful means of keeping Presidents alert to the questions bothering the attentive public. They can also occasionally inform a President about scandals, maladministration, or other irresponsible behavior in the federal government that may not otherwise have come to his attention. It is well known that President Kennedy used his frequent press conferences as important action-forcing and information-generating devices. Perhaps the greatest tribute to the utility of press conferences is that certain of our recent Presidents most avoided them amidst embarrassments with unsuccessful policies or grievous scandals.

Finally, Congress could do substantially more to keep the Presidency in line and to insist on more honest and candid Presidential public reporting. At the very least, Congress should establish standing committees on the Executive Office and Presidential operations. Most congressional committees are organized to deal with areas such as labor, agriculture, the armed services, education, and other substantive issues that are far more characteristic of the past than the present and future. If vast amounts of influence and discretionary authority have now passed to the Presidency, and if the public-relations strategies of the modern Presidency too often have subverted important principles, then it is abundantly clear that Congress should reconstitute itself so that it can oversee and investigate White House operations. What we need now are committees designed explicitly to serve as watchdogs and sentinels over White House practices. No longer can the task of overseeing vast Presidential operations be divided among dozens of committees and subcommittees, none of which looks systematically at the whole picture. What the Presidency does (and does not do) must rank among the most vital concerns of Congress. Congress and the people must have much better access to information that is too often denied to them; for Congress and the people have for too long been the victims of a public-relations script that needs vigilant scrutiny and appropriate debunking.

NOTES

[1] George Gallup, comment in *Opinion Polls*, a discussion paper published by the Center for the Study of Democratic Institutions (Santa Barbara, Calif., 1962), p. 35.

[2] Lyndon B. Johnson, *The Vantage Point* (Holt, Rinehart & Winston, 1971), p. 155.

[3] *Ibid.*, p. 157.

[4] Niccolò Machiavelli, *The Prince and the Discourses* (Modern Library, 1950 ed.), chap. 21, pp. 81 and 82.

[5] John F. Kennedy, as quoted in Hugh Sidey, *John F. Kennedy: Portrait of a President* (Atheneum, 1964), pp. 122–23. See also his entire chap. 8; and Hugh Young, Bryan Silcock, and Peter Dunn, "Why We Went to the Moon: From the Bay of Pigs to the Sea of Tranquility," *Washington Monthly* (April, 1970), pp. 28–58.

[6] Primary documentation of this Kennedy "decision" does not exist. It is related in the personal recollections of his appointments secretary and chief political counselor, Kenneth O'Donnell, in "LBJ and the Kennedys," *Life* magazine (August, 1970), pp. 51–52. His view, however, was immediately backed up by Senator Mike Mansfield.

[7] Richard Nixon, as carried in the *New York Times*, May 1, 1971.

[8] Quoted in Merriman Smith, *A White House Memoir* (Norton, 1971), p. 36.

[9] David Wise, "The Twilight of a President," *New York Times Magazine*, November 3, 1968, p. 131.

[10] Quoted in Harlan Cleveland, *The Future Executive* (Harper & Row, 1972), pp. 95–96.

[11] Stanley Kelley, *Presidential Public Relations and Political Power* (Johns Hopkins, 1956), p. 221.

IV

The Presidential Person

11

The Health of Presidents

Milton Plesur

This is not a technical analysis of Presidential ailments but, rather, a consideration of selected aspects of the physical and mental vitality of our recent chief executives to the degree that health influenced the conduct of the office.* My task is fraught with difficulties, since many illnesses in former days were undiagnosed, and in the present century the White House staff has always been prone to emphasize robust qualities of its chief occupant, except in occasional instances where illness could not be denied. Further, it is taxing to compare different personalities holding office during different times that presented problems of varying difficulties. Obviously, what was sound medical treatment in one period was considered useless, or even barbaric, with the general advance of therapeutics.

Hence, my assignment involves contradictions; four of the five Presidents rated "great" by historians in a 1962 poll had serious physical handicaps, whereas others, who were thought less capable, were physically most healthy. Some Presidents were health enthusiasts and overachievers in office, but died relatively early deaths; other more sedentary types, some burdened with overweight, lived beyond their normal expectancies. Such paradoxes complicate the task of arriving at definite conclusions on the subject of Presidential health.

And, even if it is obvious that the possibility of serious illness, incapacity, or even death will affect a President's performance in office, and possibly influence vital decisions, how can we measure the impact of ill health? Would Coolidge's performance, for example, have been less lackadaisical had he been more vital? How would Franklin D. Roosevelt have acted at Yalta had he not been the victim of advanced sclerotic disease? Would a healthy Wilson have grasped the necessity of compromise during the prolonged League of Nations debate? Inquiries such as these are sometimes regarded as excursions into trivia, but the course of history has often been linked with Presidential disorders.

In an open society, with finely honed mass media, secrecy regarding the personal life of a President is an impossibility. American voters assume that they are entitled to know everything about their elected leaders, including their health. Of course, much of the motivation for this knowledge is frankly morbid, but an examination of the number of Presidents who have been seriously ill upholds the public assumption that the right to know is important in an age when the future of civilization could depend upon a decision to use nuclear weapons.

Presidential physicians have generally been reluctant to divulge information, certainly during the President's lifetime. Perhaps in cases where public knowledge might have resulted in national panic—such as Grover Cleveland's operation for removal of a cancerous growth—secrecy is understandable. But this cannot always be justified. Wilson's doctor conspired with Mrs. Wilson to keep information about the President's health from the public; Franklin Roosevelt's physicians certainly seriously underplayed their patient's condition. The specifics of John Kennedy's adrenocortical deficit are still not known. On the other hand, every conceivable detail regarding Eisenhower's three major illnesses while in office was shared with the public. And the nation received regular medical bulletins describing Lyndon Johnson's medical problems and the progress made by Richard Nixon as he recovered from viral pneumonia. Nonetheless, the principle generally followed by the White House physicians would indicate that they and their Presidential patients have maintained that health is a private matter.[1]

Given what we do know about Presidential health, the findings are not conclusive that the burdens of the Presidency shorten life. The naked figures seems to bear out the "burden" theory. The earlier Presidents, evidently of tougher stock than their later counterparts, lived longer despite a shorter average life expectancy. Of the first eight Presidents, all except George Washington outlived the expectancy of life at their inauguration. The average age of death of the first fifteen, from Washington to Buchanan, was 74; those who served from Lincoln to the second Roosevelt lived to an average age of 63. Since the Civil War, only Cleveland, Taft, Hoover, Eisenhower, and Truman exceeded their life expectancies at the time of inauguration.[2] Nevertheless, though generalizations on the basis of only 35 deceased men are tenuous, it is true that the average duration of Presidential life has been shorter than might have been expected. Kennedy's optimistic remark about thriving under the pressure of office and Harry Truman's oft-quoted comment about "heat in the kitchen" are recalled; but most students of the office feel that the job is wearying. The late Clinton Rossiter, of Cornell University, asserted that the President would be best served by those virtues celebrated in the New Testament, *The Compleat Gentleman*, and the Handbook of the Boy Scouts of America. A chief executive, he argued, should be healthy, in the sense of being free from ailments; should possess bounce and elasticity, so as to thrive on a tough regimen of work and responsibility—and all this at a time usually past middle age, when some decline has to be expected! [3] Added to pomp and circumstance as a never-ending source of tension are physical fatigue and emotional drain. No responsible union would ever approve the President's hours of work for a "hard-hat"; and an insurance company would probably define the ordinary White House occupant as a poor insurance risk! The President must shake many hands, attempt to digest high-calorie banquet fare, attend ceremonies, and always be "center stage." No President can escape his burdens; wherever he is, the White House moves with him.

Upon the death of any President in office, the press invariably speculates on the issues of health and the burdens of office: It has often been asserted that physical fitness and relaxation were the only safeguards for Presidents, and it is true that energy or torpor, as well as relaxation habits, can be gauges to health problems.

It has recently been reported that President Nixon gave up golf as too time-consuming and much publicity was given to his conversion of the White House pool into press facilities. Bowling, swimming, and time away from Washington at the Camp David retreat or in the Florida or California sun are his diversions, but the officer with the black box containing the codes to nuclear firing follows him constantly—an unpleasant reminder that there is no escape.

Theodore Roosevelt was the most athletic of our Presidents. He enjoyed his bouts with the punching bag (ruining his eyesight because of a boxing accident), originated the fifty-mile hike, and wore off excess energy by learning jujitsu; yet, he died at sixty. Woodrow Wilson rode horses and golfed inexpertly early in his Presidency; and, under the guidance of Walter Camp, he and the Cabinet performed—as others were admonished to—their "daily dozen." Warren Harding was a horseback rider and relaxed even more around a poker table. Calvin Coolidge's exercise was limited to fishing, morning walks, and riding his celebrated electric hobby horse. Coolidge's sleep habits, amounting to about eleven hours a day, are well known, and yet he died at the same age as Theodore Roosevelt the activist. Herbert Hoover was much like James Polk, in that he seldom took extended vacations, was relatively unrelaxed, and worked long hours; but he did go fishing and did toss a medicine ball. The "Great Engineer" reached 90, whereas Polk died a few months after leaving the White House. Franklin Roosevelt derived his relaxation from swimming, poker games, and a stamp collection. Probably the most famous peripatetic President was Truman, who found his daily brisk walks, together with his piano playing and poker playing, therapeutic. And Lyndon Johnson escaped to his Texas ranch frequently for relaxation. But all that can be concluded from the foregoing examples is that positive recreational habits are necessary for Presidents in order to counteract a pressured existence, but the long-range of such habits is problematical.

Nor do Presidential battles with bulging waist lines prove very much. The elephantine Taft had a voracious appetite, and, though he dieted intermittenly, he at one point soared to about 350 pounds. Nevertheless, he lived into his seventies. Grover Cleveland hovered between 250 and 270 pounds, and yet he also reached three score and ten years. His love of wine and song, and the well-known wenching and beer bouts of his Buffalo days, added to his girth and the two or three chins he sported; but he never seemed as lethargic as Taft. In the precalorie-counting, precholestoral age, Chester Alan Arthur was famous for opulent dinners, heavy foods, and fine wines and liqueurs. The Presidential figure expanded, and he suffered from chronic indigestion, and, until recently, it was thought he died from apoplexy or chronic gall bladder disease at fifty-six—scarcely a year after he left the White House. However, the latest evidence points to Arthur's demise from Bright's Disease, a fatal kidney ailment.[4] Some of the more intimate publicity about Lyndon Johnson was his constant battle with an ever expanding waistline. His long-time cook described the White House as the perfect place to gain weight, and she and the President's physician were in constant collusion in a half-successful battle to contain the Presidential intake.

Despite the contradictory evidence we have already considered, some discussion of the sickness-prone Presidents of this century may help us in reaching some tentative conclusions about what relationship there may be between Presidential health and effectiveness in office.

Theodore Roosevelt's childhood was marked by bronchial asthma and respiratory illness, and, as is well known, he overcame these by outdoor, ranchlike routines. His love of physical exercise throughout his life was a definite carry-over from the days of building up his body by a systematic program, and his struggle against asthma was probably a vital force in shaping his future life-style. As President, he exercised strenuously at least two hours a day; and it was while boxing that he suffered a retinal hemorrhage, resulting in almost total blindness to one eye. Roosevelt was accident prone, and there were only a few parts of his body that were not injured at one time or another. In his post-Presidential years, he suffered from a would-be assassin's bullet, rheumatic problems, a tropical fever contracted while on safari, and an ear infection; but he often remarked that the White House improved his health. As the youngest President at the time of his accession, Roosevelt should have been in good health; yet his reckless manner and the number of accidents he sustained before, during, and after his Presidency must have contributed to his death at sixty.

The Presidency undoubtedly contributed to Wilson's poor health in office and to his breakdown at sixty-three. Though not as weak as once believed, he did have a history of nervous indigestion, headaches, and various gastrointestinal episodes; also, there is evidence of a mild stroke in 1906 during his Princeton years. During his years as President, his health held up until the arduous negotiations at Versailles that induced indigestion and headaches; his weakened body was finally wracked by influenza. He collapsed on his famous nationwide "swing around the circle" defending the League of Nations and suffered a serious stroke following his return to Washington. With official Washington silent and the President out of circulation, there was much uneasiness. After a frightening bladder infection (which subsided), Wilson made a partial recovery, sufficient for him to take active charge of the government once again.

Historians have been concerned about the relationship between Wilson's stroke and his state of mind. The recalcitrant attitude and sense of moral superiority he showed during his battle with the Senate over the League of Nations could possibly be interpreted as reflections of a disturbed personality. A dubious psychological study of Wilson, by Dr. Sigmund Freud and William C. Bullitt, portrays him as psychopathic at Versailles, but this book was a product of Freud's senility and Bullitt's hatred of Wilson. Basing their conclusions on Wilson's relationship with his father, they advance the thesis that Wilson was badly hampered as President. The Freud-Bullitt study was based on careless conjecture, and is probably to be entirely rejected as historical evidence. Much more sound are the conclusions of Dr. Edwin A. Weinstein, who has described Wilson's emotional instability during his illness, marked by alternating moods of euphoria and depression. Wilson, Weinstein feels, demonstrated characteristics of an anosognosic personality, in which physical manifestations and consequences of illness and incapacity are separated from the real self and given meaning in the context of values. For Wilson, illness became a moral weakness and a loss of integrity, the antidote for which was to deny incapacity for strenuous work. Despite gloomy predictions after the initial stroke and thereafter, the Wilson record is an example of the imprecise relationship between health and Presidential performance.[5]

In the nineteenth century, Presidents William H. Harrison and Zachary Taylor died from natural causes. The third President to succumb in this manner while in office was Harding. In 1923, a *Saturday Evening Post* article based on an interview with his personal physician declared that the President was not active enough, and was cramped by the formalities of a burdensome office for which, Dr. Charles E. Sawyer might have added, his patient was ill prepared. In January, 1922, Harding supposedly contracted influenza, but there is reason to suspect that, in fact, he had a slight coronary. Thereafter, he experienced increased fatigue, and a rest trip to Alaska was prescribed. When he reached Seattle, on his return home, he suffered a seizure. His personal physician, a homeopath and "Ohio Gang Crony" who, to put it charitably, was hardly a leading physician, diagnosed the ailment as an acute gastrointestinal attack caused by crabmeat—which the President, in fact, had not eaten. A few days later, in San Francisco, a new seizure was diagnosed as bronchopneumonia and circulatory failure. While in bed, listening to his wife's reading, the President quietly passed away. The official bulletin announced the cause of death as apoplexy, but some physicians felt that it was a coronary thrombosis. Harding had suffered from hypertension, angina pectoris, and an enlarged heart and had acute gastrointestinal attacks. His weight had climbed to 240 pounds; he was short of breath, and daily chores seemed to be a physical effort. The absence of an autopsy gave rise to preposterous rumors that the President took poison, was poisoned by his wife to save him from scandals about to be exposed, or even died of a venereal infection. The uncomfortable medical fact about Harding was that the physicians were unable to make a correct diagnosis from the clinical signs, and, despite the existence of the electrocardiograph since 1903, no recording was taken of Harding's heart in 1923. The popular press, in grief over Harding's death at fifty-seven, said that the burden of office killed him; but, in truth, Harding's medical history, his overindulgence in rich foods and liquor, his emotional stresses, and a severe disillusion with the office are more valid explanations.[6]

One of the most arresting of all recent Presidential medical stories is that of Franklin Roosevelt. Nearly asphyxiated at birth because of an overdose of chloroform administered to his mother, FDR was plagued all his life by a sensitive respiratory tract. A bad bronchitis attack, in 1943, was noted by some as the beginning of his failing health. His well-being had been a matter of perennial speculation ever since he first aspired to national political leadership following his contraction of polio at thirty-nine. Heavy braces on his legs kept his body upright, and, with the aid of crutches, he could take fitful steps. But Democratic Party Chairman James A. Farley met the rumors of serious ill health, in 1932, by revealing that his candidate had recently secured a king-sized life-insurance policy.

Aside from the ever present bronchial and sinus trouble, Roosevelt's medical history was uneventful, despite the constant speculation. As if in answer to the question posed by *Liberty* magazine in June, 1936, "Is President Roosevelt a well man today?" his personal physician, Dr. Ross T. McIntire, declared that the President, since taking office, had not missed a single day's work because of illness. But, in time, the pressures of protracted domestic depression and global war did drain Roosevelt's prodigious energy. Some have even contended that, in 1938, FDR suffered the first of a series of minor strokes, but this has never been supported by clinical proof.

During the fourth-term campaign of 1944, Roosevelt displayed "good health" for the critics—especially those who noted how badly he faltered in an appearance at the Bremerton Naval Yard in Washington—by riding for fifty-six minutes in an open car during a freezing Manhattan rain. The press noted that Dr. McIntire had insisted that the chief executive was not dying, nor was he even sick during 1944; in other words, the fatal stroke of April 12, 1945, was unforeseeable. The White House physician, however, did concede fatigue, but said that his patient's blood pressure was normal, and that there was no sign of arteriosclerosis.

Following the Yalta Conference, in early 1945, Vice President Truman admitted he was disturbed by the "boss's" appearance; correspondent Merriman Smith wrote that he saw the President "die" over a period of a year—a conclusion concurred in by millions who saw the most recent pictures of the President. There were undoubtedly increasing head colds; the heavy braces were abandoned; cigarettes were cut from two packs to one pack a day. Roosevelt was obviously nervous and jumpy, and had little taste for food. When he addressed Congress, upon his return from the Crimea, the marvelous voice was weaker, and the words were slurred and hurried; there were departures from the text and, for the first time, references to his braces. In short, the old Roosevelt bounce had disappeared. There was no doubt that the President was truly sick, but it has never been proved, nor is it very likely ever to be proved, that that sickness contributed to an American sell-out to the Russians at Yalta, as many critics contended. The story is that he suffered a stroke at Hyde Park in late March, 1945, and, after recovering, went to Warm Springs, where he then died of a massive cerebral hemorrhage. It seems inconceivable, however, that his personal physician would not have accompanied him if the situation was, indeed, all that precarious.

The physician who attended FDR during his last illness, Dr. Howard G. Bruenn, in an account of his relationship with the President from March, 1944, to April, 1945, reported that Roosevelt was sick in his final year, but that he was not dying; specifically, FDR was suffering from an enlarged heart, had hardening of the arteries, and his blood pressure was alarmingly high. With special care, there gradually came an improvement, however, and the campaign of 1944 passed without incident. Thus, if we interpret Bruenn correctly, the evidence indicates that the President was able to perform his duties despite hypertension and fatigue, and that his death was due to a stroke that, in view of his medical history, was clearly predictable. Dr. Bruenn's report, published a generation after FDR's death, was obviously more realistic than the optimistic and reassuring words of Dr. McIntire.

That Roosevelt was gravely ill had apparently been suspected, if not known for a certainty, by many even before his return from Yalta. Walter Lippmann, for example, in writing of the subject, asserts that, in 1944, Harry S. Truman was nominated in Chicago by a convention fully aware that it was "almost certainly choosing a president of the United States." However, those who hinted at the time that Roosevelt was not a well man were rebuked as little better than fifth columnists by the White House retinue. The Roosevelt story, then, raised many questions, and the problem of Presidential health loomed larger than ever.[7]

Eisenhower, before assuming office, was in generally good health, but, during his incumbency, he suffered three major illnesses: coronary thrombosis (1955), major surgery to correct an acute ileitis (1956), and a "small" stroke (1957). The oldest man ever to hold the office, he nevertheless survived a work load that was amazing for a man of his years and for one with his medical history. In 1956, the physicians reported that, medically, he could serve another five to ten years in office; and several years later Dr. Paul Dudley White, Ike's chief physician at the time of the coronary, wrote to me (June 21, 1970) that "Eisenhower's illnesses had no effect on the conduct of his administration other than causing temporary absences which were well handled by his many and efficient assistants."

Even before the heart attack, Eisenhower was annoyed about not being allowed, as he put it, to have a bellyache in private. After each illness, all the details were made public: People were informed of the President's blood pressure, pulse rate, and caloric intake; of the size of the damaged area around his heart; of the state of his eliminative processes, and even the size of his prostate gland.

Eisenhower, the first President to suffer from so many severe illnesses while serving, recovered from them while in office, and even came to enjoy his position in those later years. He survived for fourteen years after his first heart attack; and this makes it necessary to evaluate the whole question of physical handicaps. It might even be argued that expert medical care more than compensated for the work load.

John Kennedy had a well-publicized medical past. Despite his popularization of "vigah," vitality, and stamina, he suffered constantly from back pain as a result of a ruptured disc caused initially by an early football injury and aggravated by war wounds. Beginning in 1944, he underwent three operations on his back, one of them nearly resulting in his death. Aided by novocain treatments, he mended well enough to be pronounced in good health in 1960; but, while making a short visit to Canada the next year, he stooped to turn earth for a tree planting, and pain persisted for six months. His therapy consisted of daily baths, a special brace, prescribed calisthenics and swimming, and the famous rocking chair. His backache plagued him throughout a trip to Vienna—the one during which he had his famous confrontation with Khrushchev—but he concealed discomfort. Dr. Janet Travell, his personal physician, described the new backache as a common variety not connected with his old ailment, but she promptly limited tree planting, golfing, and romping with his children. Dr. Travell made it a point, however, to announce that there was no plan to reduce JFK's official duties.

Since Eisenhower's illnesses, frank and even intimate information about Presidential health came to be expected; but Kennedy's press aides and physcans were reluctant to discuss his problems. The back problem was common knowledge, but his adrenal glands provided more mysterious. It is not clear whether he suffered from classic Addison's disease (a hormone disorder resulting from a deficiency of the corticosteroid hormone produced from the adrenals, two glands located above the kidneys); but he did have an adrenal deficiency. Robert Kennedy denied most strenuously that his brother had Addison's disease. One cause of the disease is tuberculosis of the kidneys, but Dr. Travell stated that JFK had no visible signs of the disease and had not taken cortisone for years. (He did take, prophylactically, a cortisonelike medicine to make up for his adrenal deficiency when under stress.) Kennedy's possible adrenal problems prompted a Lyndon Johnson enthusiast, in the preconvention campaign of 1960, to assert that Kennedy would be dead if it were not for cortisone injections. The Johnson forces thus countered Kennedy's reference to their man's 1955 heart attack.[8]

Given the health experience of his predecessors, together with his own past, Lyndon Johnson furnishes another experience in Presidential medical problems. His own history included recurring bronchial illnesses and heavy colds, threatened pneumonia, surgery for the removal of his appendix, a kidney stone problem, and a 1955 coronary from which recovery took over five months. Concern for Johnson's heart began the day he became President. Back in Washington from the Dallas nightmare, he was examined and given a clean bill of health. The physicians would not predict whether he might suffer another attack, but they maintained that, after surviving so long with no trouble, he was no more likely to be stricken than someone with no history of cardiac trouble.

As President, he had a kidney stone problem, corrected by surgery, recurring bronchial illness, the removal of a wartlike growth from his hand, and a gall bladder operation in 1956. Johnson prepared the nation for this latter surgery (the announcement skillfully timed not to upset the Stock Exchange), and, after consulting with General Eisenhower, he announced his pending surgery as far in advance as possible, remaining candid with the press and the public. He also endured the removal of a benign polyp from his throat as well as the repair of an abdominal hernia; and, in 1968, it was announced that he was suffering from an intestinal ailment (diverticulosis). When chest pains and a heavy cold sent Johnson to the Naval Medical Center in 1965, this, plus his operations, caused tremors throughout the nation.

In addition to the political reasons for Johnson's historic "abdication" decision of March 31, 1968, there were also motivations of health. He recalled that the men in his family generally did not live much beyond sixty. He spoke of his own massive coronary, admitted to fatigue, and recalled Wilson's disability. The threats to his own life and Lady Bird's alleged fears that he could not survive another term may, in addition to the Tet offensive, Senator Eugene McCarthy's showing in New Hampshire, and Robert Kennedy's candidacy, have been factors in this decision. For the first time, a President referred very candidly and intimately to his own health problems, associating them with politics. And, in 1972, LBJ suffered his second coronary, and the arterio-sclerotic damage was so severe that he could not sustain a third attack in January, 1973. With Johnson's death, no ex-Presidents survive.

The Presidents discussed above were ill during their terms or were prone to sickness. In contrast to his immediate predecessors (except the healthy Truman), it is interesting to examine the health of the present Presidential incumbent, certainly one of the healthiest of all Chief Executives. Prior to the summer of 1973, when he suffered from viral pneumonia, Richard M. Nixon never missed a day's work as President, had not been hospitalized since 1960, and had in fact boasted that he never had a headache in his life. According to his physician, this is thanks, in large part, to a morning exercise program of running briskly in place 300 to 400 steps. This rather light exercise, together with some hiking, swimming, golfing, and bowling, as well as a low choles-terol spartan diet, aims at increasing his cardiac tone. In addi-tion, the President also is supposed to receive special muscle manipulation in order to stave off nervous tensions. For one who has served under Eisenhower, such health concern is obvious. Nixon is reputed to have said that, though he appreciates that the Presidency is probably the most difficult job in the world, he has not found it burdensome; indeed, he thrives on work. Nixon's aides feel that this reflects a high degree of efficiency and organizational talent.

The low-keyed, serene Nixon profile may well be related to health matters. The "cushioning" of the President and the ra-tioning of his time were justified on the grounds that he does tire easily. James Reston of the *New York Times* described Nixon as understanding well the dangers of exhaustion, but lamented the so-called work-vacations; Reston called for a "re-laxed moderation and perspective," which he frankly feels im-possible, given the Nixon chemistry. But, assuredly, Nixon is the beneficiary of all the previous publicity and knowledge about the health problems of his predecessors. Seemingly in splendid health, he exercises what caution is necessary to prevent future problems incidental to a man in his sixties.[9]

Predictions and speculation about the health of Presidents or future candidates appears not to be rewarding. Political scientist James D. Barber has suggested interesting speculations on the relationship between Presidential character, or psyche, and Presidential style. To attempt to arrive at similar conclusions from a study of physical health is more hazardous. Health is unpredictable—even in cases where there has been no previous history of illness.[10]

In today's age of media control, the tendency is to publicize the health of candidates and, indeed, generally to build them up as near supermen; hence, campaign propaganda now includes results of physical examinations. Certainly the endurance contest of politics, from the snows of New Hampshire to the heat of Chicago, proves that stamina is essential. It is important not to elect politicians who are disability-prone, and the role of the physician is crucial. There are those who feel that the candidate waives his right to confidentiality when seeking office. But the cases of Representative William F. Ryan (N.Y.), who died in 1972 during a campaign for re-election, and Senator Thomas Eagleton, who was removed as Democratic Vice-Presidential candidate that same year, raise the question: When does a physician's responsibility to the community supersede his tie to a patient? In both situations, medical testimony was either misleading or not forthcoming.

All this, however, does not mean that a President must be a perfect physical specimen; he is elected for his ability to deal with the issues and for his ability to endure the rigors of the office. As long as he is in reasonably good health, that should be enough, for many people in and out of government perform their tasks well under great handicaps. What should be of greater concern is the number of fatigue-inducing ceremonial functions that a President, as chief of state, must perform—a problem that certainly could be alleviated if there were a reassignment of functions, with, perhaps, the Vice President assuming more of the incidental duties of the Presidency.

Although Presidents are not "great" because they are sick, if any conclusion seems warranted, it is that illness tends to elevate the President in the eyes of historians and he achieves in spite of affliction. Of the five "greats," according to the 1962 Schlesinger poll, four were ill and died before the date when death might have been predicted (an average of 5.8 years less than expected). Of the six "near greats," four were ill; four, including Truman, exceeded their life expectancy. One of the sickest of this group (Jackson) lived beyond his life expectancy. This group lived, on the average, 1.44 years less than what would have been predicted. Despite the fact that eight out of eleven "great" and "near great" Presidents were ill, it is not argued that sick men make the best Presidents, or that we can recommend electing candidates with poor health. Such a statement would be folly.

It is, however, possible that sickness and even a personal struggle to avert death enhances a man's strength of character, and, hence, he becomes a better President. Perhaps the best example is Franklin Roosevelt, whose great empathy with the masses may have resulted from his own bout with polio. His optimism in the face of severe economic depression and during the war years might have been due, in part, to his personal experience in overcoming an illness that would have defeated a lesser man.

Much has been written about Presidential burdens, but it is seldom pointed out that the pressure of ordinary life, with its petty details, is eliminated from the Presidential routine: household problems, banking, taxation, travel arrangements, and so on. Moreover, the chief executive is assigned two physicians. Dr. Paul Dudley White even declared that, despite Eisenhower's illnesses, he was better off for being in the White House, with its superb care, than elsewhere. If we can say that the burden of office has not killed any President outright, we must note, however, that it has nevertheless had varying effects on different men. In the case of Harding, a weak heart, confronted by the evidence of betrayal on the part of his friends, as well as by the routine problems of office, probably caused him to succumb more quickly than it otherwise would have. In the case of Wilson, exhaustion and moral inflexibility in the end proved an uneven match for the requisites of the Presidency.

Another question is whether health problems really influence Presidential policy and style. Probably they did in the case of Theodore Roosevelt, and possibly they played a role in shaping the style of Wilson and Lincoln. But, in the cases of Franklin

Roosevelt, Eisenhower, Kennedy, and Johnson, it seems more likely that a self-disciplined personality faced up to disease. Thus, in most instances, poor health might be considered *one test* of a candidate's will, decision-making ability, initiative, and determination, rather than a formative force. By looking at the past health records of candidates, and by examining how the candidates met crises caused by illness, the public has one criterion for judgment; but how important it is, compared to other criteria, is uncertain. And how can it be said that a healthy man will be a weak President just because he never faced the test of serious illness?

Nevertheless, several suggestions can be made. Candidates might be required to have a health check-up, and findings likely to affect their performance be made public. Intimate details are not as important as general implications interpreted by a bipartisan panel of physicians. More important than the illnesses themselves would be an evaluation of how the past Presidents actually faced up to the illness, and what health problems can most likely be caused or aggravated by the Presidency. Such an investigation should be made by physicians in consultation with historians. Possibly, the public could then better judge whether a man's health problems prior to his assuming office would be of any consequence while he is in office.

Lastly, and perhaps the most important factor in a discussion of Presidential health—given all the imponderables—is the Vice President. It is obvious that in selecting candidates in the future, political parties, for many reasons, need to pay closer attention to the number-two spot. Because their running mates have generally been selected on the basis of political expediency, Presidents have not always been able to rely on them to continue their policies in case of ill health or in the eventuality of Presidential death. For example, Vice President Adlai Stevenson did not enjoy President Cleveland's trust at the time Cleveland was operated on for cancer and when the silver crisis in the 1890's was at its height; and Woodrow Wilson refused all overtures of help from Thomas R. Marshall in 1919 and 1920, because he regarded Marshall as an Indiana nobody. The Twenty-fifth Amedment may have settled most questions of physical disability of Presidents, but it can do nothing about incompatibility of the Vice President and a possible lack of mutual trust. But because the Vice President is always but one heartbeat from the Oval Office, the number-two man is an essential factor in assessing the President's health. All that is implied here is that, since Presidential health is such an imponderable, as much attention should be paid as possible to the selection of a compatible and healthy running mate.

Medical and health problems are complex and dynamic influences and, in ways all too little realized, help shape the institution of the Presidency. The physical and mental strains of decision-making, especially in today's complicated world, render this question pertinent, even though it is impossible to reach definite conclusions. Mortals that they are, practically all Presidents have somehow been affected in the execution of state policy by some affliction, disease, or medical problem. And, because of the very fact that so many of the better Chief Executives were among the most ill, the entire subject takes on an importance of more than passing interest.

NOTES

* General works dealing with the subject of Presidential health are Rudolph Marx, *The Health of the Presidents* (New York, 1960), an interestingly written, even detectivetory approach to the subject; and Karl Wold, *Mr. President—How Is Your Health?* (Saint Paul and Minneapolis, 1948). These books are generally not documented, they are uncritical, and they make little attempt to relate the subject to the social and cultural factors involved. An excellent article on Presidential physicians containing sources and a description of most Presidential illnesses is Charles A. Roos, "Physicians to the Presidents, and Their Patients: A Biobibliography," *Bulletin of the Medical Library Association*, XLIX (July, 1961), 291–360.

[1] Several perceptive articles on the relation between public and private information on Presidential health problems are David D. Rutstein, M.D., "Doctors and Politics," *Atlantic Monthly*, CXCVIII (August, 1956), 32–36; Jonas B. Robitscher, J.D., M.D., "Public Life and Private Information," *Journal of the American Medical Association*, CCII (October 30, 1967), 398–400; and Michael J. Halberstram, "Who's Medically Fit for the White House?" *New York Times Magazine* (October 22, 1972), 39, 100–102, 106, 108.

[2] Louis I. Dublin, "Vital Statistics," *American Journal of Public Health*, XVIII (February, 1928), 216–17; Frank L. Griffin, Jr., "Actuarial Note:

Mortality of United States Presidents and Certain Other Federal Officers," *Transactions of the Actuarial Society of America*, XLI (October, 1940), 487–91; and *Statistical Bulletins of the Metropolitan Life Insurance Company*, (October, 1946), 1–3; (September, 1967), 2–4; (April, 1969), 3–4. See also Thomas A. Bailey, *Presidential Greatness* (New York, 1966), pp. 340–43, 170–72.

3 Clinton Rossiter, *The American Presidency* (New York, 1962), pp. 179–81.

4 Thomas C. Reeves, "Chester Alan Arthur and the Presidency" (unpublished manuscript), pp. 15–16.

5 See Edwin A, Weinstein, M.D., "Denial of Presidential Disability: A Case Study of Woodrow Wilson," *Psychiatry*, XXX (November, 1967), 376–91; Alexander L. George and Juliette L. George, *Woodrow Wilson and Colonel House: A Personality Study* (New York, 1956); and Sigmund Freud and William C. Bullitt, *Thomas Woodrow Wilson, Twenty-eighth President of the United States: A Psychological Study* (Boston, 1966).

6 Carl W. Ackerman, "How the President Keeps Well: An Interview with Brigadier General Charles Elmer Sawyer," *Saturday Evening Post*, CXCV (May 5, 1923), 46, 48; and "President's Illness and Death," *Review of Reviews*, LXVIII (September, 1923), 226–32.

7 Ross T. McIntire, "Did U.S. Elect a Dying President?" *U.S. News & World Report*, XXX (March 23, 1951), 19–22; and *White House Physician* (New York, 1946), pp. 3, 14–17, 53–54, 67–68, 76, 235–39; Herman E. Bateman, "Observations on President Roosevelt's Health During World War II," *Mississippi Valley Historical Review*, XLIII (June, 1956), 82–102; A. Merriman Smith, *Thank You, Mr. President: A White House Notebook* (New York, 1946), pp. 133–44, 175–88, 202–3; James M. Burns, "FDR: The Untold Story of His Last Year," *Saturday Review*, LIII (April 11, 1970), 12–15, 39, an excellent analysis of the possible effects of Roosevelt's illness on world events; Howard J. Bruenn, M.D., "Clinical Notes on the Illness and Death of President Franklin D. Roosevelt," *Annals of Internal Medicine*, LXXII (April, 1970), 579–91, a detailed account by the physician who saw FDR during his last year and who attended him at the time of death; and Walter Lippmann, in a comment, *Saturday Evening Post*, CCXVII (May 19, 1945), 108.

8 John Nichols, "President Kennedy's Adrenals," *Journal of the American Medical Association*, CCI (July 10, 1967), 115–16; "Management of Adrenocortical Insufficiency During Surgery," *Archives of Surgery*, LXXI (November, 1955), 737–42; and *New York Times*, October 21, 1954.

9 "How Nixon's White House Works," *Time*, XCV (June 8, 1970), 15–16; James Reston, "Fiery Run, Va.—Who's for a Vacation?" *New York Times*, June 7, 1970; and "The President's Health: Interview with White House Physician," *U.S. News & World Report*, LXVII (November 24, 1969), 39–40.

10 See James D. Barber, *The Presidential Character: Predicting Performance in the White House* (Englewood Cliffs, N.J., 1972), especially chaps. 7–12, on FDR, Truman, Kennedy, and Nixon.

12

Man, Mood, and the Presidency

James David Barber

Every leader with any understanding of what he is about knows that he has two jobs: to move the enterprise forward and to keep his people happy. Often, these tasks interfere with one another. The press for action disrupts the harmony of the team, or the price of a happy organization may be lassitude. The trick is to make of these two problems two resources, to reinforce the thrust for action with high morale and to make achievement a source of satisfaction. But that is hard to bring off; most leaders fail at it.

In our peculiar Presidency, one way of working this out is precluded: the division of labor. Studies of small decision-making groups have frequently discovered two leaders, one who emphasizes the objective tasks, another who handles the group's emotional life, the pair of them Mutt-and-Jeffing their way to success. To a degree, the assignment of the Vice President to "politics" is a try in this direction. But in the main, we lean on the President for leadership in making the government work and in making us happy about our country. We elect a politician and insist that he also be a king. The British solution probably never was available to us; in any case, President Washington, by his superb performance as monarch, quashed for all time the idea of the President as a mere clerk to execute the will of the Congress. One man, in full sight of us all, must, if he is to succeed, bless us with inspiration as he goads us to action.

A second solution is alternation: The President is King for a while and then shifts to being politician for a while, and back again. President Nixon has this propensity, I think, and it has contributed to all the uncertainties observers have felt in char acterizing a man who is now the very image of calm self-restraint, now the independent fighter. His emphasis on time and timing reinforces this adaptive technique, as does, in a much more fundamental way, his memory of the contrasting styles of his parents. But it is a dangerous game; once it is understood—once the public perceives it—its effectiveness wanes and what sticks is an impression of shiftiness.

I think we need a larger time frame to get at the basic relation between the man in the White House and the mood of the country, and I want to develop, in this essay, an interpretation of the recent Presidential past and emerging future in the context of such a larger frame. I think we have seen, in Kennedy, Johnson, and Nixon so far, a series of failures, traceable to interesting causes, in meeting the emotional demands Americans place on the Presidency. And I believe we may be able to use some simple psychological concepts to project the more likely implications for the next few years. To get at the topic requires, first, a closer look both at the nature of the emotions surrounding the Presidency and at the psychological implications of the passage of time.

Americans look to their President to satisfy at least three sets of needs. First is the need for reassurance. It is clear, in studies of reactions to the death of Presidents (McKinley, Garfield, Harding, Roosevelt, as well as Kennedy) and in the propensity of children to want to believe the President is a good man, that people turn to the President for a sense that things will be all right; that in the midst of trouble is a core of serenity, and that our ordinary ease will be sustained. Harding had this appeal down pat, with his normalcy and his ability to "bloviate" the common clichés so reassuringly to an emotionally exhausted citizenry. People want to be taken care of; they place ultimate responsibility for that on the President.

Beyond reassurance, people want a sense of progress and action. The contradiction may be only a trivially logical one—part of what was reassuring about FDR was the feeling that he was taking effective action, moving forward with some kind of program, at least at first. But at times the people react against "do nothing" government and more specifically against a President who seems to be holding the office but not playing the role. There was some of that feeling against Eisenhower, a questioning of his political competence and drive amidst a general aura of respect and affection. The President is supposed to be a take-charge man, a doer, a turner of the wheels, a producer of progress, even if that means some sacrifice of serenity.

Then people want a sense of legitimacy from and in the Presidency. Again, there is an apparent contradiction: He should be a master politician who is above politics. He should have a right to his place and a rightful way of acting in it. The respectability—even religiosity—of the office has to be protected by a man who presents himself as defender of the faith. There is more to this than dignity, though, more than an air of propriety. The President is expected to personify our betterness in an inspiring way, to express in what he does and is (not just in what he says) a moral idealism that, in much of the public mind, is the very opposite of "politics."

I think close study would show that Franklin Roosevelt, Truman, and Eisenhower, in somewhat different ways, exemplified these themes. For all his deviousness, Roosevelt was a master reassurer (no slouch as a mover and shaker, either, or as king-hero to most). His humor, his air of patrician calm, his simplicity of expression, and his masterful use of intimacy over the radio calmed a trembling nation even when his policies were faltering badly. People who were politically aware then have that memory with them, that model to hold up against the current reassurers. Indeed, to those who grew up with Roosevelt, from 1933 to 1945, the office and the man seemed to grow together into one thing, one oaken trunk of stability in the midst of national and world chaos.

Truman put great store in maintaining the dignity of the office; but, of course, his strength was his fighting courage in the face of adversity. To the "average man" (for or against him),

Truman was a quite satisfactory battler—direct, open, definite, aggressive, persistent, unswerved in his pursuits—or so he seemed. Even his intense personal loyalties, which eventually sullied his image as a legitimator, fit the picture of a man who stuck to his guns. And he decided; he seemed to know where he was going and how to get there, without a lot of delicate hesitation. He left behind a memory of the President as a man moving strong and straight toward a goal. That was not just the way Harry acted. That was Harry himself.

Eisenhower's very bumbling seemed to confirm his legitimacy. The 1950's word for him was "sincere," and, if his idealism took expression in mimicable form, its content struck home to a people ready for spiritual uplift. What other politician could have said what Ike did—about the duty he felt to serve his country, about his second crusade—and be believed? Truman angrily dismissed Ike's promise to go to Korea as a publicity gimmick; what politician today could make that seem a straight-forward attempt to end a war? Ike was believed, and believed in, as a President-King-archbishop of an American brand. Much of his moral indignation went into justifying *not* taking action in various circumstances, in retreating from the roiling political tides. But that was all right with the public. By 1956, all other reasons for preferring him paled in comparison with the simple statement of preference itself—"I like Ike"; and he left the office barely touched by the Adams scandal. He left a legacy, a memory trace that reminds us that, whatever else a President should be, he should be a damn good man.

Reassurance, action, legitimacy—at least a *sense* of those—encompass most of what Americans want to feel about their President. The people want those feelings so much that they will get projected onto a new President until he proves himself other-wise. Americans want and need to believe that the ordinary men they elevate to the Presidency (or might elevate) are "Lincoln-esque"—bearers of the torch, benevolent leaders. All this they try to confirm in the allegiance they pay the man as he takes office. From that high point, he tends, as John Mueller has shown so strikingly, to descend in a remarkably regular curve, broken by upward leaps in popular esteem when crisis comes to remind us of the uniqueness of his charge. (Possibly, there is some deep and wide current in the public mind that wants to experience vicariously the tragic drama of a king falling, which requires setting him up high in the first place.) In any case, the criteria of emotional evaluation, as distinguished from evaluation of his policies and practices considered objectively, do not seem to change much. He ought to keep us safely in his care. He ought to get the country moving. And he ought to inspire our higher selves with an example of principled goodness.

If we consider these needs as motives, what happens when they are frustrated? If the need is superficial, frustration will, eventually, eliminate or at least trivialize it—people will stop worrying about it and turn to other things. But, though most American political motives are shallow, as shown by general lack of interest in, or emotional attachment to, political activity and information, those centered in the President are different—much more intense, much more persistent. If the need is intense and persistent, frustration will not easily dispel it. Up to a point, the longer gratification is delayed, the more drive accumulates, the less sufficient minor gratifications become in satisfying the need. There is a building up, a heightening, of expectation, an increase in demand for satisfaction. Typically, the person probes around for substitutes—for example, in aggressive behavior. But the broad and simple pattern is probably the right one: Frustrate an important need now and you only intensify the demand for its satisfaction later.

I think the public has experienced, in the last three Presidencies, a good deal of disappointment in their desires for Presidential reassurance, activism, and legitimacy. They also have been disappointed in some dimensions of public policy objectively considered, but I do not see any very unambiguous connection between the actual achievements of an Administration, in policy terms, and its success or failure along this emotional dimension. Whatever their "real" accomplishments, Kennedy, Johnson, and Nixon have, in different ways, let us down, frustrated our fundamental needs for kingliness in the White House.

The modal response to Kennedy once elected was, I think, centered in his activist image. He was the young prince elevated to the throne, insisting that his predecessor's standards were not good enough for a new generation, promising forward motion with a new vitality. People were ready to give him a chance. But, from the start, there was something vaguely unsatisfying about Kennedy as fighter for progress. He had that edge of restrained rage that comes through so effectively on television. But he was, or seemed, iron and ice, not fire and brimstone. Many appreciated him who could not quite identify with him. One could get angry beside Harry Truman; one could only get indignant beside John Kennedy—or so it seemed at a distance. Then came the practical restraints. Empowered in a narrow victory, he had to move cautiously in Washington, waiting out the congressional elders, learning that they could not be pushed as easily as the campaign politicians. Results came slowly; for high adventure, the public had to make do with the Peace Corps and the space program, both of them probes away from the tangle of home politics. The Kennedy Administration seemed to shape itself not so much around a team of fighting partisans as around a technology, a rational, statistical approach to mechanized decision-making. It is hard for people to find excitement in a new accounting system. In many of these ways, President Kennedy, though he remained a vessel of hope and good intentions, came across as too cool, too slick, too stylish to rile up America between the Appalachians and Lake Tahoe. The people rushed, figuratively, to his side in crisis, but that seemed more a dutiful rally than a heartfelt leap into the fray.

Then came the sharp horror of the assassination, for which disappointment is too pale a word. But, clearly, one aspect of that was dashed hopes, the sudden curtaining of the drama of President Kennedy as leader of the nation's progressive, activist forces. This was the ultimate disappointment.

Lyndon Johnson came on as the dedicated, determined continuer. A good deal of early speculation concerned his background as a wheeler and dealer and his adequacy to fill John Kennedy's shoes. But I think there was another feeling: Something desperately immoral had happened, a gigantic disruption of tradition. People were perhaps less interested in what Johnson would continue than that he would continue, would uphold and sustain the government's legitimate succession. Johnson quickly picked up these themes. For all his colorful private conversation, he presented himself to the public as Old Reliable, as Preacher Lyndon—interestingly, more in the Eisenhower than in the Roosevelt mode. His war on poverty and his championing of civil rights were advanced as highly moralized stands on principle. At a deeper level, Lyndon Johnson may have suffered the strains of intense personal ambition and power-hunger, may have experienced some desperate need to confirm himself as a real person with his own preferences rather than a mere compromiser. But his public rhetoric reached out for the people's need to believe that their President embodied American values. Possibly, part of the interpretation of his incredible win against Goldwater was that Johnson, in contrast, seemed to be upholding the traditional principles against some bizarre and uncertain threat from the right. Johnson would be the National President, the voice from the White House calling on the people to do the right thing.

I think he saw the Vietnam war that way. At least to the public, he passed quickly over the details of possible compromises with the enemy to get to the main points: honor, coming to the aid of victims of aggression, standing up for what you believe in. But, in the end, much like that other President Johnson of a century earlier, Lyndon Johnson frustrated the popular need for legitimacy. The credibility gap cracked open under his feet and no amount of preaching could close it. People moved from suspicion to despair, with much help from the press and television. His popularity plummeted, and the forces of youthful idealism took out after him. In the end, he gave the impression of a leader at bay, grasping at resignation on principle as a way to reassert his personal legitimacy, only to have that dismissed as a calculated ploy. For all his ponderous moralizing, Johnson came to stand in the mind of much of the public as a moral pariah. The point is not the justice or injustice of that characterization, but that it represented a failure, despite immense effort, to satisfy the people's need for sincerity and simple idealism in the Presidency.

It is too early yet to be perfectly sure about Richard Nixon's

resonance with the emotional tides around the Presidency, but he
began with "lowered voices," a plea for peace and quiet echoing
Harding's normalcy. I think he sensed the national desire for a
surcease of anxiety—the need for reassurance—and wanted to
meet that by conveying an impression of calm, professional,
unideological rulership. He seemed to shy away from dramatics,
even as he was announcing various historic firsts. His Cabinet
had no famous heroes or villains; he had to describe their "extra
dimensions" to the nation. He meant to get on with the task and
be judged by results to be achieved with quiet efficiency.

By now, it is obvious that Nixon has not succeeeded in reassuring the nation. Indeed, his regime itself has crumbled away
in the floods of Watergate, and his personal credibility has
reached an all-time low. Much as many people may want to
believe Nixon—even to foist some sort of heroic greatness upon
him—that feeling now competes with harsh experience, from
the shocks of the Cambodian invasion to the indictment of several
top aides. As poll after poll shows declining confidence, few
Americans are left with the sense that they can drop their
emotional guard and leave the troubles up to him. Uncertainty
about just who Nixon is and where he is going adds to the
national anxiety, and not only in the nervous Northeast. Here
again, then, the people have been disappointed in their hope
and expectation that the President could help still the palpita-
tions of a scared country.

Disappointment with the President is not, to say the least, the
root cause of our current national turmoil. Nor does the fault
of it necessarily lie in some personal moral flaw in the President
himself. It is one factor, one more on top of all the others,
reinforcing politically unhealthy tendencies, and it can happen
to the best of men. Its larger implication is that stored-up needs
for reassurance, activism, and legitimacy—for emotional suste-
nance from the White House—can emerge to distort political
choices and divert energies from productive action. These bottled-
up, frustrated needs make it harder to find Presidential candidates who could satisfy them and, at the same time, produce
genuine social progress. On the other hand, a candidate who
combined this variety of "charisma" with extraordinary com-

petence in policy-making would be an immense national resource.

Insofar as the man's character and style are factors in the equation, the lack of fit between President and public mood is not hard to fathom. The President's character was formed in another era, modeled after old-fashioned heroes of the past. His style was, in many cases, an invention of his early political emergence, suited to the time he found himself politically, but almost inevitably, out of kilter with the present. I think it is possible to find out the main thrust of a political character once we discern his rate of political activity and his affective stance toward that activity—basically, whether he works hard or takes it easy, and whether he generally seems to like what he does or to suffer through it. The combination produces four types, four gross simplifications of a much more complex reality, nevertheless useful in estimating the fit between man and office. His style is a later accretion; I have argued, with some evidence, that the clearest clue to style—the way the man manages his political rhetoric, interpersonal relations, and decision-making— is to be found in his first independent political success, that time when he found a special way to make words, other people, and work pay off in personal success, usually in late adolescence or early adulthood.

I have developed these connections in *The Presidential Character: Predicting Performance in the White House.* The point here is a temporal one: People are trained for leadership long before they assume it, and therefore are always, to a degree, regressive in their attempts to adapt to the present. In a fast-moving political culture that can be a source of important strain, of disparity between the man's and the nation's ways of life.

Perhaps another set of factors contributing to the President's troubles in meeting the public's emotional needs is the increasing rationalization of politics. The process of electing a President has become a high-powered business enterprise, a technical, organized, systematic production. The strong focus on getting elected has somehow increasingly divorced that problem from the problem of governing. For all the manipulation of sentiment, the election process has acquired a technocratic tone that seems to work against emotional expression. The resonance between candidate and people is shallow, temporary and calculated—and known to be calculated. The steam has gone out of the drama; what is left is the image of the clean machine, the blinking computer. Undoubtedly, television has helped this along, with its emphasis on cool wit rather than belly laughs, mild disdain rather than free anger.

Similarly, in governing as in campaigning, there is the elevation of technique over value. Despite a good deal of emotive language, the picture of government run by a combination of technocrats and clever political manipulators comes through. Perhaps this is best symbolized in the physical White House: no longer a pleasant shrine, but a plantation façade hiding a political factory.

These and other culture developments make it ever harder to articulate convincingly the religious-emotional themes that have for so long been a part of our politics. The result is a a symbolic thrashing around—with the flag, for example—in search of some heartfelt connection between government and people. Given the centrality of the Presidency to our political emotions, the chances that these feelings will fasten themselves to the President and Presidential candidates are great. They are even greater after a period of emotional disappointment, of accumulating frustration. For these reasons, I think we will see a search for candidates who can elicit strong emotional responses from the public. A cool image on television will not be enough; nor will piling up delegate votes through local issue primaries or chicken dinnering suffice. The connection will not be made by a candidate who supposes that the more social turmoil there is, the calmer he should come across.

People are hungry for a hero, one who fits the new age. Soon they will find one. A good deal is riding on the question whether they will find a demagogue or a democrat as they search out a way to link their passions to their government.

V

Presidential Performance and Accountability

13

Presidents, Congress, and the Legislative Functions

Hugh G. Gallagher

Once upon a time, there was a President who was master of all he surveyed. The people round him—the white, the black, the yellow, the halt, the lame, the poor, even the farmers—loved him. He commanded huge majorities in Congress; they hastened to do his bidding. He did battle with the Supreme Court and, in the end, always won. The press was devoted to him. He dined with Kings and heads of state. He was the master politician of the age. He was the commander in chief, the economist, the diplomat, the mediator, the legislator, the father of us all. He gave us confidence when all was despair. He led us to victory when defeat loomed large. All news, all events emanated from the White House, in fact, from the President himself.

This President was Franklin D. Roosevelt and this, unfairly summarized perhaps, was his concept of the Presidency. It was certainly not the image of the Presidency held by his predecessors. Beard said that Roosevelt, in his Administration, changed the concept of the President's role more than had all the previous Presidents lumped together. Beard was not wrong.

Roosevelt sold us all his bill of goods. As political scientist Thomas E. Cronin has pointed out, FDR's concept of his office has now come to be universally accepted. We are taught in

school that the President is the most powerful man on earth
—head of state, head of party, chief legislator, and so on and so
forth. All Presidents since FDR are measured by this standard
and are found wanting. The men who have tried hardest to
imitate this Rooseveltian image have been the least successful
of postwar Presidents: Kennedy, Johnson, and Nixon. Kennedy
failed with Congress and learned, only under great pressure, the
hazards of nuclear foreign policy. Johnson, though outstanding
in many areas—legislation, for one—failed in his manic persever-
ance to be all things to all people in the FDR manner. Nixon
has been the saddest case of all.

The "FDR Presidency" is beyond the capability of any man
to fill, especially in this post-nuclear, cybernetic, synergistic
age. It was, in fact, beyond the ability of any man in the time
of FDR. Roosevelt seemed to be doing all those things, filling
all those roles. But, in fact, he was not. No man in history,
perhaps, was better equipped to fill them all, but, in fact, he
did not. He was many things, one of them being a consummate
actor. He wasn't guiding the wave, controlling its crest; he just
thought he was—and he made us think so, too.

If FDR is set aside as a separate matter—a unique case—as one
President out of thirty-six, it is possible to place the Presidency
in a more realistic perspective with Congress. If we stop looking
at the President as some sort of colossus towering over Congress
and the country and look at him, instead, as the man he is,
we find him at the head of a co-equal branch of our national
government. He may propose legislation, in the State of the
Union message or otherwise. His proposals will be received by
Congress, and, depending on a host of variables, Congress will
give its attention to them.

Sometimes he is more influential, sometimes less influential,
with Congress as it considers legislation. Sometimes his legislative
proposals are innovative, sometimes not. Sometimes his authority
is great in one policy area but not in others. Our system of
government is not a see-saw, with the President up while Congress
is down. It is a system with separation of executive and legislative
powers. In regard to his legislative powers, the President is
a constitutional monarch with hardly more authority over Congress than Elizabeth II has over Parliament.

In the years since FDR, the executive branch has run amuck. The various departments have grown in size and responsibility, the executive office of the President has grown; the White House staff itself is larger now than the whole Washington government was under Hoover. But this growth of the executive branch of government does not mean a growth in the power of the President. Far from it.

The President is not strong but weak: He has lost control of the departments, of domestic policy, and, as we see in Watergate, even his own House. He has retreated into foreign policy, but even there he must share his authority with Congress.

So much attention has been given, in recent years, to the growth of executive power that an essential point has been overlooked. It is true the executive branch has taken upon itself extraordinary powers—war, peace, control of the economy. This does not mean, however, that the man elected by the people to the Presidency can actually wield these powers. He does not rule, he reigns—with the deplorable result that no one responsive to the people governs the country.

It is axiomatic that, sooner or later, all Presidents come to hate Congress. They have reason to do so. During the course of Presidential campaigns, the country is encouraged to hold the last President responsible for what has happened in his Administration and to expect the new President to produce on his promises in the new Administration. Clearly and repeatedly, Congress comes between the President and the expectations of the people. This leads to Presidential frustration of a high order.

After the messianic hundred days and then some, even Roosevelt's relations with the Congress settled down into the normal bad. After the great purge effort of 1938, they became worse and continued so until his death. After 1938, with the exception of declarations of war and other necessities, FDR received little congressional support for his innovative legislative and social proposals. It is true that Congress gave him the executive powers he sought in order to direct the war, but not fast enough to suit him. In a peculiar address to Congress, rather chilling in its overtone, Roosevelt said, in 1942, "in event that the Congress should fail to act adequately, I shall accept the responsibility and will act. . . . I have given the most thoughtful consideration to meeting this issue without further reference to Congress . . . when the war is won the powers under which I act automatically revert to the people to whom they belong."

Many a President has threatened to horsewhip congressmen, but this is, I believe, the only time a President has stood in the halls of Congress and threatened to abolish it.

Harry Truman, originally a Senate club member if ever there was one, ended up making his living by giving hell to the eightieth "Do Nothing Congress"—actually, a most responsible, productive session. Lyndon Johnson, after that *annus mirabilis* of 1964, during which he conducted Congress through its most productive session in history, came to despise congressional criticism. He was at length to be driven from the White House because of it. "Go ask Walter Lippmann for your appropriation," LBJ was overheard growling to a senator who had questioned his Vietnam policy.

There is very little left by which a President can reward a friend in Congress. Patronage and the Post Office are not the help they once were. An opportunity to share the Presidential publicity spotlight for a few moments at a bill-signing ceremony is nice but brief, and there are other ways to obtain publicity. A Presidential campaign swing through a member's district just before election is supposed to be of value, but anyone who has lived through such an exercise must have his doubts. The value of Presidential endorsements, always debatable, have in recent years become largely discredited.

So, although the President has little to trade, he has a desperate need for congressional cooperation. Congress can undo him at every turn. It can make his program appear successful by approving it and funding it; it can turn it into disgrace by harassment, underfunding, and overinvestigation.

No wonder Congress so often produces a Presidential rage of impotence. It is built into the System—it is the System—and we can perhaps take comfort in the thought that it is not new. When the Senate rejected not only his first but his second nomination to the Supreme Court, President Nixon lashed out, accusing the Senate of action vicious, false, and hypocritical. It is, he said, the "constitutional responsibility of the President to appoint members of the Court." The Senate's rejection of the nominations amounted to the substitution of the Senate's "own subjective judgment for that of the one person entrusted by the Constitution with the power of appointment . . . the fact remains, under the Constitution it is the duty of the President to appoint and of the Senate to advise and consent." Failure to consent, he said, placed the "traditional constitutional balance in jeopardy."

John Tyler, tenth President of the United States, would have had great sympathy with President Nixon's frustration, for certaintly John Tyler was the all-time champion of bad relations with his Congress. A fine and decent Virginian, he became President by mistake, upon the death of William Henry Harrison, who died of a chill contracted while giving a much too lengthy inaugural address. Tyler had broken with the Jacksonian Democrats to accept second place on the Whig ticket with Harrison. The Whigs thought he would bring Virginia with him. He failed to do so. He was not a Whig. He thus came to the White House with virtually no party support in Congress. There ensued three zany years in the history of the Republic.

When Harrison died, the congressional Whigs confidently expected Tyler to serve as acting President only. They soon found out how mistaken they were: "I am the President and am responsible for my Administration."

The President vetoed the Bank Bill. The Congress promptly passed another Bank Bill. The President vetoed it. The House of Representatives drew up a Bill of Indictment with intent to impeach the President. The President protested by message—a message the House refused to receive, let alone consider. The President's Cabinet resigned en masse, excepting only Webster, who had his own Presidential ambitions. The charade reached its zenith—or perhaps nadir—over Senate confirmation of Tyler's appointments. In the last session of his Administration, the Senate rejected four Cabinet nominations, four Supreme Court nominations, nominations of ministers to France and Brazil, five marshals, one attorney, fourteen deputy postmasters, thirty-one custom officials, four receivers of public money, and four registrars of land offices. These figures must of necessity be approximate. The records are confused because several of the nominations were submitted and rejected a number of times.

President Tyler was a stubborn man.

On the last night of the session, as was the custom of the day, Tyler went to the President's Room adjacent to the Senate chamber, ready for battle. That night, the Senate received and rejected three times the nomination of Caleb Cushing to be the Secretary of the Treasury. Similarly, that night Henry A. Wise was nominated three times and rejected three times as minister to France. Old Senator Benton reported that "nominations and rejections flew backwards and forwards as in a game of shuttlecock—the same nomination in several instances being rejected . . . within the same hour."

Never was a President more badly treated by a Congress.

And perhaps it can fairly be said that never was a Congress more badly treated by a President than in the actions of Abraham Lincoln. At the beginning of the Civil War, the President purposefully delayed calling Congress into session to avoid the criticisms and delays that Congress invariably produces. To save the Union, President Lincoln used powers he did not have, knowingly and repeatedly overstepping the Constitution.

In a statement, breathtaking and sweeping, to Senator Chandler, Lincoln said, "I conceive that I may, in an emergency, do things on military grounds which cannot constitutionally be done by the Congress." Roosevelt threatened to assume powers held by Congress, but, until Nixon, only Lincoln claimed powers held neither by Congress nor by the President. No wonder Senator Wade said the country was going to hell.

President Lincoln called up troops, drafted men, and spent unappropriated money. He used his own friends to carry unappropriated money from the Treasury to pay arms and ammunition makers. He interned persons of suspected loyalty and abolished habeas corpus.

As a politician, a candidate, and a President, it was his theory to watch and wait for the big event and to ignore the small, entangling ones. Utilizing his concept of his war powers, against the advice of his Cabinet, without consulting Congress, he issued the Emancipation Proclamation. This action, its moral significance aside, abolished without compensation, at one fell swoop, considerably more than a billion dollars of personal property held by American citizens. He issued his Proclamation even as the Congress was considering legislation of its own to provide for the freeing of the slaves.

As war President, Lincoln dictated the terms of the peace. He appointed military governors without congressional approval and declared what terms and procedures must be satisfied before returning Southern states could take up their places in Congress and the Union. He was preparing to implement his Reconstruction program (which he had prepared without consulting Congress) at the time of his assassination. Lincoln saved the Union, but upset the comity between the President and Congress for a generation.

We have allowed strong Presidents like Lincoln to assume sweeping powers in times of great crisis. After the crisis, Congress has always moved to reassert itself, to bring the President down to size, to redress the balance. The danger of allowing a President like Lincoln to act without regard to constitutional restraints in a great crisis is that lesser men may take Lincoln as precedent in lesser causes.

In general, and from the beginning, the President and his Administration have always had to lobby Congress to obtain what they wished. Secretary of the Treasury Alexander Hamilton thought of himself as President Washington's Prime Minister and for five years lobbied Congress to obtain approval of the President's program. Congress has, from the beginning, been indignant at such interference in the legislative process.

The business of rallying support for the Administration in a tight vote is an extraordinarily difficult thing to categorize. It involves all the things we read about in textbooks and newspapers: patronage, judgeships, projects, grants, bargains with labor, pressure from industry, swaps of support of dubious programs, appeals to one's higher instincts—and the President can play a central role. President Cleveland was once busy dispensing patronage in exchange for votes. When told he would not win until hell froze over, he replied with some confidence, "Hell will freeze over in exactly twenty-four hours."

Woodrow Wilson is widely believed to have been the first

modern President to utilize his officials to lobby Congress in any consistent, continuing manner. Albert Sydney Burleson, Wilson's Postmaster General, used the President's Room off the Senate chamber for his office as he lobbied the Wilson program through the Senate. Upon occasion, this Room has seen Presidents themselves pleading for their program. Harding used it during his extraordinary efforts to defeat the Soldier's Bonus Bill. President Grant lobbied in favor of his Santo Domingo Treaty from it.

Presidents have actually taken their lobbying to the floor of the Senate and occasionally to the floor of the House. There is nothing in the Senate rules that allows the President to speak. He has, however, never been denied the opportunity. President Harding spoke directly to the Senate as it was considering the Bonus Bill. In one extraordinary moment, President Hoover pleaded with a unresponsive Congress for passage of his tax bill. In the depth of the Depression and the depth of his despair, he appeared late one night, without previous notice, before the Senate to plead that "in your hands at this moment is the answer to the question whether Democracy has the capacity to act speedily enough to save itself in an emergency." In this case, the Democratic Congress cooperated. Otherwise, it was congressional politics as usual until Roosevelt took office.

The best-known case of an incumbent President appearing before a congressional committee was unexpected, unannounced. The Joint Committee on the Conduct of the War was considering, in secret session, reports of treason within President Lincoln's immediate family. Lincoln walked in, to the astonishment and dismay of the Committee, told its members there were no traitors in the White House, turned, and left. This killed the investigation.

Presidential efforts at influencing committee investigations or congressional actions are seldom that effective. Probably the basic reason for this, trite as it may be, is that the President is a short-termer, while Congress, like the Civil Service, is a career. Of the thirty-six Presidents preceding Nixon, only eleven, or fewer than one-third, have been elected to two consecutive terms. The popular conception that incumbent Presidents tend to be re-elected is just not true. It was true through the first forty-eight years of the Republic, when five of the seven Presidents were re-elected. Since then, there have been twenty-nine Presidents, and only six of these have been elected to two consecutive terms. Four were wartime leaders (Lincoln, McKinley, Wilson, and Roosevelt), and two were beloved war heroes (Grant and Eisenhower).

This is important to the balance of power between the executive and the legislative. Congressional leaders, with their years of seniority, full of "stubbornness and penicillin," as Senator Eugene McCarthy once put it, are cunning with experience. They have seen Presidents come and go, but they remain. If a new President does not get his legislative program—and, since TR, all Presidents have had a program—approved by Congress in his first two years, he won't get it approved at all. Woodrow Wilson pointed this out, and FDR used to quote Wilson on the subject, although, as his term wore on, he stretched Wilson's two years to four. In any case, by that time Congress has decided what it likes and will approve and what it will not. The President, without experience or very much influence, is seldom able to revive a program once bogged down in a recalcitrant Congress.

It is my impression that, on the whole, Congress has been more innovative and creative in proposing legislation than has the President. Even though subject to numberless exceptions, excuses, an explanations, this statement is defendable.

The root reason for its truth is a simple one. There is, after all, a basic difference between what it is that the two branches do. To garble a Bernard Shaw quotation, the Administration looks at things the way they are and tries to improve them; Congress looks at the way things should be and tries to achieve them.

There are intelligent, able men in both branches of government. Those in the executive branch are intent to keep things from flying apart or from grinding at last to a full stop. The Administration tries to administer rather than to innovate. Its people react to events. Congress has the opportunity to act, not react; to create events. It can create new institutions, it can abolish old ones. It is not limited, like the Administration, to adjusting or perfecting the existing machinery of government.

Congress attracts intelligent men. It would not do so if it

were but an empty honor. Intelligent men would not be content merely to ratify the President's ideas, appropriate him money, and go home. There are over 500 members of Congress (including the Vice-President). Not all of them may be intelligent, but all of them carry a degree of ambition. This combination of intelligence, ambition, and place provides an encouragement to creativity. The disparate many in Congress are struggling for the respect of their peers, the approval of their constituents, and national recognition. This brings about a congressional search that never ceases. Members and their staffs are ever looking for the issues that will catch on the bandwagon that is going to go, the Big One. They are anxious for an interview on *Meet the Press*, an article in *Parade*, an item on the front page of the *New York Times*.

The story of each piece of legislation is different, but all arise out of a complicated struggle of powers and ambitions, inspiration, public interest, and re-election.

An innovative proposal will come from one or two or several voices in Congress. It may be an old proposal brought to life again, like revenue sharing and the direct election of the President—ideas that date back at least to Andrew Jackson's first State of the Union message. They may be new ideas fresh from a sociology course or the mind of a congressman. The idea, once expressed, may cause discussion. If it is taken up by the press, debated by the intelligentsia, deplored by the establishment, there may come, in due course, serious congressional attention to the proposal. Hearings will be held. More discussion will be generated, radicals will support it, the establishment will continue to oppose it. At some point, it passes from heresy to dogma. It receives the Presidential imprimatur; it is mentioned in the State of the Union message and becomes part of the official Presidential legislative program.

The State of the Union message in which this program is set forth is largely an empty institution. It consists normally of harmless homilies, one or two headline-grabbing innovative proposals, and a list of legislative items that, though not new, carry reasonable prospects of passage into law. These serve to maintain a fairly respectable Presidential batting average. The message is usually universally ignored the week after it is given.

There is no sadder task than reading through the messages of past years. For example: Lyndon Johnson made it an annual practice to pledge a massive clean-up of the Potomac River to make it a model for the nation's rivers. And public-health officials annually advise Washingtonians that their model river remains a cesspool, a mortal peril to upturned canoeists.

The writing and preparation of the actual bills and amendments have become a profession, and each branch of our government now has its experts in legislative preparation and interpretation.

The camaraderie that in many cases has grown up between the professional staff of a congressional committee and the career staff of the agency over which the committee has jurisdiction is a source of uneasiness both to the White House and to members of Congress—and properly so.

Each Senate and House committee is staffed with persons of specialized knowledge in the area of the committee's competence. Each executive department and agency has its corresponding staff of legislative counsel and liaison. Over the years, they develop a working relationship that continues no matter what the election results. To check this intimacy, there is, within the executive office of the President, the Office of Management and Budget, a group of dedicated men with that "passion for anonymity" defined by Louis Brownlow. These men perform a service called "Legislative Reference." They are not political, they do not make policy. It is their duty to see that the legislative statements, testimony, and reports emanating from all the many executive agencies reflect Administration policy, are consistent, and are not contradictory. They serve as a clearing house, a court of appeal, a traffic cop. It is not their duty to question Administration policy: simply, to see that it is applied, to interpret and implement it throughout government. "Policy" itself is supposedly made across the street, in the White House, by the politicians, perhaps by the President himself. In fact, there are many times when there is *no* policy, and it is made consciously or unconsciously by the nonpolitical civil servants of Legislative Reference. These men see Presidents come and go, and they have no great respect for the ability of the White House staff, whether it be Republican or Democratic. So, in the absence of policy, they make it—in order to keep the executive end of legislation functioning. They make it one way until someone tells them to make it another.

In this strange and shifting world of legislative policy, authority is there to be used by those who take it. Legislative Reference in OMB has the advantage and wiliness that come from years of experience. Actually, they can be—and have been—overruled, by a ribbon clerk in the White House who claims to be, and occasionally may be, close to the President. Most junior White House clerks, however, do not know they can do this, and, by the time they learn, they are usually on their way back to private business or wherever they came from.

Confrontation within an Administration, of course, depends on the character of the Administration. In recent Administrations, not including the present, the secretary of any department had the right to reject the dicta of the Office of Management and Budget on legislation or, indeed, on anything else. He could appeal directly to the President. This was done, often enough, in a state of high dudgeon. The strength, importance, and utility of the OMB depended on the ability of its director to get to the President *first*. A wise President supports his director, for the Office of Management and Budget offers his one last, sad hope of retaining control over that vast bureaucracy, the U.S. Government. Over the past years, there have been reports that even OMB has lost its grip and that the Executive Office of the President, as wildly proliferating as any coral reef, is itself out of control.

If Watergate means anything, it is that this is indeed the case. The men around the President appeared to distrust not only their departments but their own colleagues in OMB. Our executive branch is now so large that perhaps there is no way to make it efficient and responsive to the President. Certainly, the Nixon men's attempt to create a tight little government within the government, a group of "loyal" men who could be trusted to do what the agencies and OMB could not, is only demonstration of the lack of Presidential direction and control over the executive branch.

The President himself, in search of legislative achievement, must buck Congress, the established Civil Service, the departments, and now the executive office itself. No wonder John Kennedy is reported to have said that he found "no pleasure" in the job.

Once a proposal has become part of the President's program, it gains in stature. Lobbyists and interest groups—including states, cities, and localities, federal agencies, and commissions—struggle over its terms. The professional syndicates take over—that is, the organizations, the clients, the lobbyists, the civil servants, the philanthropists, and the congressmen who are bound together by a common interest in education, mental health, SST, or whatever. The bill may become a partisan issue. Democrats and Republicans vie to develop, according to their lights, a more acceptable version of the measure. Finally, it is passed, and its sponsors and cosponsors are invited to the White House to participate in the Presidential signing ceremony. The President passes out pens to all concerned and makes a moving statement on the progress thus achieved, a statement carried by all major networks on their evening news program. And this is how the original idea of Congressman "X" becomes a major achievement in the record of the Administration of the President.

In 1946, Dr. Lawrence Chamberlain of Columbia University published his book *The President, Congress and Legislation*. Professor Chamberlain analyzes the legislative history of ninety major pieces of legislation passed by Congress between the years 1880 and 1940. He chooses measures in the fields of business, tariff, labor, national defense, agriculture, federal credit, banking and currency, immigration, conservation, and railroads. Over the sixty years studied—including the New Deal years—Chamberlain found, "Of the entire ninety laws no less than seventy-seven traced their ancestry directly to bills which originally had been introduced without Administration sponsorship." He says, rather quietly, "These figures do not support the thesis that Congress is unimportant in the formulation of major legislation." It was Chamberlain's contention that the creative role of Congress could not be denied, even in the major pieces of Roosevelt legislation: the National Industrial Recovery Act, the Securities and Exchange Act, the Agricultural Adjustment Act, the National Labor Relations Act, the Fair Labor Standards Act, the Social Security Act. "Most of the great mass of regulatory Legislation of the past decade, popularly dubbed 'New Deal Legislation,' had a well defined prenatal history extending back several years before it was espoused by the Roosevelt Administration. This is true not only of the more conventional fields such as banking, railroads and taxation but of the newer areas of social security, holding company regulation and security control." Ronald C. Moe and Stephen C. Teel of San Diego State College have done a valuable update of the Chamberlain study. Their results are published in the September, 1970, *Political Science Quarterly*. Their appraisal of Congress through the 1960's confirms Chamberlain's observation—Congress remains the innovator.

Judgment and selection are necessarily subjective. With this caveat, I list some bills essentially of congressional origin in recent years:

The Area Redevelopment Act of 1961 (Douglas)
The Taft-Hartley Labor Management Relations Act of 1947 (Taft-Hartley)
The Labor Management Reporting and Disclosure Act of 1959 (Landrum-Griffin)
The Interstate Highways System (Gore)
The Federal Merchant Marine Program (Magnuson-Bartlett)
The Atomic Energy Act of 1946 (McMahon)
The National Aeronautics and Space Act of 1958 (Anderson-Johnson)
Civil Rights Legislation (Kefauver *et al.*)
The Cold War GI Bill of Rights (Yarborough)
Consumer Legislation (Magnuson)
The National Environmental Policy Act (Muskie-Jackson)
Anti-Pollution Legislation (Muskie)
The War on Hunger (McGovern)
The Anti-ABM Movement (Symington)
The Anti-SST Movement (Proxmire)
The Atomic Test Ban Treaty (Humphrey)
The Disarmament Agency (Humphrey)
The Peace Corps (Neuberger-Reuss)
Health Care (Hill)
Education (Morse)

And of course the areas of taxes, import duties, and immigration have always been Congress's.

Moe and Teel also take note of what I consider a most interesting and significant development. The President has found it increasingly difficult to exert leadership over the executive branch and its policies, let alone compete with or lead Congress as chief legislator. It appears that the President increasingly tends to retreat into foreign policy and world affairs—areas over which he has clear constitutional and historical dominion. Because of the exigencies of great power and H-bomb missile technology, perhaps this is unavoidable, but every President since 1940 has devoted more time to foreign affairs than he has to domestic matters.

After the recent debacle in Vietnam, the cries became general that Congress has relinquished its "traditional and constitutional" responsibility to share foreign-policy-making with the President. This is said as though the President had deliberately and impudently seized powers in the field hitherto held by Congress. Such is just not the case.

Cecil Crabb, Jr., summarized what has been happening since World War II. "A striking phenomenen associated with the control of foreign relations in recent American history is the expanded role of Congress in virtually all phases of external affairs." Moe and Teel quote Crabb and list the areas of dominance—economic-aid policy, military assistance, agricultural-surplus disposal, location of facilities, immigration and tariff policies. To this list I would add several other specific items—the Nuclear Test Ban Treaty; the approval and withdrawal of the Gulf of Tonkin Resolution; the Lebanese and Quemoy and Matsu Resolutions; the Fulbright Vietnam hearings, televised nationwide; the Pearl Harbor hearings after World War II; the hearings on the Dominican Republic invasion; and the congressional investigation into the Pentagon Papers.

In spite of President Nixon's brilliant innovations in foreign policy, Congress continues to have its way. The Senate insists on amendment to the SALT treaty; it blocks the Russian trade *détente*. Congress forces the President to cease Cambodian bombing. Such things demonstate to the world, as did Wood-

row Wilson's Senate, that the President *alone* cannot commit
the United States to a foreign policy.

Even with regard to Vietnam, Congress condoned the President's policy by appropriation and resolution. When it withdrew
its support, America's active involvement came to a halt. This
simply demonstrates that Congress plays a substantial role in
American foreign policy–making, a role larger than that of confirming ambassadors and ratifying treaties. The President may
have more power to act on his own initiative in this area, but,
even here, he is a limited constitutional monarch, with no more
control over Congress than over his own departments.

The President of the United States has many titles. Chief
legislator is one of them. It is a paper title.

Congress legislates, and, except in rare instances, the President
has little to say about it. The origins of most of the innovative
legislation in the last ten years, or the last century, can be found
in Congress.

Presidents, like Kings, provide a handy chronology. They are
easy to remember. The personality of a King is more memorable
than the multitudes of a Parliament. To identify a measure as
part of the Kennedy New Frontier program is to fix it in times
as a silver spoon is fixed as Georgian. In most cases, upon
examination the Kennedy Administration had about as much
to do with the initiation of the proposal as the Georges had to
do with the design and craftsmanship of the spoon.

Congress is a small and diverse body. It is a career. It is run
by old men at the top, with the young men at the bottom. The
old have the experience of age; the young have the ideas of
youth. These ideas are sifted by experience, and what results is
usually timely and responsive.

Congress is close enough to the people to determine when
change is necessary and, unlike the executive bureaucracy, small
enough to provide it.

Do not worry too much about Congress. It is doing its job.
If anyone is in trouble, it is the President, who is more in danger
of losing control over his own executive branch than he is in
a position to seize control over the legislative branch of our

federal government. As the size and responsibilities of the federal government grow, the President's lack of control grows apace.

The Presidency is a weak office. It always has been. Only very few men have transcended its weakness.

In 1838, James Fenimore Cooper wrote, "As a rule, there is far more danger that the President of the United States will render the office less efficient than was intended, than that he will exercise an authority dangerous to the liberties of the country."

This is still the case.

14

Presidents as Chief Executives

Thomas E. Cronin*

What ever happened to the New Frontier, the Great Society, and the New American Revolution? Afflicted though they may be with a case of crisis of confidence, Americans have, for the most part, grown callously accustomed to Presidential promises that go unfulfilled. Presidential proclamations of a long series of wars—on domestic poverty, crime, pollution, hunger, cancer, et cetera—seem to have had only a marginal impact on the problems singled out for attention. But neither Presidents nor the public objects much to losing these wars, in contrast to the way we do a foreign war.

Despite the fact that our most recent Presidents have been activist and purposeful, relatively "strong" Presidents, we nevertheless have witnessed a decade in which domestic public policy has been the orphan of Presidential attention. And, beyond that, White House–level monitoring and evaluation of domestic public policies have been haphazard and inadequate—not employed when needed and often not offering much help when employed. This essay will suggest some reasons why this has been the case, some implications it has for national policy-making, and what, if anything, might be done about it.

* Though the first draft of this essay was delivered as a dialogue paper at the Center for the Study of Democratic Institutions, much of the research for it was done while the author was associated with the Brookings Institution. The author is grateful to both institutions for the support and encouragement tendered him for writing and rewriting this paper.

On the basis of the record of the 1960's and the Kennedy, Johnson, and Nixon Presidencies, it may be helpful to think about the American Presidency as consisting of four sub-Presidencies: a foreign-policy Presidency, an aggregate-economics Presidency, a domestic-policy Presidency, and, finally, a symbolic and moral leadership Presidency. These are, obviously, not mutually exclusive categories. For example, domestic policy, in the final analysis, normally can be reduced to economic terms, or "who gains—who loses." By aggregate-economics, I refer to a concern for the macroeconomic problems of monetary and fiscal policy, concern for unemployment, inflation, interest rates, cost-of-living index, the stock market, taxing levels, balance of gold, and trade and tariff policies, as opposed to the more explicitly "domestic-policy" concerns of education, ecology, health, housing, welfare, and, in general, the quality of life and social justice. In fact, successes in one sub-Presidency generally, though not always, provide extra Presidential resources and credit for the others. At least in recent years, Presidents have found their staffs and their Cabinets increasingly differentiated and compartmentalized along these same four lines. Each of these sub-Presidencies competes with the others for Presidential time and energy; the net effect has been that the administration of domestic policy and, to a lesser extent, the development of domestic policy have been subordinate to the other sub-Presidencies.

Recent Presidents have spent their available "policy time" predominantly on national-security and foreign-policy matters. Several former White House aides estimate that their President spent as much as 60 per cent, or two-thirds, of his time exclusively on national-security activities or foreign-policy crises. This has not necessarily been by Presidential choice. While both President Kennedy and Nixon had a history of being personally more interested in issues of foreign policy, it is equally clear that Lyndon Johnson was not initially so predisposed. Nixon, for example, according to his aides, would much rather be in meetings with Henry Kissinger planning the future of the world than in negotiations with Wilbur Mills or in meetings with the H.U.D. and Interior secretaries about housing and environmental pollution problems. It is quite easy to believe that President

Johnson would have been content to go on passing domestic legislation as if his operational code vis-à-vis Congress were "We shall overwhelm!" Regardless of these leanings, Johnson, as is now well known, became literally consumed with national security and military policy and their politics.

It is almost taken for granted now that Presidents are, first and foremost, national-security managers and foreign-policy—alliance negotiators. These responsibilities cannot be delegated; they are executive in character and Presidential by constitutional fiat as well as by long tradition. Not surprisingly, the Presidential schedule is crowded with foreign-policy trips, summit meetings, conferences with visiting heads of government and foreign ministers, and continuous working sessions with national-security counselors, foreign-policy Cabinet advisers, and military officials. The next largest portion of Presidential policy time is spent on economic-policy issues. It is impossible today for a President to hide from the highly visible and quantitatively hard economic indicators: stock-market indicators, unemployment rates, cost-of-living index, commodity prices, interest rates, inflation rates, tax levels, and so forth. These figures are now available to everyone and become inexorably linked with how the public judges the sitting President. Americans now expect their White House to cope aggressively and imaginatively with economic distress, to offer workable economic game plans, and to use the nation's budget as an instrument for ensuring a healthy *and* growing economy.

Besides attending to foreign-policy and economic issues, we also want our Presidents to serve as teachers, as moral leaders, and, occasionally, as folk heroes, as symbolic leaders summoning us as a society to higher achievements. In this role of political leader and teacher, a President develops and sustains the nation's sense of purpose and attempts to reaffirm the nation's credibility and legitimacy. Such efforts at Presidential pedagogy or Presidential public relations, together with the President's occasional forays into partisan politics, absorb sizable portions of Presidential energy.

What time remains for thoughtful design and implementation of Presidential domestic policies? Very little. Here, too, emergencies such as strikes, riots, or natural disasters tend to siphon off the most time. Moreover, Presidents and their staffs are almost always more keenly interested in generating new policy ideas than in the more tedious and usually frustrating job of putting legislatively approved policies into operation or improved operation. In contrast to the well-known box-score ratings of Presidential success in dealing with Congress, no such box-scores or similar incentive ratings exist in the area of program evaluation and administration.

In interviews with fifty former White House aides, it turned out that not one of them praised the quality of White House domestic-policy monitoring and evaluation! Those expressing some modest satisfaction were foreign-policy staff aides, and they carefully noted that they were speaking only in reference to foreign-policy activities. More than one-quarter of the aides, however, thought White House policy-evaluation and -monitoring capabilities were mediocre, and nearly two-thirds responded that, in their experience, such capabilities were "poor," "terrible," or virtually nonexistent. Let a few from each of the recent Administrations speak for themselves.

From the Kennedy Administration:

> *There is never enough time to think profoundly about policy evaluation and the like at the White House. It is always too much in a rush, moving from one thing to the next. It is just about all you can do to get things started. The burden of the presidency is to get things started. The presidency is not an executive agency with clout to carry out the goals of the president. It perhaps ought to have been done, but we didn't have time for it, we just didn't work that way. The Bureau of the Budget did some reviewing of programs, but even they didn't do much along these lines.*

> *We didn't have that good a system for monitoring programs. . . . We just didn't have the people or the right training. Little serious attention was ever given to evaluation and monitoring; we just never really did it thoroughly,*

*partly because so little of the President's legislation passed
and partly because JFK was a bad administrator.*

*JFK used to receive about an 80-page compilation of weekly
reports from the various departments and agencies to brief
him on controversies or trouble spots (for example, on the
Billie Sol Estes affair); essentially these were progress reports—but not much follow-through occurred. Kennedy basically felt that the people he appointed would do the coordination and implementation of his policies. Kennedy was
not particularly well organized himself; he wasn't by nature
a good disciplinarian, especially when the people were beyond his staff, and out of his sight.*

From the Johnson Administration:

*You aren't going to get evaluation or monitoring in the
normal sense of those terms. . . . Most White House staff
are engaged in generating new programs, not looking at old
programs. You soon forget about programs that were started
earlier or even programs begun earlier by your own administration. That's not going to change much, given the way
the White House staff operates and the way in which its
reward system works.*

*Johnson was really a Legislator; he was never very involved
in administration or even keenly aware of administrative
implications.*

*The Presidency is a very fragile and under-equipped
Office. There is very little intelligent or systematic evaluation and very little monitoring of policies. In fact, there was
a terribly weak information system—if even it can be called
that. The PPBS [Planning, Programming and Budget Sys-
tem] system was badly needed and it may help, but its impact has thus far been very modest indeed. . . . Not only is
the presidency weak in policy analysis, the White House
stands precariously atop . . . a bottom-heavy administrative
system, consisting of departments and agencies equipped
with resources, clientele and historical baggage that con-*

tinually threatens to out-think and out-run the tenuous policy management capabilities of the White House.

From the Nixon Administration:

> *Well, in all candor, we are very weak in this area. So many of the programs which we inherited are of the type that we did not know whether they worked or not. Very little in the way of evaluation was done during the 1960s. Sure, there has been a lot of waste in model cities, the war on poverty, or in the programs established by the Elementary and Secondary Education Act—but we didn't have proper monitoring or useful evaluation intelligence on them. And Congress gives us an especially hard time because they claim that the same people who run the programs do the evaluating, so Congress cuts rather than adds to our funds for these purposes. We have tried to rely on cabinet committees, but most of these, unless the president chairs them, turn into a lot of squabbling and even though this is the heart of our newly fashioned domestic council process, these committees never get much done.*

> *It hasn't been a very good record in this area. Communications from the White House take so long to get out, and an equally long time in coming back. It is not uncommon for White House policy directives to take up to, or as long as, a year before they really get down to the action level in the departments where they are charged with carrying policy out. . . . We don't pressure the federal agencies forcefully enough to come up with hard data and figures except occasionally for presidential speeches, but that is hardly enough, and hardly the right occasion for systematic attention to program progress. The Domestic Council setup has helped, but considerable improvements in policy management and planning are needed.*

The size of government and the size of the federal role in domestic concerns has so expanded that the personal involvement of the President has shrunk correspondingly. From 1930 to 1970, the nation's population rose from 123 million to over 205 million; the GNP rose from $90 billion to $977 billion; government expenditures on the domestic side alone rose from $2.7 billion to $116.3 billion. Federal grant-in-aid programs rose from a handful to over 500, and the number of federal civil servants went from 600,000 to nearly 3 million. Scores of federal agencies work with some 81,000 entities of government at all levels around the country. Federally funded research and development has also accelerated: from $100 million in the late 1930's to about $16 billion in 1972, with sometimes as much as 80 per cent done outside of government, under contract.

Newly elected Presidents are obviously caught in a difficult choice-making situation. In campaigning, they promised change, they pledged new domestic programs, and they implied that they would use the full resources and powers of the office to bring about change. But, upon entry into office, a President finds that his budgets are virtually unchangeable for the next year and a half; and, even then, the percentage of controllable federal expenditures is exceedingly small. Presidents learn, too, that it takes a long time, sometimes a four-, five- or six-year period, to translate new ideas into policy language, mobilize public and congressional support, secure adequate funding, and steer a measure into operation. One can see why (though I disagree) both Presidents Johnson and Nixon flirted with the notion of a six-year Presidential term. The tendency is to seek short-cuts and, if possible, to go around the existing federal bureaucracies in order to press new programs into operation. As Frederick Mosher has aptly observed, "Political executives, under unrelenting pressure from elements in the society and dissatisfied with the answers available from the established bureaucracy, tend to develop and utilize machinery directly responsible to them for developing new programs and changing old ones." This is happening at all levels of government and in several areas of policy, but it appears in a pronounced way when one examines contemporary Presidential participation in national domestic-policy affairs.

One of the most crucial of Presidential responsibilities is to gain control over the existing bureaucracies and make them work

with and for the White House. Most recent Presidents have
resisted this. Lacking confidence in old-line bureaucracies, and
fearing that programs will get buried in the encrusted, custodial
hands of the seemingly inert federal-agency structure, Presidents
have sought short-cuts and frequently set up new agencies, or
transferred yet a few more policy-development or operational
activities to the "front office," that is, within the executive office.
Such, for example, has been the response, in the Nixon Administration, to pollution, civil rights, drugs, volunteerism, cancer, and telecommunications. But one cannot bypass or ignore
the federal bureaucracy without costs. If the White House is
to have any impact on existing policies that are run by the
federal bureaucracy, the President and his top lieutenants have
little choice but to become extremely familiar with the routines
of government—the budget, the personnel system, the Presidential
advisory system, the public-information function, the legislative
clearance and liaison processes, and so forth. These are both the
"guts" and the tools of government.

We are left, then, with the following questions: Why have so
many Presidents concerned themselves so little with gaining control over the sprawling executive-branch departments that, in
turn, are so critical to domestic public policy? And why have
recent Presidencies been so especially frustrated in this regard?

There is a great residual of respect toward the Presidency
both in Washington and in the federal agencies throughout the
country. But this respect for what the President can do is predi-
cated on the fact that the Presidential voice can be heard and
believed as authentic, not just through second-level staff voices.
Otherwise, federal civil servants feel that they must protect their
"rational" and "professional" interests from White House interference. For a fairly sizable number of government professionals,
White House staff interference and influence with their operations is viewed as very degrading (and sometimes even illegal).

Hence, the burden on Presidents themselves becomes enormous.
Trained and experienced as politicians, they must now, quite
late in their careers, acquire a sense and feel for managerial
problems and learn, however best they can, the skills of effective
organizational leadership. Not surprisingly, many Presidents

prove ill suited to the task of winning control of the immense organization that theoretically is at their command. Examples from corporate life are relevant. It is not uncommon for a top business executive to note that it requires three, four, or even five years to become genuinely a member of the management team. As a recent president of General Electric put it, "The board of directors made me president of the company in 1950, but it took four years before the organization gave me the same honor." One also is reminded of Harry Truman's celebrated complaint, "I thought I was the President, but when it comes to these bureaucracies, I can't make 'em do a damn thing!" Close watchers of the White House, however, say that every President complains about the cumbersome size and the troublesomeness of the federal executive establishment. Truman's complaint is merely par for the course. Kennedy made the same complaint a little more elegantly. And Lyndon Johnson a little less elegantly.

REALITIES AND CIRCUMSTANCES

Presidential neglect of domestic policy cannot be easily explained. Nor would simply more time spent on domestic policy ensure that the great domestic wars that have been declared will be won. And that the capacity for the federal government to provide leadership in this area is now open to serious question is not to imply that this will always be the case. Let us examine a variety of converging realities that contribute to this orphaned state of domestic policy.

One reality—or perhaps I should say one *un*reality—is the way the American people view their Presidency. With the New Deal Presidency firmly fixed in memory, and no doubt with the passage of time, we now expect our Presidents to be vigorous and moral leaders, who can steel our moral will, move the country forward, bring about dramatic and swift policy changes, and slay the dragons of crisis. An FDR halo effect has measurably shaped public attitudes toward the Presidency, persisting even today. In the arena of national and international leadership, FDR upstaged all comers, as he robustly magnified the personal and heroic role of a competent and confident leader in the context of tumultuous times. The vision, and perhaps the illusion, is that, if only we can identify the *right* man, our loftiest aspirations can and will be accomplished. Certainly radio and television, and the emergence of the United States as a strategic nuclear power, have, indeed, made the Presidency a job of far greater prominence than it was in the days of Coolidge and before. But it seems to me that our textbook writers and many of our journalists have egregiously oversimplified and exaggerated the capabilities of the modern Presidency for policy accomplishment. The typical "textbook Presidency" conveys an inflated and unrealistic interpretation of Presidential competence, omniscience, and beneficence. The textbook version implies that there is virtually no limit to what the President can do; in the words of the late Clinton Rossiter, "He is, rather, a kind of magnificent lion who can roam widely and do great deeds so long as he does not try to break loose from his broad reservation." Another problem of the "textbook Presidency" is the misguided faith that is associated with the Presidency—for example, Theodore White, in one of his *The Making of the President* series: "So many and so able are the President's advisers of the permanent services of Defense, State, Treasury, Agriculture, that when crisis happens all necessary information is instantly available, all alternate courses already plotted."

On balance, more consensus than contention has characterized the literature on the American Presidency. The verdict: Only the President is, or can be, the architect of national policy, and only he, by attacking problems and crises head on and interpreting his powers expansively, can be the engine of change to move this nation forward. By symbolizing the past and future greatness of America and radiating inspirational confidence, a President can pull the nation together while directing us toward the fulfillment of the American Dream. In lieu of a national church or a royalty, the White House has become almost a national shrine and the Presidency somewhat superhuman.

But the country, in the 1930's and early 1940's, had been jolted by stark and truculent crises—the Depression and Pearl Harbor in particular—that so permeated society and so challenged the "business as usual" routines that the nation willingly accepted, if not cried out for, aggressive leadership and dramatic policy proposals. The nation may well be experiencing crises of as great significance today, though of perhaps more subtle quality; but the American people have never been jolted as severely or as visibly as they were during the 1930's and early 1940's. Today, in contrast, the American people seem concerned mainly about personal problems, such as arthritis, whether their son makes the local Little League team, or whether their daughter will be accepted by a good college. Personal energies are far more likely to be invested in relieving one's front lawn of crab-grass, participating in a local bowling league, or watching a Sunday afternoon football game than in worrying about public-policy questions of the day. To be sure, there was resentment and outrage over the prolonged war in Vietnam, and a certain concern for inflation and unemployment, but, otherwise, we seem to be living in a period of "business as usual."

Not insignificant, too, is the fact that those issues that do arouse attention tend far more often, such as in the cases cited above, to be in the foreign-policy and economic-policy spheres as opposed to domestic policy. In the absence of physical and dramatic crisis, important national-policy change is seldom swift in the making. On several occasions during the 1960's, the policy struggles that frustrated successive Presidents have come to naught, or have been realized only in the most compromised versions, because the requests for programatic changes have been highly controversial, and a viable coalition of support has not yet been put together. And, as is well known, our system of government is distinctly weighted in favor of the *status quo* and against easy or swift domestic-policy change. Mobilization of support for important policy reform is just as much a Presidential responsi-bility as proclaiming the need for this reform. Presidents Ken-nedy and Johnson sometimes acted as if they expected a public ground swell to occur once they announced, by press release, that X or Y was their legislative program, their remedy for "fixing" the ills of domestic society. But proclaiming or making policy by press release was not enough. Even "getting the laws on the books" was not enough. Programs had to be properly designed and funded, and systematic attention needed to be devoted to developing managerial and bureaucratic organizations necessary for the implementation of these laws. (Even then Presidential dependency on state and local authorities made for an uneven, if not totally impossible, performance for many national undertakings.) All this took time—far more time than is suggested in the standard textbook description of the American Presidency.

Political analyst Richard Scammon suggests a far more realistic, albeit a more dispiriting, commentary about how nationalpolicy change currently takes place:

> . . . *there really aren't any new solutions. There are modifications, adjustments. Most good ideas have already been thought of. You don't really come into a situation like this with a totally new concept. You improve this, polish up that. You take a plan that was discarded four years ago, and you pull it out and look at it. And maybe you salvage Points One, Eleven, and Twenty-nine. As the circumstance changes, it suddenly becomes more applicable than it was.*

Roosevelt, of course, knew all this and practiced it. But, since then, in our ever eager quest for moral leadership and for the reassurance of authoritative helmsmen, we expect, sometimes, that Presidents can do everything. Part of the problem is no doubt related to the way campaigns are conducted and to the intensive hard sell or oversell seemingly demanded of candidates. So embellished are some of our expectations that we virtually push the candidates into poses akin to the second coming of FDR. Necessarily adopting the language of promise and sloganism, candidates and their publicists vie to outdo each other as they pledge that they will accomplish objectives that are either near impossible or unlikely. In short, Presidential elections generate a vast number of policy-change hopes, and people often gain an impression that a new President, or newly re-elected President, can achieve changes that verge on the miraculous.

Textbook Presidency expectations held by the public and often reinforced by the press encourage the notion that where the President should be involved is where he can make dramatic, swift, personal choices. John Kennedy's missile-crisis episode or Richard Nixon's China trip suits the expectation and image. Then, of course, there is a difference in the types of perceived potential defeats, and this no doubt shapes a President's thinking and time allocations. As Kennedy said, the "the big difference is between a bill being defeated and the country being wiped out." Foreign affairs had always interested Kennedy more than domestic. And, according to his close aide, Theodore Sorensen, "they occupied far more of his time and energy as President. They received from him far more attention to detail, to the shaping of alternatives, to the course of a proposal from origin to execution."

But the point to be appreciated is that it is more "Presidential" to be concerned with, or preoccupied with, foreign or economic development than with the complicated no-win or minus-sum entanglements present in most domestic-policy fights. President Eisenhower, who deliberately shied away from domestic-policy activism, seemed to escape with the fewest liabilities, at least as recorded in the national public-opinion polls. Then, too, some Presidents turn to foreign-policy matters as if in recognition that they are unlikely to get major legislation accepted in the Congress. Foreign policy looms up as an area in which the constraints seem less present; where, despite the complaints about the State Department, the bureaucracies are more susceptible to Presidential influence, and the Congress is decidedly more willing to delegate policy-making discretion to the executive. And, of course, as the fourth sub-Presidency mentioned earlier—symbolic and moral leadership—is emphasized, which is necessarily the case if the President wishes to live up to textbook Presidency expectations, it, too, takes time away from what might otherwise be given to domestic policy and its management.

Another circumstance that measurably affects Presidential domestic-policy performance is the manner in which Presidents must delegate responsibility. The appointment prerogative is clearly the most central of Presidential resources, yet it is very frequently wasted or misused.

Presidents spend two or three years running for the Presidency, only to find out that the people they needed and courted during the campaign—delegates, newsmen, fat cats, political-machine operatives—are quite different in character and experience from those needed to staff and manage the federal executive branch. Seldom does the candidate get to spend time with experts or professional leaders for serious discussions of domestic public policy. To be sure, experts occasionally prepare "white papers" for the candidate, but these often are superficial and are rarely fully understood by the candidate. And the participating experts frequently become disappointed, if not disillusioned, by the relationship. Rarely does the Presidential candidate think about the complexities of managing the federal government or confer with prospective and potential managers of his major executive-branch departments. Hence, a John Kennedy, upon election, exclaimed, "People, people, people! I don't know any people [for the Cabinet and so forth]. I only know voters! How am I going to fill those 1,200 jobs?" Kennedy appointed a Cabinet almost half of whom he had not known before. This point bears repetition: The people needed to win the Presidency are not the same ones needed to govern the nation.

And, in the rush and frenzy of the post-election months, a surprisingly large number of sub-Cabinet appointments are made by Presidential subordinates, with only the most limited Presidential awareness of whether the man is properly matched for the policy (that is, whether he agrees with the President) and managerial requisites of the position. And patronage factors enter into domestic-policy appointments far more than is the case in national-security or economic-policy positions. The ironic reality is that, when the President has the opportunity to appoint the largest number of people to his Administration and enjoys the greatest drawing power, he has the least time available for this than at any other point in his Administration. Later, when he occasionally might have some spare time for careful recruitment and selection, he has fewer vacancies to fill and less drawing power.

Presidents have repeatedly made mistakes in naming Cabinet heads, regulatory commission members, and Supreme Court nominees. Too many Presidential appointees are chosen on the basis of highly subjective judgments, or because of political patronage, or for geographical representation, and from too limited a field of choice. Many have had no experience in management. As one former Presidential counselor has written recently, "Those with supervisory responsibility frequently have difficulty in recognizing the significance and scope of that responsibility and are inclined to divorce themselves from institutional management through close identification with their subordinates." And, once on board, the new role is often very difficult to learn rapidly. Norton Long once suggested, "In this respect, much of our politics resembles a continuous performance of the Battle of Bull Run with new actors for each show and a minimal build-up of knowledge from the experience."

Presidents seem to take a special interest in high appointments in the Defense and State departments. And positions in the Justice and Treasury departments are often filled on the basis of close professional or policy ties with the department heads. But, in the other domestic departments, the quality and thoughtfulness of the selection process can be quite another matter. Several Nixon White House aides said that, in the first two years of their Administration, patronage and recruiting efforts amounted to a virtual disaster. Even the President was reported as having said that he had made serious mistakes in this area. Kennedy and Johnson aides similarly remarked that their so-called talent hunts and executive identification efforts were more haphazard and accidental than they ever should have been.

Complicating all this is the circumstance that, other than the Vice Presidency, the Senate is, and for the last ten or fifteen years has been, the only real Presidency "on-deck circle," while the governor's office has become less of a viable course to the White House. At one point in 1971, 10 per cent of the Senate were candidates for the Democratic nomination in 1972! There are a few obvious reasons for this. One is that senators can more easily and frequently gain experience in, or at least exposure to, foreign-policy issues than can governors, and national security has become a continually important issue in Presidential elections. Senators can absent themselves from their Senate responsibilities and travel abroad far more easily than can governors.

If they are members of one of the variety of national-security or military-affairs committees, they can gain considerable familiarity with foreign-policy issues. What matters is that they can prepare themselves as specialists (or at least seem to prepare themselves) about world affairs and international trouble spots. Perhaps a more important advantage for the modern senator is that he is not held accountable to the public for policy failures and public dissatisfactions. It is the contemporary governor who must raise state taxes, or who presides over controversial battles over welfare, medical, and higher-education expenditures; it is the governor who, in many states, now has to inform his citizenry that public services, such as universities and state parks, must face budget reductions. These are not the types of actions upon which national political careers and Presidential campaigns are easily launched.

Yet, it is the governors rather than the senators who can gain the best-detailed and first-hand apprenticeship as domestic-policy executives (especially the governors of large heterogeneous states). Senators, in comparison to governors, have small staffs and few managerial challenges. Senators are used to operating in an arena in which the bill-signing ceremony is the culmination of the policy-making process. Governors and Presidents learn that this is hardly the case. Thus, in a Presidential election, we frequently end up guessing at the candidate's abilities as an executive or as an effective domestic-policy leader rather than relying on already tested leadership.

No President, of course, will be judged a success solely on his ability to attract able managers and place them in the appropriate positions in his Administration. But it is increasingly clear that a President who will, of necessity, have to delegate so much of his discretion in national-policy matters to his top managers in the executive departments will not be served well unless he sets very high standards in the area of recruitment and talent search. As John Macy has concluded, "Reliance on the party faithful, the longtime friend, the available job seeker or even the in-line career official can no longer serve as exclusive sources for such posts." It would be helpful if Presidential candidates could outline their staffing standards and their search and selection ideas during their campaigns—but this has not been the case and, one suspects, is one of those many important criteria for Presidency selection that will continue to be appraised after rather than before the fact. But organizational ability to recruit able people, to strengthen their hand once they are in the Administration, and to provide the proper mix of communication and motivation to them is an ability that, ironically, has been as superficially developed as it is potentially strategic.

A third circumstance related to Presidential neglect of domestic policy lies in the important but generally ill-understood distinction between "inner" and "outer" Cabinets. The inner Cabinet consists of the Cabinet officials who head the departments of Defense, State, Justice, and Treasury, together with a few ranking White House staff counselors, especially the assistant for National Security Affairs and the director of the Office of Management and Budget. The outer Cabinet is essentially the domestic cabinet, composed of the departments of Labor, Commerce, Agriculture, Interior, HEW, HUD, and Transportation, as well as lesser domestic agencies. These are the "service," "clientele," and, in the eyes of the White House, "advocate" departments.

Because, in recent years, Presidents have increasingly found that they have so little time to spend with the outer Cabinet members, they, in effect, have relegated the bulk of communications and oversight responsibilities in this area to a few White House aides and the budget director. These staff aides enjoy access to the President for presenting occasional new policy ideas, but the outer-Cabinet chiefs find they have little access either for discussions of new proposals or for administrative problems. Rapport between Presidents and their domestic department heads weakens as Presidents, in frustration, turn more and more to their close, trusted staff aides to settle jurisdictional and interdepartmental conflicts. Confusion grows over where domestic-policy leadership rests, and whether or to what extent it exists in the departments, in the Office of Management and Budget, or with the White House aides. Staff and line distinctions become blurred, the White House staff grows, and the estrangement between the domestic-department heads and the White House staff continues.

In the early 1960's, President Kennedy and his staff tried to get his outer departments to come up with innovative proposals for legislation. But, according to Kennedy aides, they usually came up with very weak "interest group types of claims, very parochial, more-of-the-same types of proposals." As a result, domestic-policy formation was brought into the White House proper. More staff jobs were created and the program-development role of the Bureau of the Budget expanded. The White House and executive-office aides became increasingly involved not only in program development but, subsequently, in getting these programs launched and coordinated. To an extent, these Presidential aides transformed the White House into an action agency, if not exactly a department itself.

President Johnson extended this relationship, relying so heavily on his top domestic staff aides and his budget directors that they occasionally were known as the "Over-Secretaries" of the domestic departments. The domestic-program departments began to lose the capacity to sharpen up their programs as well as to maintain close working relations with the President. (This was not as often or as much the case, however, with State, Defense, Justice, or Treasury.) This produced, among other things, a sense of insecurity and unease among many of the domestic-department heads. Lyndon Johnson's memoirs confirm what many of his aides and Cabinet members have said in private— namely, that he seldom sat down for substantive policy discussions with the domestic Cabinet, while, in contrast, spending vast amounts of time with his national-security Cabinet heads. Foreign-policy matters are discussed six or seven times as much as domestic-policy concerns. While making only passing reference to most of his former domestic-department heads, President Johnson makes more than a hundred citations of his reliance on, and deliberations with, Secretary Dean Rusk.

It is, of course, not novel that domestic-department heads become upset at key White House aides and the budget director. Their departments more often have the controversial budgetary appeals and fights and more frequently experience more prolonged conflicts with the Congress and with mayors and governors. Presidents always risk the possibility of raising their fences too high between themselves and their outer Cabinet, but this becomes more the case in a period of endless foreign and economic crises. In the words of one Johnson White House lieutenant, the "cabinet became a joke, it was never used for anything near what could be called presidential listening or consultation."

When they did get a chance to see the President, they were tempted, if not actually forced, to perform in the compromising advocacy role. A former sub-Cabinet official sums up the problem this way:

One basic problem lies in the fact that domestic cabinet members are so rarely with the president than when they do have a chance to see him they have to advocate and plug their departmental program in an almost emotional style trying to make a plea for expanded appropriations or some new departmental proposal. But precisely at such times, the senior White House aide present can adopt or strike a pose as the more objective, rational statesman taking a non-advocate and more "presidential" position—all of which leaves the domestic cabinet member appearing like a salesman or lobbyist rather than part of the President's team. But the cabinet member seldom has a chance to make his points or his case—the White House aide knows on the other hand that he can see the president later that day or the next, and so can afford to play a more reasonable and restrained role in such meetings. Such role casting clearly favors the staff man while placing the cabinet member in a most uneasy position.

Tension readily builds up between domestic staff advisers to a President and the Cabinet members who head up the domestic departments. The White House aides enjoy better access to the President. They are continually looking for ways to save the President's time and gradually come to believe that they possess much more objective understanding of what it is that the President wants to accomplish. At the same time, however, the Cabinet head is the one who has to live day in and day out with the managerial responsibilities for his large department. He is the one who has to sell and explain his departmental programs to Congress and the public, and, of course, to his own department. It is the Cabinet member who is more exposed to, and is responsible for coping with, the multitude of claims from organized interest groups in his department's area. Not unreasonably, most domestic-cabinet members believe that they, too, know what Presidential policy is or should be. To be sure, this same phenomenon occurs with respect to foreign- and economic-policy development—but the scope of the problem is considerably less in those areas both because of the smaller number of departments and agencies involved and because recent Presidents have been more successful in sharing with, or conveying to, the inner-Cabinet members a Presidential perspective.

Interviews with a sample of domestic-Cabinet members who served during the 1961–71 period yields abundant evidence that most of them felt removed from the White House and believed that the mechanisms for resolving interdepartmental and White House–departmental conflicts were considerably less than adequate. Their resentment is obvious.

From a Johnson Cabinet member:

My own feeling is that the President's top domestic aids never understood staff-line distinctions and as a result many mistakes and frustrations resulted. They looked upon their intrusions into departmental affairs as "power plays." I am opposed to the White House staff acting as a staff of super planners and coordinators. There should be much more reliance on collaborative cabinet leadership. Under LBJ, there was far too much unconscionable confusion and hectic activity surrounding important domestic policy initiatives and as a result many of the programs flopped.

From a Kennedy-Johnson Cabinet member:

Kennedy had my policy area way down on his agenda. The White House people, especially the President, left me alone! It was a pleasant relationship, though his top aides were tough keepers of the door. So often was I kept away that when I wanted to see JFK I would have to talk to him on the run . . . or on a trip. There is a tendency on the inside to guard the president too much—they develop considerable power by tightening up the ring around the president. They all play on the fact that he hasn't any time for this or that, etc. . . . But a good cabinet member—one who isn't just filling some political niche—can be a very excellent corrective to the White House "hot house" staff who are confined there and are virtually locked up fourteen hours a day. . . . The President needs to hear from his cabinet. . . .

President should occasionally sit down in a leisurely way with his cabinet members and listen and ask that important question: "what do you think?" But this occured very rarely with either President Kennedy or Johnson.

In retrospect, all of the past three presidents have spent too much time on foreign affairs. They all felt that's where the action is and that's how they could be judged in the history books.

From a Kennedy-Johnson Cabinet-level administrator:

Recent presidents have let their White House political and personal aides go far too far in pressing administrators to do things they shouldn't. Too many of them are trying to make administrators squirm. There are too many aides at the White House who are just looking for a headline for the president. You have to guard against those types. There is just too much of it and presidents are guilty of letting it continue—they don't sufficiently realize that you have to have confidence in your department administrators. Perhaps it is due to the fact that they have never been administrators —they spent all their time in the Senate.

From Walter J. Hickel's 1971 memoir "Who Owns America?"

There was an "isolation of thought" developing [in the Nixon Presidency]. In early 1970, I was conscious of a deep-

ening malaise inside the Administration—a sense of vague uneasiness. Others in the Cabinet shared my feelings that some of the White House staff were stepping up their efforts to filter contacts between the Cabinet and the President. It appeared that an effort was being made to centralize conrol of all executive branch activities of the government immediately within the White House, utilizing the various departments—represented by secretaries at the cabinet level —merely as clearing houses for White House policy, rather than as action agencies.

Should a department—for example, Interior—develop policy for those activities under its control, submit those ideas to the White House for approval or disapproval, then follow through at the administrative level? Or, as some of the White House personnel seemed to want it, should a department wait only for marching orders to be issued by the Executive Mansion?

In the absence of Presidential time and attention, domestic-policy matters become delegated to White House aides, and they, in turn, attempt to provide domestic-policy leadership and coordination over and among the many splendid, but often many splintered, federal domestic departments and agencies. This sometimes works and sometimes proves inadequate. But it nevertheless seems to be an increasingly persisting reality. It deserves to be recognized as a circumstance with which Presidents must live, for they are not likely to enjoy much of a letup from the pressures of foreign-policy issues or economy management. At the same time, however, it is apparent that recent Presidents have not adequately compensated for the intensity and extent to which this development has taken hold.

It is not now enough to have a small band of staff lawyers manage the nation's domestic policy. Seldom have the White House aides had much experience in organizing or managing large, complex enterprises, and White House aides too often mirror Presidential dispositions to accentuate new ideas and pass new bills, to the neglect of concern for implementation or departmental management responsibilities. White House aides, in this regard, supplement or reinforce Presidential leanings rather than serve as a counterbalance.

In brief, Presidential relations with the domestic-Cabinet officials have frequently been ambiguous, ill defined, and unsatisfactory. By the end of the 1960's, the domestic departments were highly distrusted by both Democratic and Republican White Houses. Departmental lack of sensitivity to the Presidential perspective became exacerbated. Departmental lack of experience in generating new programs and negotiating policy adjustments with the President inhibited their performance in dealing with the White House. It was as if a vicious cycle of circumstances repeatedly contributed to the further deterioration of the possibilities for sensible and effective Presidential domestic-policy leadership.

A fourth persisting circumstance is that much of what recent Administrations have attempted has lacked a clarity of purpose and has been accompanied by only the most meager efforts at analytical planning; it is as if the White House often does not know what it wants. A sure way of losing control over domestic agencies is not knowing what it is that you want to accomplish. But, as James Q. Wilson reminds us, "Thinking clearly about goals is a tough assignment for a political system that has been held together in great part by compromise, ambiguity, and contradiction."

Presidential domestic-policy initiatives in recent years appear to have been particularly afflicted by that Washington disease known as multimissionitis. First, the domestic "innovation" has several parents or sponsors, each of which wants a different aspect of the policy emphasized. Then there is the almost inevitable congressional compromise and logrolling process, wherein several related but distinct objectives are somehow mashed into one hybrid measure, all of which get written into sufficiently obtuse language that not only permits but actually invites professional bureaucracies and local authorities to bend it to their own preconceived and usually self-serving ends. With the passage of time, it becomes difficult to distinguish the original purposes of a program from those that have been added for pragmatic or political reasons. Frequently, as noted by Morris and Rein, "An institution can become so preoccupied with marginal activities which enhance its prestige that it neglects the less visible work which makes up its true purpose."

Within the executive branch, reporting is often superficial or misleading: Hard indicators of domestic-policy performance are difficult to come by; what measurements are available are frequently not transmitted accurately or swiftly to the White House. Until recently, domestic agencies have routinely "measured" their performance by adding up program inputs—that is, the number of dollars spent, the number of people employed, the number of local projects in operation, and so forth. Departmental officials had not been trained or required to view their programs in terms of outcomes, that is, performance results, or to have their impact compared to alternative ways of achieving the intended policy goals. Basic audit and evaluation procedures are often so neglected that bureau officials are not even sure of how much money is being spent on one subprogram as opposed to another and are sometimes unable to talk in terms of end product costs—that is, how much it costs to produce what they are in the business of producing.

The measurement problem sometimes occurs because departmental officials purposely want to camouflage the real costs of their operations. But the problem stems partly from the fact that it is difficult to develop outcome or impact measures in many domestic-policy areas. In contrast to the relatively hard economic indicators that are available to describe unemployment, the cost of living, or mortgage rates, it is more difficult to measure whether poor children are learning faster and whether they will be more employable, or whether there has been real progress in civil rights or in reforming the criminal justice system. Sometimes, it is nearly impossible to relate government expenditures with policy outcomes or to be very precise about which factors are the causal agents of social changes when change can be noticed.

Rarely, during the 1960's, did the White House engage in serious policy experimentation and planning. The political incentive system seemed, if anything, to propel energies in an opposite direction. Pass now, plan later! Presidents and congressional leaders were eager for fast results and rarely appreciated the often considerable need for more analysis, testing, and small-scale pilot experiments. They felt they were elected not just to study and research policies but to put them into operation!

Henry Fairlie, a shrewd English observer of American political life in the 1960's, paints an even more disquieting picture. In his splendid, albeit overstated, *The Kennedy Promise,* he sums up this period and its politics as a reeling politics of expectation, crisis, and confrontation. He suggests that the Kennedy brothers, for example, practiced a method of politics which was exacting beyond the nation's capacity, calling the American people to a feverishness of expectation which had prepared their imaginations only for crisis; each crisis to be met only by confrontation:

> ... *in practice [President Kennedy] exalted the "extraordinary powers' of his office: in word and in deed, he inflamed the people with an exaggerated promise of what a politician —what the President—what politics—what the Presidency— could achieve. This disillusionment, when it came, was turned against his successor, but it is a reasonable assumption that, if he had been elected for a second term, it would have been turned with some force against him. He had strained the American people too far with the politics of expectation which he practised, and at some point they would have confronted him eyeball to eyeball, asking that the promise should be realized; and one does not know how he would have reacted.*

The congressional process usually reinforces this resistance or inattentiveness to systematic planning and policy evaluation. To some extent, this is justified because of the notorious lack of quality in so many government reports. Congress grows suspicious of so-called evaluations that are essentially public-relations advertisements But, though congressional staffing has improved in recent yeaı much of what passes for congressional oversight, in hearings and investigations, is inadequate. Moreover, though the General Accounting Office attached to the Congress has recently experienced a quantum jump in the quality of its work, it does not now contribute to preimplementation policy evaluation, and its postimplementation studies contribute mainly at the margins of the fundamental questions.

Bureau chiefs and sub-Cabinet officials in the domestic departments can learn, if they are willing, about the extent to which programs are being carried out and what obstacles the programs run up against. But such information is much harder for the White House or the Office of Management and Budget to come by. Reports coming from departmental bureaus and agencies are particularly suspect, since the success of the programs they administer, to a considerable extent, puts their own performance on the line. And, despite the vast expansion of the Presidential advisory system in the 1960's, the White House often was not properly staffed to digest available policy intelligence when it was available, let alone put it to effective use. Complicating all this is the fact that, as Victor Navasky has recently written, "It is an unwritten law of annual report writing in the federal bureaucracy that every agency's statistics are better than those of the previous year and far better than those of the previous administration, so the statistics trotted out at such moments prove nothing." Much the same could be said about the liabilities of any easy acceptance of information coming from Presidential advisory councils, interdepartmental committees, or congressional hearings.

Several recommendations have been at least implicitly raised in the previous discussion: the obvious need for better White House–departmental communications, more imaginative and systematic use of the appointment prerogative, and a major upgrading of internal reporting within the federal executive branch. But some skepticism is warranted, for it is far easier to propose what appear to be common-sense reform suggestions than to know whether such investments of time or alterations in structure will measurably improve the quality of policy performance. The circumstances outlined in this essay are persistent and not easy candidates for reform. Moreover, reforms in one branch of government can often have reverberating, unanticipated effects, changing the strength or health of other parts of our highly interrelated policy-making and political system.

I believe, though, that there are several modest and concrete proposals that emerge out of the examination of the contemporary Presidency as a domestic-policy executive. Such proposals must, first of all, recognize the obvious: that Presidents will invariably feel more hedged-in and hamstrung in domestic-policy reform areas than in most of their other responsibilities; and that, in all likelihood, Presidents will continue to be preoccupied with foreign-policy crises, a variety of pressing economic emergencies, and symbolic obligations that will deny time that might otherwise be given to domestic-policy planing and administration.

First, it might be helpful if we could disabuse ourselves of inflated expectations of what Presidents, acting alone, can accomplish. A strong case can be made that we have for too long expected that Presidents are able to do just about anything, and that, therefore, all our energies should be spent nominating our favorite man as a Presidential candidate or electing the best man running. To be sure, these efforts are always important. But measurable policy changes and reform do not customarily occur from the top down. It was never expected that we should elect an omnipotent and benevolent superhuman and then vest all our hopes in his wisdom and omniscience. There have to be outside forces promoting prolonged, persistent, and often grass-roots campaigns and pressures to create widespread support for national-policy change.

Contemporary policy studies suggests that the more we learn about Presidential policy performance in varying policy subsystems, the more apparent it becomes that Presidents only rarely accomplish policy outcomes that can be credited as distinct personal achievements. More realistically, the Presidency serves as a broker for a few party priorities and as a strategically situated and important participant among vast numbers of policy entrepreneurs and political leaders. More often than not, a President's personal policy views are essentially moderate and only vaguely refined. When in office, however, he finds himself constantly surrounded by people who have "high-energy" interests and investments in specific policy options. Those who want to bring about significant and lasting policy reforms will have to organize, conduct very thorough analyses of what it is they want to achieve, and spend large amounts of time mobilizing support as a counterweight to existing vested interests. Occasional participation in Presidential election campaigns is hardly enough to help sustain the type of political support required if major change is likely to be brought about. Textbook generalizations about the importance of elections and the men elected are misleading to the extent that they underemphasize that our system is weighted against change unless sustained, long-term efforts are mounted to bring pressure on the system and, not least of all, upon the Presidency.

Second, there is a vital need for the creation of an Office of Policy Planning and Program Evaluation, to be located in the executive office of the President but preferably detached from the President's personal staff as well as from the Office of Management and Budget. This staff should be concerned with problem identification and with the development of better indicators of policy progress in the area of social and domestic concerns. The President needs such a unit, also, as an in-house experimentation center that can, either alone or in concert with outside research agencies, conduct small-scale experiments testing alternative policy options prior to launching grand-scale enterprises.

A similar office, which might be called the Office of Legislative Policy Evaluation, ought to be created as an adjunct service for the Congress, separate from the existing GAO but perhaps within the Congressional Research Service. This office would be charged with elevating the quality of analysis that is given to executive-branch policy proposals as well as for reviewing new ideas and proposed amendments being considered by various members of Congress. This office should have wide latitude for relying on outside research that could be encouraged in universities, research and development institutions, and the like. The conventional format of asking congressional-hearing witnesses, who come at their own expense and are often very unprepared, to discuss the complicated policy implication of pending legislation stands in need of a major overhaul, with the explicit aim of upgrading the quality of analysis, data, and expertise that are potentially so important to the proper execution of the legislative function.

These proposed offices may strike some readers as a clear invitation for duplication and overlap. This may well be the case. But the beneficial effects of competition between these two evaluation offices to the two elective branches should far outweigh the incidental overlap or extra expenditures. Both branches need vastly improved policy information and guidance. To give these resources only to one branch may be to erode the necessary base of influence for the other to remain a separate but significant partner in the national-policy–making enterprise.

Political leaders at both ends of Pennsylvania Avenue have for too long permitted "policy research" and "program assessments" to be carried out by either the same people who administer the programs being evaluated or by departmentally appointed advisory panels that more often than not are beholden, or incestuously tied, to the interests of the bureau officials. It is past time for both Congress and the White House to turn this situation around and capitalize on the growing availability of professional policy analysts. The Congressional Office of Legislative Policy Evaluation might also take advantage of large numbers of Capitol Hill career staff assistants and committee personnel who often find that their work loads vary with the season or with the cycle of interests in certain policy areas. Such people might be lent to the Office of Legislative Policy Evaluation for short-term assignments when they are not being fully employed by their committee or congressman; and, by this exchange, many of these people who have had only limited training in substantive policy evaluation would receive a certain amount of in-service training in systematic policy research, while contributing to the availability of more systematic thinking on domestic issues. Although much remains to be done in improving the quality of education in this area, the very establishment of these two proposed offices will serve to highlight the need for better analysis as well as the future possibilities in the development of governmental learning systems.

Third, there is an important need for a first-class, management-consultant organization within the executive office of the President. There are, to be sure, severe limitations on the effectiveness of government reorganizations or structural remedies. Organization seldom stands in the way of able people, and rarely can reorganizational efforts convert mediocrity into excellence. Yet, so many of the time-consuming problems visited upon the White House or faced by the domestic-department heads concern complex jurisdictional questions of overlap and coordination. During the 1960's, the White House and the Office of Management and Budget were in no position to offer sustained professional advice to the President or the Cabinet members in this area. As one Johnson Cabinet member told me, "If there had been a high-level and competent consulting agency available to me, I would have had it in use every day, full time!"

These management specialists should be available for both Presidential and Cabinet-member use. They should also be available to the President for short-term assignments, as trouble shooters or expediters in intradepartmental or intergovernmental controversies. White House aides with already sizable policy portfolios usually do not have the appropriate time to devote to the intricate negotiations and bargains that so frequently must be conducted along these lines. Too often, these responsibilities get placed upon the youthful White House staff aides who often are too inexperienced to cope with the organizational and technical questions of making bureaucracies function. Then, too, these same White House aides have often earned the enmity of the Cabinet officials in previous negotiations over legislation and budget decisions, and, hence, their credibility proves an obstacle in such managerial arbitration assignments. Obviously, policy and management concerns can never be entirely separated, but professional specialization in this particular area at the executive office is clearly warranted.

Finally, consolidation of several of the domestic-Cabinet–level departments makes sense. Cabinet reorganization will not solve everything and, perhaps, will contribute little in the way of immediate visible improvement. But it is clear that domestic-Cabinet heads have not enjoyed close working relations with the White House, have been forced into behaving as advocates and adversaries to the White House, and have often been unable to bring their departments into cooperative arrangements with allied departments, with which they necessarily intersect. The real conflict in these relationships is not between the President and the Cabinet head as much as it is between special and general interests. Several task-force and study groups have now advised both Presidents Johnson and Nixon that it is the weak, narrowly focused Cabinet positions that are a threat and a disservice to the President, since their occupants are now too dependent upon parochial bureaus in their departments to serve as counselors and representatives of the Presidential interest—however individually loyal they may want to be. In oversimplified terms, the greatest strains are between those who are narrowly devoted to specific functional programs supported by particularistic elites and clienteles, on the one hand, and those who seek to manage and coordinate a range of particular policies to achieve more general, or "public," policy objectives, on the other.

President Nixon's 1971 reorganization proposals deserve consideration, although they are merely one variation of the type of consolidation that might take place. Even with a reduction of domestic departments and Cabinet positions, no Cabinet member will ever see issues and problems exactly as a President does, just as the present inner-Cabinet officers never act entirely as pure counselors to the White House. But reduction of the now seven domestic departments, and social related agencies and offices, into three or four, more broad-ranging departments would enhance the possibility that more jurisdictional conflicts could be resolved within departments, while, at the same time, strengthening the hand of domestic-Cabinet members vis-à-vis special interests. Submerging special interests into multiple-interest departments will be effectively accomplished only if the departmental secretary position and its office are considerably strengthened and equipped with both the tools and the authority to manage the department. These new Cabinet positions will also need enhanced rapport with, and confidence from, the President if they are going to be effective in presiding over large and more heterogeneous departments. But the President would hardly be well served if this were not to be the case; for (1) he cannot afford, politically, to become too removed from important policy conflicts, and (2) he is the major immediate beneficiary in trying to make such a reorganization work.

Reforming the Presidency is, of course, not a neutral goal.

Special interests and other branches will quite naturally resist. Presidents need flexibility in designing their Presidency in the manner that suits their own style of operating. While all of the recommendations above offer the possibility for increasing Presidential leadership capacities in the area of domestic policy, none of them will measurably alter the fact that the burdens on the Presidency are nearly impossible; expectations on Presidents to lead us to easy victories will probably always exceed the realistic possibilities.

15

On Bringing Presidents to Heel

Rexford G. Tugwell

Anyone who takes seriously the prevailing concern about the pre-eminence of the Presidency, and who accepts the necessity for change, must deal with the stubborn difficulties inherent in the alternatives proposed by critics. Certainly, executive operations have been enlarged, and this understandably has provoked strong reactions. It may be useful to summarize the complaints most often heard and, this done, look briefly at the suggested curtailments of the President's powers.

If it is concluded that the office has accumulated too many duties and has too much authority—perhaps the most frequent charge—such questions must be asked as: Where have the duties, and the authority to carry them out, come from? Why were they allocated to the President? To whom should they be entrusted, or with whom should they be shared if they are to be reduced?

If it is concluded that recent accumulations have caused a systematic neglect of traditional domestic duties—as is unquestionably true—then it has to be asked how the neglect can be remedied without, at the same time, risking the national security. This latter responsibility especially, it will be said, cannot be put aside for any other consideration.

Concerning the domestic duties of the office, the theory of the

Constitution is that the President, through his departmental heads, will actually administer all the government's operations. But Presidents are no longer able to follow agricultural, medical, or space research; they cannot judge the sufficiency of the government's elaborate welfare services, the effectiveness of its correctional efforts, or the adequacy of its efforts to curb exploitations of natural resources. Nor can they inform themselves, in any but the most superficial way, about progress in the sciences or the arts. Appointed officials act "for the President" in these and many other matters; but it is a fiction that they do so under his direction. In fact, as everyone knows, their relations with interested legislators are closer than any they have with the President. To this extent, in many matters, legislators replace executives.

If, however, the usual assumptions concerning the distribution of power are no longer valid, it is mistaken to conclude that the President is no longer actually the chief executive. What must be understood is that he can no longer be the government's *administrator*. This is a distinction frequently either neglected or ignored.

The most pervasive criticisms of the President as chief executive, however, center not on those constitutionally assigned duties he seems to neglect but on the manner in which he conducts those affairs he does manage. Critics allege that he behaves as a dictator, consulting only his close personal aides. It is only fair to ask such critics how decisions can be made otherwise in the prevailing circumstances. Ought decisions to be concluded by a group, each having an equal vote, as is done by the Supreme Court, thus spreading both the management and the responsibility? Aside from questions of constitutionality, this method would involve an expectation of unanimity among several decision-makers. If agreement should not be reached, could the public be expected to have confidence in the policies agreed upon by a majority, with a minority of dissenters? Would it not be suspected that the minority may have been right, and that a wrong policy had been adopted? If this were so, might not the Presidency be paralyzed when it most needs to be capable of acting?

Particularly on the part of congressional committees probing the behavior of the administering branch, there is some attempt to break through closed decision-making by demanding access to the exchanges among Presidential subordinates in the course of formulating policies. Such data have almost always been formally withheld. (They are often leaked or stolen, however; and then commentators end up as the judges of what is properly made public.) This withholding of information is a cause of repeated irritation and leads periodically to acidulous debates; all recent Presidents, and most department heads, have been attacked for such refusals. They are decried as further evidence of a progression toward dictatorship. Actually, of course, they are not new. Many Presidents have refused disclosure of data used for arriving at decisions. They have also refused to release the contingency plans required for possible future action.

The secrecy surrounding Presidential decision-making becomes even more important because of the frequent assertion that the President has intruded into the province of the legislature. He is not supposed to *make* laws, some complain, only to *execute* them; but, for many years, he has gone beyond the constitutional directive to "recommend . . . such measures as he shall judge necessary and expedient" and has used a variety of means to see that they are adopted. This includes a formidable lobbying staff and the use of his immense resources for bargaining.

Considering the accepted theory that Congress is to make laws and the President to execute them, it is amazing to what extent the rule is denied by the facts. Legislation is more apt to originate in the executive branch; and it is quite customary for legislators, under the rubric of oversight, to interest themselves in administration. Among the important pieces of legislation originating with the President there come to mind the TVA, AAA, and NRA of the New Deal, the supporting legislation for the cold war, and both the establishment and, later, disestablishment of the Great Society in numerous, separate acts. Congress has, in effect, been reduced to approving, disapproving, or negotiating for amendments. What would be the alternative, in view of the nature of the legislative process? Would it be to confine the President closely to the Constitution's "recommendation," prohibiting actual legislative proposals as well as maneuvers on his part to get them passed? If so, who would then originate projects, recalling that the President is still his party's head, with a fixed, four-year term, and recalling, also, the discouraging immobility of Congress as it is now organized?

At this late time, it is unlikely that the President will be excluded from the originating of legislation.

This, however, is not the main concern of the critics. Their bitterest protest is that the President, proclaiming an emergency or asking a concerned—perhaps frightened—Congress to declare one, assumes that his powers as commander in chief allow him to use the armed forces at his discretion, thereby making, at an extreme, what amounts to war without consultation; or, short of that, to dominate relations with other nations by brandishing the nation's military might.

It is frequently complained that there has been a growing tendency to ignore the "declaration of war" phrase in the Constitution. This was true of earlier, frequent interventions in Latin America, as well as of more consequential ones in Korea and Southeast Asia, not to mention incidents such as the temporary occupation of Lebanon and Santo Domingo. In all of them, the armed forces were deployed without the "declaration" mentioned in the Constitution and without much "consultation." Critics have demanded an end to executive war-making—and even to use of the military in making foreign policy. But they do not satisfactorily explain what might happen in a situation known to threaten the national security if instant action were not taken. Would they, for instance, really find a Communist government in Santo Domingo desirable? Or were they, when the question was being debated, opposed to support of the South Vietnamese, so widely considered a bulwark against Communist aggression? It was, it will be recalled, a time of excited concern about the "free world" and its vulnerability to subversion as well as actual attack. Self-determination was an accepted liberal cause.

The alternative most often put forward is that all relevant information concerning crises be submitted to Congress, together with a request for legislation drafted by the legislators. Presumably, this would require inquiries in both houses, then processing by committees, followed by debate. What would emerge, however, would be the product of a process unlikely to offer a solution to the problem. It would almost certainly be worse than legislative consideration of a definite proposal already put together by Presidential assistants.

There is another explanation concerning the delegation of powers to the President. The most skeptical critics are compelled to recognize that wars no longer begin by the slow deployment of troops, the gradual taking up of adversary positions, and, finally, when diplomacy fails, by the outbreak of fighting. In World War I, a whole year elapsed after the declaration of war before the armed forces could be prepared for deployment. Less time was required for engagement in World War II, but that was because Roosevelt had forced the pace of rearming—against an opposition of such strength that it was nearly successful. Recognizing that delayed reaction might result in fatal consequences, prolonged argument might, in certain circumstances, be fatal. The abdication of Congress in such circumstances is necessary to survival.

Critics who deny this usually do so in times of relative tranquillity, and, faced with a demand for alternatives, tend to avoid the real issue. They are, of course, able to argue that such emergencies are avoidable and would not occur if more wisdom were used in shaping peacetime policies. This, however, would require much more than restraints imposed by congressional committees; it would, indeed, require participation in the conduct of negotiations. The difficulties involved in this have been obvious since the Articles of Confederation were abandoned for the present Constitution. Possibly, these might be overcome, but only by more drastic changes than are usually contemplated.

A further complaint is that no crucial foreign-policy decisions ought to be made by only one man, with no advice from peers. But where are these peers to be found in the American system? It could be argued, perhaps, that both the cold war and its abrupt ending were responses to popular desires; but it is also true that neither was preceded by any but personal and exclusive conclusions. The President was one man, and he alone made both momentous decisions.

In the past, irritation about this was less because of a tradition that politics ended "at the water's edge," with members of all factions agreeing to close ranks behind the President in his dealings with other nations. Indeed, a generation ago, it was a custom never to mention foreign affairs in national campaigns. In 1932, for instance, Roosevelt assiduously avoided any reference to the pressure for settlement of the war debts, the impending World Economic Conference, and even the question of joining the League of Nations. The precedent had been established by his predecessors and was generally observed, except when war threatened, or when difficult and unpopular settlements had to be made.

The assumption that foreign affairs are exempt from politics was made untenable after Roosevelt, however, by the many differences concerning such issues as the containment of Communism, the ambitions of American businesses to become international, and the support of self-determination for other nations —not to mention continual controversy as the many obligations of the United States as a great power appeared to expand indefinitely. Indeed, they were enlarged by every President after World War II until 1968. *Pax Americana* used to be confined to neighboring nations embraced by the Monroe Doctrine. It was extended, after 1945, to other continents and other seas. This was perhaps a consequence of American campaigns during the war on the continents of both Asia and Europe and of a two-ocean fleet to control the waters reaching those shores. At any rate, the policy afterward took the armed forces, in new engagements, into Southeast Asia, the Mediterranean, the Indian Ocean, and Africa—a responsibility that eventually strained even the immense resources of the American economy and became a furiously debated issue no candidate could ignore. The Nixon Doctrine of withdrawal was an admission that the massive postwar obligations had become insupportable. The extension of these responsibilities had been largely a Presidential initiative; retreat from them was likewise an exclusively Presidential decision.

The extension of partisan politics to foreign relations reinforces another concern of some critics: that the President, having been a party candidate, remains a party man. They suggest that some other way of choosing Presidents must at least be considered, one that ensures the support essential to leadership and provides the lead-time necessary for national policy-making, but avoids the divisiveness inherent in party politics.

There is certainly a dilemma here: A candidate, after a partisan campaign, suddenly becomes President of all the people, not just the leader of his party. This, if regarded as an absolute, would separate him from the permanent organization needed for party control, if not for his own re-election. The maintenance of party solidarity in the legislature and elsewhere admittedly makes for easier passage into law of whatever program seems to have been approved by the President's election.

That these abandonments of political ties are often more talked about than acted on, however, is shown by the party's influence in choosing the White House entourage. If it is assumed that, once in office, he is President of all the people, how is it that members of other parties or independent opponents are so generally excluded from employment?

And a final question: Does this partisan selection process result in the best possible President? It is charged that most Presidents have not been the best available selections for the awesome duties they must assume, and there is much evidence that this is so. Historians generally agree that those who cannot be rated as successful far outnumber those considered to have been adequate or near adequate. If this is a reliable assessment, it brings into question the whole selection process and opens a vast area of democratic dogma to exploration. It goes not only to the determination of qualifications for suffrage but to the electoral processes. But does anyone demand that the electorate be purged, or that nominations come under federal law?

A Pattern

It is not intended here to imply that, in all controversies about policy, Presidents have been wise; but a pattern does seem to exist: Repeated assumptions of power are followed each time by a chorus of criticism. No President escapes furious castigation.

The critics, however, are conspicuously negative. The means they offer for reducing the powers of the President and easing the differences between his power and that of the other branches are hopelessly inadequate for the purpose. More drastic changes are needed than are offered as alternatives.

There are, to summarize, specific complaints of dictatorial behavior; invasion of legislative prerogatives; inadmissible uses of the armed forces; monopolization of new governmental concerns —the economy, welfare, consumer protection, environmental dangers, scientific and cultural activities; and even the control of discussion about public policy. There are other complaints as well, some variations of these, and some combinations of several. Each has a tendency to gather others about itself, and usually, as complaints mount, all are justified by the assiduously conducted campaigns of political antagonists.

Presidents are so exposed, and so apt to make decisions with consequences found intolerable by vociferous critics, that the heroic stature of their first months almost inevitably becomes diminished so seriously as to make them antiheroes before they have been long in the White House.

Some years ago, it might have seemed exaggerated to speak of a crisis in constitutional divisions of power, but suddenly, during Johnson's Administration, such a concern did not seem exaggerated at all. Something, it was agreed, must be done about the Presidency; but the suggestions most often heard were neither useful appraisals nor workable correctives. Mostly, the offerings were palliatives. Even after a quarter-century of growing distrust, nothing really remedial emerged.

This meant that Nixon, after the deplorable history of the Johnson years, would not even be permitted to try new approaches if his detractors could prevent it, and very often they could. He was more inventive than his predecessors. He delegated many of his duties and concentrated on his own judgment about policies, with such information as his helpers provided. When he emerged from his characteristic solitary sessions with such startling decisions as the reversal of the quarter-century policy of containment and of traditional economic *laissez faire*, his critics were infuriated but speechless, since he had clearly co-opted the issues they had hoped would embarrass him and perhaps defeat him for re-election.

The dangers in his procedural changes were, of course, illustrated by the discovery that he had chosen unprincipled subordinates and allowed them too much authority; but it had at least been an effort to solve the central problem of decision-making. It was clear after Watergate that another method would have to be tried.

Would Nixon's method have been improved by the confrontation so ardently advocated as a corrective to his solitary habit? Who would confront him? Only members of Congress were in a position to do so; and it must be said that debates did take place. He lost most of those on domestic matters and won most of those on foreign policy; but Presidents have usually had this experience. It would certainly have been more agreeable to the press if it had been known in advance that he intended to propose new initiatives; but there did have to be a feeling-out process; and, if he had been repulsed in the midst of public furor, it could hardly have furthered the cause of peace.

On certain issues, there had obviously been compromise with congressional leaders in advance. Because of this, some parts of the President's program were canceled by other parts. The likelihood that his economic measures would cure inflation was as doubtful as their effect on unemployment; but relief from either or both would have been even more remote if he had waited for debate with peers—whoever they might be. If arrangement for confrontation had existed, his chance of making any effort at all would have been prevented. In any case, it would have been too late; the confronters would have disagreed in about the same proportion as the dissenters did when he announced the effort, and their power of delay would have been fatally effective.

When, in his attempt to control inflation, he used a permissive law passed earlier to absolve Congress of responsibility for economic distresses, there was a stunning effect. When he announced an immediate freeze on both wages and prices, it was recognized that debate would have made these measures far less effective. This, indeed, was an example of the need for Presidential freedom in emergency. With the emergency already recognized, he was able to move into a deteriorating situation and establish a block. Discussion could follow; if it had preceded action, chaos might well have ensued.

It soon became clear that the economic troubles were the result of mistaken policies of long standing. These were not amenable to emergency reversal; but something did have to be done, and the President had to do it. Corrective measures would run deep and be bitterly opposed. His critics, however, paid little attention to past mistakes. They were acidulous about the handling of the crisis and chary of helpful suggestions about alternatives.

CONFRONTATION CONSIDERED

In the instance of the price and wage freeze, it was a fortuitous circumstance that an emergency formally recognized by Congress existed. If Congress had not acted, the President might have felt forced to move anyway, without explicit authorization; other Presidents had done so. Nevertheless, legislators' criticisms, if not foreclosed, were weakened by their attempt to embarrass him. They had expected to be able to say at election time that he had refused to use the authority so freely conferred.

This same problem of defining an emergency confused the Supreme Court when it was deciding whether Truman, as President, had acted within his powers in seizing certain steel mills paralyzed by strikes during the Korean war. Several justices wrote separate and differing opinions, none notable for logic or reasonableness, concerning constitutional justification for the use of emergency powers. What was demonstrated by the Court's indecision, and became clearer afterward, was that emergencies, together with procedures for meeting them, needed constitutional definition. That is to say, the President should not be able to designate any situation as an emergency and then define his own powers while it lasts; but neither should it depend on congressional consent or public confrontation. Sometimes, Congress simply abandons responsibility; its leaders recognize that there are times when events make argumentation either impossible or undesirable.

The Constitution has no provision for such a circumstance.

It has to be concluded, from repeated experiences with situations requiring executive action without consultation, that definition, however much needed, is not likely to come from those within the system or those who have made adjustments in it favorable to themselves, that is, from anyone in office or from outsiders who have mutually supporting relations with them. They prefer the present indefinition. The critics are not "constructive" in any understood meaning of the word.

Changes will have to originate with those who are concerned, but who are not committed to vested interests, traditional institutions, or popular preferences; and they will have to be constitutional. Suggestions—and there are many—must show, in the case of the economy, for instance, how to escape from the contrast between enormous potential and constricted performance without the use of such dictatorial measures as the freeze of 1971. The economy has long been capable of achieving, year after year, twice or three times its actual growth. That such a consistent advance is possible is shown by its having been attained repeatedly. Government is staffed with a personnel and furnished with laws and appropriations that ought to make agriculture and industry as productive in tranquil times as they are in times of war, when the incentive is conspicuously greater. Actually, most of the organized groups in the economy, except when under Presidential discipline, have a propensity for stifling the others. No power has been available, except in emergency, to bring about the needed coordination among these conflicting interests.

Regulations affecting travel, communication, and other facilities and limits on prices and wages have been imposed a number of times during wars and depressions. They have been accepted as necessary sometimes, but frequently they have been resisted or evaded. During World War II, the Office of Price Administration, with an army of employees, had only limited success in controlling black markets; and other agencies had even less effect in allocating capital and materials. Especially toward the end of the war, the regulations were largely ignored. There was never any assurance that what was being done had constitutional justification, and so punishment for violations could never be really adequate; restrictions were apt to be regarded as arbitrary and unwarranted limitations on freedom. The agencies imposing them were constantly reluctant to risk legal tests. The Nixon economic regulations were no more successful than preceding ones, and for the same reasons.

As for the wider complaint that Presidents are becoming more dictatorial even when there is no emergency, and that there should be adversary proceedings before important policies are decided, there are obvious difficulties.

Aside from the now fixed tradition that, on most issues, the President proposes and the Congress consents or does not consent, his proposals do have airings. Congressional committees hold hearings, and opponents are quite willing to argue their positions on television. Legislation submitted by the White House is almost always modified, often drastically. Administration lobbyists have been increased in number because of this perennial opposition. Unless it is proposed that the President himself be required to appear and defend his proposals, there is not much more to be done in this way. Even if it should be ignored that his appearance would be inconsistent with the separation principle, there is the consideration that the chief of state would be involved in caustic exchanges with political detractors—spectacles likely to defame an office there is some reason for protecting from embarrassment.

The economic crisis of August, 1971, was one of those clearly requiring extraordinary measures, and they were followed at once by extraordinary appeals not only for support but also for voluntary compliance, because it was so widely doubted that the powers to be used were enforceable. The President made appearances, sometimes running to half a dozen a day, before immense crowds and on television, arguing his position and asking for cooperation.

It has to be recognized that every minute of every Presidential day is occupied by the duties of office. Something else has to be neglected for such extraordinary efforts. Those who would insist on open debates at his critics' convenience, and presumably at length, before decisions on policy innovations are taken would force the neglect of still more duties. It is already well known that, even in quiet times, the President knows what goes on in the departments only as he is told in rare conferences with their heads; and his directions to them are channeled through his subordinates, who, it is suspected, are really their originators. Only the more serious problems are even known about by him, and then only when trouble impends. His knowledge is so superficial that mistakes of judgment are not just likely but, indeed, probable.

At the most extreme, critics suggest confrontation concerning all important policies, domestic as well as foreign, thus putting the President in the position of defending many determinations he cannot possibly be informed about. Actually, what happens at present is that subterranean relations are established between congressional committees and bureau or agency chiefs, the President and his office being bypassed. Confrontation would be ineffective in reducing this undercover bargaining. If it did take place, it would be superficial and unreal on both sides.

It is not, of course, about domestic issues that the demand for Presidential response to critics mostly arises; it is about foreign policy, the commitments made for the nation by its chief of state. The most controversial of these, in recent years, concerned the use of the armed forces. It is argued that, before these forces are deployed abroad, the President should consult with others. Those others, unless there should be constitutional change, would be legislators. The legislators could not well be *all* 535 senators and representatives. They would, presumably, be the members of the committees, most importantly their chairmen, assigned to deal with foreign policy.

The fact is, however, that committee chairmen already argue with the President, and with his lobbyists, especially when majorities are not of the President's party. This is well known; but it is evidently not enough for advocates of confrontation. They would prevent the President from acting without explicit consent, even after an effort at justification. By the time hearings are held and debates occur, they say, commitment has already been made. Certainly, it could not be contended that hearings, as traditionally conducted, have the effect sought. Committeemen frequently are patently partisan. They are more often interested in promoting themselves or their parties than in clarifying issues, and, of course, what they get from Presidential defenders is not offered in good faith, either.

The frequently repeated suggestion that the defeated candidate in the last election be given a legislative seat and adequate means for informing himself, with the purpose of opposing the incumbent, assumes that the duty of legislators is not to pass laws but to contest those proposed by the President. To accept this scheme would also be to abandon the theory that, once elected, a President represents all the people, not only those who voted for him. Since this is an essential attribute of a chief of state, it would seem to be a denial of an important tenet of our Constitution.

Here, it must be noted that there are enormous differences between crises requiring instant response and gradually developing ones requiring permanent changes in policy. The slowly developing ones may, if neglected, turn into emergencies; but they ought to be preceded by discussion of alternate suggestions for remedy, and they usually are.

Concerning long-range commitments, the lack of adequate consultation is, without any doubt, something requiring remedy. When a new general position is adopted, not previously debated and not generally understood, it ought not to be effectuated until there is substantial consent. Lacking this, there will sooner or later be acrimonious dissent. How is this to be arranged? Or, to put it another way, how is the President to know whether he has approval? It is not enough to depend on campaign debates; many important issues are never touched in the quadrennial appeals, one reason being that the candidate who is assured by the polls that he is in the lead will avoid advocacy of any policy likely to arouse the opposition of any large group of voters— ethnic, economic, social, or other—and so will come to office without instructions from the electorate. Similarly, the candidate who is running behind is likely to concentrate on criticisms ("throw the rascals out") and will be even more likely to avoid proposals for any substantial change.

Because he has made no commitments or, at the most, only very general ones, and because he will have four years in office anyway, a President feels free to adopt policies not previously debated. He may even make dispositions certain to alter relations with other nations; and these may, at the most extreme, amount to alliances or provocations leading to rupture. Presidents will do this believing they are acting in the best interest of the nation, and because they believe themselves chosen to make just such decisions.

Those who complain of such Presidential exclusiveness and who advocate confrontation are in a weak position if they are unwilling to designate those with whom the President should be required to argue and the conditions requiring such discussions. Some have done this; but they characteristically refuse to go outside present institutional limits, and this confines them to demanding that he consult legislators, or some of them—usually the committeemen who deal with foreign relations. It is to most people an appalling thought that the senators who are heard from most often, as things are, should have a decisive voice in really vital matters. Their chosen role is critical, their habit probing, their purpose exposure, their attitude self-righteous. They represent districts or states, not the whole nation, as does the President. When things go wrong, they become invisible. Something quite different from this is needed—but it *is* needed.

As for the confrontation with peers, there is a curious refusal to say who these peers might be. If they do not exist in any part of Congress as it is now constituted, their creation would obviously require constitutional amendment. If that should happen, would the newly created peers be associate Presidents, would they be a court of appraisal—or what? How would such a group operate? Would its members actually share the President's decision-making, perhaps voting on policies to be adopted? Nothing less would seem to suffice.

Perhaps what is being edged toward is a plural, or collegiate, Presidency. This is a well-understood arrangement and one that is not new to political literature. It even exists in smaller countries—Switzerland, for instance, where it is so successful that there is no desire for change. Plurality would provide one species of confrontation. Policies would be discussed among a group of whatever size was decided on. It would not, however, satisfy minorities who could never be sure that their point of view had been adequately represented. It would also suffer from the same lack of unity that reduces the authority of the Supreme Court. When four members dissent from the majority opinion of five, the fallibility of judgment, and even the possibility of future reversal, is all too obvious.

Yet, it has become impossible for the President to meet his constitutional responsibilities. The burden and complexity have outrun his human capacities. Perhaps plurality will have to be turned to as the only real alternative. As things are, the President has no one to share his responsibility. Only he represents all the people. The creation of peers would require that they have the same representative legitimacy. No constitutional amendment to effectuate such a change is suggested by the critics; but what it must be like is quite obvious. Others at his level of authority must be chosen. Why is it that the advocates of confrontation avoid this conclusion?

CREDIBILITY

Is the President justified in deception when, in his judgment, it is necessary in the public interest? This is by now a familiar question. It is evident that what men of honor would not do in their private capacities they frequently do in their public ones. All find themselves, sooner or later, compelled to choose; and they all choose at least to dissimulate if not so often to deceive.

Credibility became a familiar word during the Johnson Administration; and "credibility gap" was used to describe the claim that what was being told to the public by the President and his associates was untrue. Since there was nothing novel about this, the charge had its force from the flagrancy of the particular offense. It had to do with an extremely unpopular foreign involvement; and exposure of deception was too well authenticated for effective denial.

Operations in Southeast Asia were being portrayed in ways calculated to support policies and actions decided on and carried through both by military and civilian officials; and approval was unlikely if the facts about the situation were understood by

the public. Reporters in the battle areas and around head-
quarters insisted that damaging facts were being concealed. The
invasion, they consistently maintained, was going badly. Both
the strategy and the tactics were mistaken. Decisions were made
in secrecy and then denied (such as the support of small armies
in Laos and Cambodia); and both people and land in the areas
of engagement were being ruthlessly sacrificed.

An accumulation of distrust, going back far beyond his Administration, caused a fiercely critical examination of Johnson's
performance. In addition, concerning Johnson, there was also
the complaint that massive intervention in Santo Domingo had
been undertaken for quite another reason than that offered in
explanation: that the lives and properties of U.S. citizens had to
be protected. It was plain enough, reporters said—and they were
echoed by commentators, legislators, and others—that his real
purpose had been to prevent another Communist takeover, such
as had been allowed to occur in Cuba. If this was the reason,
he succeeded; but those who were offended by his avoidance of
frankness were not disposed to allow him any credit for the
result, even if they agreed that another Communist enclave in
the Caribbean would be intolerable. The obviously false explanation was a grievance they were not disposed to give up; the
habit of deception was becoming too evident.

Complaints about the cover-ups concerning Southeast Asia
were, of course, more consequential; but they were of the same
nature. In spite of massive evidence, Johnson refused to admit
that there had been grievous errors in decision-making and
execution. The list of his sins became a long one and tended,
moreover, to be exaggerated. There was a concerted search for
the bad news he was trying to conceal. Naturally, it was found;
and his discredit eventually became politically insupportable,
making it impossible for him to continue in office.

Everyone with a moderately long memory knew, however, that
these defensive Presidential representations had become characteristic of the office. Deceptions had only become more professional. Their use to defend a costly and unpopular foreign
involvement was peculiarly offensive to legislative critics, who
were not entirely innocent themselves. It was suddenly discovered

that legions of public-relations men attached to the military were engaged in interpretation of repeated failures as a succession of victories. So few, in fact, were deceived that persistence in keeping on with attempts to deceive seemed an insult to public intelligence. What had been a well-understood and fairly tolerable style of defending executive behavior became, in Johnson's case, so exaggerated as to be wholly unacceptable.

Besides, it began to be noted, this kind of manipulation was not peculiar to the military. The same sorts of specialists were attached to other agencies of government. They were, in effect, being paid by the taxpayers to befuddle rather than to inform them. This was more reprehensible than the similar operations of large corporations. They, of course, could deduct such expenses from their tax bills, and so charge them to consumers who were being deceived; but their operations were not quite so direct, nor did they have so obvious a bearing on public policy.

Legislators, as well as administrators, were implicated. They had been busy building up similar public-relations staffs, so that they could hardly object to the President's or even to those proliferating in the executive departments. The difference was that the President was regarded as responsible for decisions and for the explanation of them by his subordinates. Blame washed over the White House in a rising flood; so did resentment that such massive attempts had been made to explain it away. The public-relations men attached to legislators won this battle with those defending the President.

It would not be at all difficult to list manifestly self-serving statements issued in numerous Administrations since Washington's—in practically all of them, in fact. Approaches to both World Wars, for instance, were marked by hardly forgivable declarations by Wilson and Roosevelt that they were firm opponents of involvement. They would not send American boys to fight in foreign wars, they said; and it appeared soon afterward that they had intended all along to do just that.

Retrospect turns up this kind of thing too late, in most instances, to be really embarrassing; or, if what was done appears to have been wise and farsighted, the deceptions are forgotten or forgiven. Neither Wilson nor Roosevelt suffered politically:

Wilson was justified by victory and the Kaiser's abdication; Roosevelt's repeated declarations that he only meant to defend the nation were forgotten after Pearl Harbor and were excused as part of his foresighted approach to joining the Allies and achieving victory.

Even in domestic matters, deceptions of the same sort occur. They may be illustrated by the conspiracy among officials to conceal the depressing statistics of unemployment and business failures between 1929 and 1933. Frances Perkins, Roosevelt's Commissioner of Labor in New York State, exposed with ruthless satisfaction the minimization of what was rapidly becoming a national disaster. The exposure played some part in Roosevelt's first campaign for the Presidency.

Roosevelt, in his turn, however, made grossly exaggerated predictions that a bizarre "re-employment agreement" would result in the immediate resumption of business activity. Within months, of course, he had to preside over its quiet burial. He also conducted an adventure in manipulating the market for gold as a cure for the country's paralysis. Within months he recommended the fixing of a price, and it was accepted by Congress. The public never really knew what had been done. He told them that everything was going well, even as policies were being abandoned.

Considering what a long list there is of such representations by Presidents of actions whose failure they have preferred not to disclose, how often they have tortured the facts into justifications, and how often they have actually been untruthful, it must be concluded that, as a rule, Presidents do not hesitate to deceive when it seems necessary to get their way or to defend themselves. This is not attributable to faults of character or to doubtful personal morals. With one or two exceptions, they have been upright men who found themselves in positions that offered them no alternative. It must be expected that future Presidents, given similar circumstances, will behave in the same way.

The alternative most frequently suggested is the obvious one: Make deceptions impossible by arranging for disclosure of the facts. This, of course, neglects the aphorism that truth is elusive and appears different to different people. There is also the well-known propensity for self-deception, heightened by the weight of great responsibility. Presidents usually seem to believe what they say, even when it is patently false; and this weakness is apparently worsened when national interests are involved. It is probable that they do not regard themselves as taking moral risks, even in outright lying, if essential purposes are to be served. In such situations, preferred beliefs or settled convictions appear to be extremely resistant to controverting evidence; and since, in complex matters, it is possible to claim exclusive knowledge, and often the support of dependent experts, a chosen policy is easy enough to defend—until it collides with reality and collapses!

An illustration on the grandest scale is available in the quarter-century of hostility to Communism after Roosevelt's death. It was supported by massive compilations of evidence that a nation given over to Communism could not succeed. During that period, however, the Soviet Union grew in strength, until it finally became an undisputed superpower and challenged the position of the United States in the world. But, given the widespread—almost unanimous—assumption of the system's weakness embedded in American opinion, no political leader saw fit to associate Soviet growth with virtue. The system was manifestly capable of progress because it had progressed; but, in American opinion—reinforced by Presidential rhetoric—it continued to be at once feeble and dangerously strong.

There arises a question: Where, in all that time, were newspapers, magazines, and television broadcasters, who so often profess devotion to informing the public? If the public had the right to know, its right was not respected. When successive Presidents reiterated their interpretation of events, they were joined almost unanimously by communicators. This long deception was certainly assisted by a failure of reporting.

It is even more revealing to ask where were the legislators who had at least some knowledge of growing Russian power? They were even more assiduous than Presidents in disseminating a deception that must eventually be revealed for what it was.

There are so many illustrations of official deception, and of the concurrence of those who might have objected, that Johnson's departures from veracity concerning Southeast Asia appear in perspective as no different in kind, and very little worse in effect, than familiar ones in the past. Truman justifying the use of the atomic bomb by concealing efforts of the Japanese to surrender; Eisenhower plainly lying about overflights of Russia by spy planes; Kennedy sending troops to Vietnam disguised (for the benefit of the public) as observers (or perhaps advisers)—these are only a few recent incidents of this kind. None of those was unknown to legislators or reporters. Apparently, it is only when hostility to a policy becomes general that the media begin to find and disseminate evidence that the public is being deceived.

So long as the shapers of public opinion have strong preferences about policy and use the instruments they control to support those preferences, they will not serve as a source of public enlightenment. When they prefer one candidate to others, or find an official agreeable to their interests, they do not complain about "credibility gaps" and violations of the "public's right to know." It is all too evident that newspapers and television will not, in all circumstances, expose the elaborate fictions of Presidents defending doubtful policies. They have biases and interests of their own, and they have their own means of protecting them. Morality becomes an issue much more easily when Presidential behavior is displeasing to them.

INCOMPETENCE

Americans find it almost impossible to admit, despite incontrovertible evidence, that the present selection system sometimes results in the election of Presidents who, however upright, are simply incompetent for what is expected of them, and often of Presidents whose abilities are much inferior to those of some of their contemporaries who were available. Some were incompetent even for the far simpler Presidential duties before the great wars and the Depression. Van Buren, Harrison, Taylor, Fillmore, Pierce, and Buchanan—the line preceding the Civil War—all failed to reach even a minimum standard of effectiveness. After Lincoln, there were Andrew Johnson, Grant, Hayes,

Garfield, and Arthur. Then, after Theodore Roosevelt, there were (omitting Wilson) Taft, Harding, and Coolidge; and after Franklin D. Roosevelt, there was Truman. All these are usually judged to have been less than adequate for the office.

No one, at this distance, would defend any one of these as the best available choice. To take Harding and Coolidge, for illustrative purposes, recall what the consequences were. Harding demeaned the office and left a record of scandal; Coolidge passively allowed the economic catastrophe to develop that swamped his successor, Hoover. Instead of Harding, Governor Lowden of Illinois was an available alternative, an able and trusted state executive, but not likely to have been amenable to control by the Old Guard of his party. The instance of Coolidge is somewhat less illustrative, because, as Vice President, he succeeded at Harding's death; but, at the next election (1924), he was preferred to John W. Davis, the Democratic nominee, and, before that, had been preferred to several Republicans for the nomination, any one of whom—Hoover or Hughes, for instance —was highly visible and, moreover, known to be more competent.

These Presidents were selected in a process with no other constitutional legitimization than that in the Twelfth Amendment (ratified in 1804 to supplement sections 2 and 3 of Article II in the original), providing that electors choosen in the states would meet and make choices later to be counted in Washington.

The framers of the Constitution did not anticipate any such gradual degradation of representation as has taken place. Since, in their time, only a small percentage of the adult male citizens could vote (at most 15 per cent), the select few were to choose a still more select group in each state as electors, and these were to make the final choice. When suffrage was extended, first to nonproperty owners, then to former slaves, to women, and, finally, to eighteen-year-olds, the entirely new situations made changes in procedures obviously necessary; but none was provided for by amendment.

When, from a few voters—leading citizens in each community —the choice in elections passed to the millions newly enfranchised, new kinds of appeals had to be made. The wealthy and wellborn have different standards from what those who are poor and undistinguished have. The electors, when they were actually functioning, had chosen Adams. It is doubtful whether any of the early Presidents, except Washington and perhaps Jefferson, too, would have been nominated at any time after 1838; and certainly the original electoral college would not have chosen half or more of the succession that began then—perhaps none of them, since the successes in that line had, besides unexpected abilities, the necessary touch of demagoguery and a willingness to compromise with the demands of the bosses.

The original electoral college soon fell into desuetude because of the rise of parties; but it continued to exist, functioning in a pro forma way. The electors no longer exercised any choice. The substitute process consisted of conventions to nominate candidates and nationwide voting in a contest among them for votes, so that electors have been reduced to merely registering the result in their respective states.

What explains the curious disarray of election procedure is this growth, without legitimization, of an entirely new selection process to take the place of the one originally provided for in the Constitution. Direct election has been proposed over and over again, but no proposal has been adopted by Congress for submission to the states as a constitutional amendment. Even if one had been adopted, however, and ratified, the quality of the candidates chosen by the conventions would not have been improved.

There were some years, in the early nineteenth century, when congressional caucuses provided candidates. These were superseded by conventions called by various organizations, and gradually took on forms provided for by their own resolutions. They thus made laws for themselves. They were nearly always controlled by small groups of professional politicians, usually state or city bosses; and the candidates they provided were mostly mediocre.

Some delegates to these conventions now come from states with Presidential primaries; but many of these primaries do no more than indicate preferences, and the selection of candidates has remained, on the whole, a closely held privilege of those who, by assiduous management of local party machinery, are able to have themselves designated as delegates. Conventions tend to become bargaining sessions among these self-chosen power brokers, who settle finally on a candidate they believe will take advice concerning policy and will distribute favors according to the agreements reached at the convention. They prefer one who has at least a chance to win; but this is often less important to them than are the fortunes of their local organizations.

A process controlled in such ways is bound to produce a high percentage of incompetent Presidents. It is not always convenient to select from among the possibilities a person who will promise not to disturb the existing arrangement of privileges; but one is often found. It has lately become essential as well for him to have access to the huge funds necessary to conduct modern campaigns. It is understood that there will be some sort of compensation for campaign contributions, or at least that the interests of those making them will not be jeopardized. The professionals realize this, of course, and the subtle corruption of candidates made possible by contributions to party funds begins at the outset of the selection process. No one will be put forward who is unacceptable to those financing his campaign.

Such a set of requirements promises nothing in the way of managership for the vast service departments of government, for the making of foreign policies, or for the complex business of achieving stability in a privately managed economy. The infrequent exceptions to the rule of mediocrity—Wilson, Hoover, and the Roosevelts, for instance—are accounted for by unusual circumstances: Theodore Roosevelt by the death of McKinley; Wilson by a split in the Republican party; Hoover by his great wartime reputation as an administrator; and Franklin D. Roosevelt by the discrediting effect on Hoover of the Great Depression. The exceptions do not vitiate the rule.

It is often pointed out that ten of the largest contributors to Nixon's campaign funds became ambassadors, but so did the most generous of Roosevelt's financial backers. Besides, the Cabinets of both Presidents were largely chosen to please the conservative elders of their respective parties. Their Administrations were indifferently equipped for their tasks.

Turning from senatorial activities to administration requires a most unlikely transformation. The management of a bureaucracy comprising perhaps thousands of careerists will be, at best, nominal; the agency heads will inevitably outmaneuver a politician-secretary. Presidential orders transmitted through such channels become more mysteriously changed to suit the bureaucracy's preferences. Policies persist from one Administration to another remarkably unchanged. Resistance to change is also reinforced by the alliances between bureaucrats and the appropriate congressmen. Altogether, it requires a most sophisticated and determined President to effect any changes at all.

At the very time when most can be accomplished, new Presidents, even those who have had long experience, are apt to be incapable of getting anything done. This was conspicuously true of Truman and Kennedy, for instance; but Eisenhower, also, did not discover for a long time how different being President was from being a general. Johnson was an exception, of course, but his notable honeymoon record is accounted for by the overwhelming majority of liberal legislators who came into office when he did. His ability to carry Congress with him stopped abruptly in 1966, when the midterm elections returned the Old Guard and their army of lobbyists to power. Nixon's early difficulties were of a different sort. He was much more experienced and realistic, but had a hostile Congress to contend with and an unusually rapacious coterie of campaign contributors who expected returns in government favors. This is only to speak of legislative accomplishments. As an administrator, neither Johnson nor Nixon appeared to have much interest in faithful execution. Johnson's spate of welfare laws proved to be badly coordinated, and many became objects of ridicule; they seemed to Nixon, in his time, ready for transformation by the simplistic formula of "revenue sharing." His success in this was no greater than Johnson's in his war on poverty.

Since the probability that the present selection process will produce mediocre Presidents is high, why has it been allowed to develop and to continue? The answer is, of course, that it is natural to an enormously expanded electorate more or less at the mercy of those with special interests to be served and with control of the mass media. Party membership is open; loyalists become fewer and fewer; and those who are unreliable have no standing in the organized nucleus. The masses of voters cannot be counted on for support, and they have no influence at nominating conventions, except as the polls give some indication of their preferences.

BETTER PRESIDENTS

To provide the United States with a Presidency competent for the responsibilities it must carry, fairly obvious changes will have to be made. They will be drastic—that is to say, constitutional—and will not only affect the processes of selection and the activities of the office but also alter the position of the Presidency within the government.

The processes of selection will have to be freed of the obligations incurred by present financing necessities. That is to say, campaign funds will have to be public. No individual and no interest can be allowed to hold the office in its debt. Equally important, the workings of the whole party system will have to be democratized, so that anyone with political talents will be able to begin at the local level and rise to positions of more and more responsibility.

Having made it less likely that Hardings and Coolidges will become Presidents, the more capable incumbents will have to be relieved of all duties not essential for the President himself to carry—specifically, administration of the proliferating service functions characteristic of the welfare state. This will allow him time and energy for the unavoidable duties, those having to do with the security and good prospects of the nation.

For these major tasks, he must have the support of his wide constituency and the assistance of peers. He will have been elected by all the people. He must keep their trust by sounding their wishes and by explaining his formulations of policy. He must also have the critical appraisal and the cooperation of the legislative branch. These can be had only by assuring, in the selection process, that some part, at least, of the legislature will be chosen for the same reasons as he himself and with the same ends in view.

A President, as things are, succeeds or fails largely because he can or cannot persuade Congress to accept his leadership and assist in developing common policies. The legislature, however, is so positioned that it has other aims, different from those of the President. He represents all the people; members of Congress represent smaller, localized constituencies. Congressmen, in the belief that their time and effort are best spent in pleasing their constituents, inevitably form an opposition, and one intensified by the likelihood that a majority of them will belong to another party. If some representatives were elected at large, and on the same ticket with the President, cooperation rather than obstruction would be more likely.

The President, being responsible for dealings with other nations and for future domestic policies, should be given the assistance of a planning agency devoted not only to the calculations necessary for the formulation of national needs and the resources available for meeting them, but also to bringing into its deliberations the expertise of the scientific and technological community. Thus reinforced, Presidents could exert leadership with greater confidence that large mistakes would be avoided and future prosperity made more likely.

Decisions arising out of recurring environmental and technological changes must now be made by Presidents alone, and largely on the basis of instinct tempered only by the advice of department heads and intelligence services. Because of this situation, there have been costly errors, such as the depopulation of the American countryside and the proliferation of urban slums, or, again, the undertaking of the long and exhausting cold war, which led into the involvement in Southeast Asia.

Such decisions could benefit from reliance on a peer group for advice, but the President now has no peers. It is suggested that the Senate, having been originally the result of compromise and being unnecessary for legislation, should be transformed into a House of National Concern. If its members were appointed from panels of citizens with proven ability, and were forbidden any other employment, they would be as nearly peers of the President as could be devised without actually making them voting associates. A select body of these senators might be chosen to join in certain of his crucial decisions, such as the deployment of the armed forces abroad or in far waters, thus avoiding the near approach to dictatorship clearly developing in recent years.

These changes are indeed drastic, and they require changes in a basic law that has been essentially unchanged for nearly two centuries, except for the extrapolations of the Supreme Court. That law might regain its credibility and usefulness by such a reconstitution.

The Contributors

REXFORD G. TUGWELL, a former Professor of Political Economy and Planning at Columbia University and the University of Chicago, was a member of President Franklin D. Roosevelt's "Brains Trust." Later, he was Under Secretary of Agriculture and the wartime Governor of Puerto Rico. Currently a Senior Fellow at the Center for the Study of Democratic Institutions, he is author of more than a score of books, among which are *The Democratic Roosevelt, The Brains Trust, The Enlargement of the Presidency, In Search of Roosevelt, A Model Constitution,* and his latest, *The Emerging Constitution.*

THOMAS E. CRONIN, a graduate of Holy Cross and Stanford University, has been a White House Fellow and a faculty member at the University of North Carolina (Chapel Hill). He has authored numerous articles and books on the Presidency, including *The Presidency Advisory System* and *The State of the Presidency.* Recently, he has been conducting research in political science at both the Brookings Institution and the Center for the Study of Democratic Institutions.

C. HERMAN PRITCHETT, Professor of Political Science at the University of California, Santa Barbara, was formerly Chairman of the Department of Political Science at the University of Chicago. He was President of the American Political Science Association in 1963–64. A specialist in American constitutional law and the judicial process, he is the author of some ten books and many articles on the Supreme Court and American constitutional issues.

FRANCIS G. HUTCHINS, Lecturer on Government at Harvard University, is the author of *India's Revolution: Gandhi and the Quit-India Movement* and *The Illusion of Permanence: British Imperialism in India*. He has also written a number of articles dealing with American and South Asian politics. Currently, he is a Research Fellow at the Institute for Advanced Study, Princeton, New Jersey.

LOUIS FISHER is the author of *President and Congress: Power and Policy*. A contributor to numerous journals and popular magazines, Dr. Fisher received his doctorate from the New School for Social Research and taught for three years at Queens College. He is at present with the Congressional Research Service of the Library of Congress. The views he expresses in his essay are his own, not necessarily those of the Congressional Research Service.

ADOLF A. BERLE, the late noted New York lawyer, served several Presidents in numerous advisory capacities, among them as Assistant Secretary of State and Ambassador to Brazil. His several books include *The Modern Corporation and Private Property* (with Gardiner C. Means), *New Directions in the New World*, and *Power*. From 1927 to 1964, he was a professor of Corporation Law at the Columbia University Law School. He died in 1972.

ARTHUR SCHLESINGER, JR., who was a Presidential Assistant from 1961 to 1964, is now Albert Schweitzer Professor of Humanities at City University of New York. Among his many books are the three volumes of *The Age of Roosevelt, The Age of Jackson,* and *A Thousand Days: John F. Kennedy in the White House,* of which the last two received Pulitzer Prizes. His most recent book is *The Imperial Presidency*.

GEORGE E. REEDY, former White House Press Secretary and former Staff Director of the Senate Democratic Policy Committee, is now Dean and Nieman Professor of the College of Journalism, Marquette University. He is the author of *The Twilight of the Presidency* and *The Presidency in Flux*.

JOHN E. MUELLER, Professor of Political Science at the University of Rochester, is the author of *War, Presidents and Public Opinion* and the editor of *Approaches to Measurement in International Relations*. He has also published articles on such subjects as foreign and defense policy, voting behavior, and the politics of fluoridation.

DANIEL P. MOYNIHAN, who is U.S. Ambassador to India, was a member of the sub-Cabinets of Presidents Kennedy and Johnson and—until his return to the John Fitzgerald Kennedy School of Government at Harvard in 1971—of the Cabinet of President Nixon. He is the author of *Maximum Feasible Misunderstanding* and *Beyond the Melting Pot* (with Nathan Glazer). He has also been a frequent contributor to *Commentary* and *The Public Interest*.

MILTON PLESUR, Professor of History at the State University of New York at Buffalo, is the author of a monograph, *America's Outward Thrust: Approaches to Foreign Affairs, 1865–1890,* as well as a number of articles. He has also edited three collections— *The 1920's: Problems and Paradoxes; Intellectual Alienation in the 1920's;* and *Creating an American Empire, 1865–1914.*

JAMES DAVID BARBER is the author of *The Presidential Character: Predicting Performance in the White House*. He has been Professor of Political Science at Yale University, Guest Scholar at the Brookings Institution, and a Fellow at the Center for Advanced Study in the Behavioral Sciences at Stanford. Currently, he is Professor and Chairman of the Department of Political Science at Duke University.

HUGH G. GALLAGHER is the author of *Advise and Obstruct: The Role of the United States Senate in Foreign Policy Decisions* and the recently published *ETOK: A Story of Eskimo Power.* Currently Washington Representative of British Petroleum, he has worked in the Office of Legislative Reference, Bureau of the Budget, and for Congressman Aspinall and Senator Carroll of Colorado and the late Senator Bartlett of Alaska. He holds degrees from Claremont Men's College and Oxford University, where he was a Marshall Scholar.

Bibliography

This listing of the important monographs and studies of the Presidency as an institution makes no attempt to be exhaustive. Rather it is offered for readers who want to know the standard works in the field as well as those which develop at greater length some of the themes that have been assessed and reappraised in this anthology.

ALLISON, GRAHAM T., *Essence of Decision: Explaining the Cuban Missile Crisis* (Little, Brown, 1971).

ANDERSON, PATRICK, *The Presidents' Men* (Doubleday, 1968).

BAILEY, THOMAS A., *Presidential Greatness* (Appleton-Century, 1966).

BARBER, JAMES DAVID, *The Presidential Character* (Prentice-Hall, 1972).

——— (ed.), *Choosing a President* (Prentice-Hall, 1974).

BERGER, RAOUL, *Impeachment: The Constitutional Problems* (Harvard University Press, 1973).

BINKLEY, WILFRED E., *President and Congress*, 3d rev. ed. (Vintage, 1962).

BRANT, IRVING, *Impeachment: Trials and Errors* (Knopf, 1972).

BRODER, DAVID S., *The Party's Over* (Harper and Row, 1971).

BROWNLOW, LOUIS, *The President and the Presidency* (University of Chicago Press, 1949).

BUNDY, MCGEORGE, *The Strength of Government* (Harvard University Press, 1968).

BURNS, JAMES M., *Presidential Government* (Houghton Mifflin, 1973).

CHAMBERLAIN, LAWRENCE H., *The President, Congress and Legislation* (Columbia University Press, 1946).

CLARK, KEITH, and LAURENCE LEGERE (eds.), *The President and the Management of National Security* (Praeger, 1969).

COCHRAN, BERT, *Harry Truman and the Crisis Presidency* (Funk and Wagnalls, 1973).

CORNWELL, ELMER E., *Presidential Leadership of Public Opinion* (University of Indiana Press, 1962).

CORWIN, EDWARD S., *The President: Office and Powers* (New York University Press, 1940).

COTTER, C. P., and J. M. SMITH, *Powers of the President During National Crises* (Public Affairs Press, 1961).

CRONIN, THOMAS E., *The State of the Presidency* (Brookings Institution, 1974).

CRONIN, THOMAS E., and SANFORD D. GREENBERG (eds.), *The Presidential Advisory System* (Harper and Row, 1969).

DESTLER, I. M., *Presidents, Bureaucrats and Foreign Policy* (Princeton University Press, 1972).

DONOVAN, JOHN C., *The Policy-Makers* (Pegasus, 1970).

DUNN, DELMER D., *Financing Presidential Campaigns* (Brookings Institution, 1972).

FAIRLIE, HENRY, *The Kennedy Promise: The Politics of Expectation* (Doubleday, 1973).

FENNO, RICHARD F., *The President's Cabinet* (Vintage, 1959).

FINER, HERMAN, *The Presidency, Crisis and Regeneration* (University of Chicago Press, 1960).

FISHER, LOUIS, *President and Congress* (Free Press, 1972).

GOLDMAN, ERIC F., *The Tragedy of Lyndon Johnson* (Knopf, 1969).

GRABNER, DORIS, *Public Opinion, the President and Foreign Policy* (Holt, Rinehart and Winston, 1968).

HALBERSTAM, DAVID, *The Best and the Brightest* (Random House, 1972).

HARGROVE, ERWIN C., *Presidential Leadership* (Macmillan, 1966).

HELLER, FRANCIS, *The Presidency* (Random House, 1960).

HENRY, LAURIN L., *Presidential Transitions* (Brookings Institution, 1960).

HERRING, PENDLETON, *Presidential Leadership* (Farrar and Rhinehart, 1940).

HOFSTADTER, RICHARD, *The American Political Tradition* (Vintage, 1948).

HOLTZMAN, ABRAHAM, *Legislative Liaison: Executive Leadership in Congress* (Rand McNally, 1970).

HOOPES, TOWNSEND, *The Limits of Intervention* (McKay, 1969).

HUGHES, EMMET JOHN, *The Living Presidency* (Coward, McCann and Geoghegan, 1973).

————, *The Oreal of Power* (Dell, 1962).

HYMAN, SIDNEY, *The American President* (Harper, 1954).

JAMES, DOROTHY B., *The Contemporary Presidency* (Pegasus, 1969).

JANIS, IRVING L., *Victims of Groupthink* (Houghton Mifflin, 1972).

JOHNSON, DONALD B., and JACK L. WALKER (eds.), *The Dynamics of the American Presidency* (Wiley, 1974).

JOHNSON, LYNDON B., *The Vantage Point* (Holt, Rinehart and Winston, 1971).

KALLENBACH, JOSEPH E., *The American Chief Executive* (Harper and Row, 1966).

KENNEDY, ROBERT F., *Thirteen Days: A Memoir of the Cuban Missile Crisis* (Norton, 1969).

KOENIG, LOUIS, *The Chief Executive* (Harcourt, Brace and World, 1968).

LASKI, HAROLD J., *The American Presidency* (Grosset and Dunlap, 1940).

MCCONNELL, GRANT, *Steel and the Presidency* (Norton, 1963).

————, *The Modern Presidency* (St. Martin's, 1967).

MCGINNISS, JOE, *The Selling of the President 1968* (Trident Press, 1969).

MATTHEWS, DONALD R. (ed.), *Perspectives on Presidential Selection* (Brookings Institution, 1973).

MILTON, GEORGE F., *The Use of Presidential Power* (Little, Brown, 1944).

MOE, RONALD C. (ed.), *Congress and the President* (Goodyear 1971).

MORGAN, RUTH P., *The President and Civil Rights* (St. Martin's, 1970).

MOYNIHAN, DANIEL P., *The Politics of a Guaranteed Income* (Random House, 1973).

MUELLER, JOHN E., *War, Presidents and Public Opinion* (Wiley, 1973).

NEUSTADT, RICHARD E., *Alliance Politics* (Columbia University Press, 1970).

————, *Presidential Power* (Wiley, 1960).

PATTERSON, C. P., *Presidential Government in the United States* (University of North Carolina Press, 1947).

PIERCE, NEAL R., *The People's President* (Clarion, 1968).

POLLARD, JAMES F., *The Presidents and the Press* (Public Affairs Press, 1964).

POLSBY, NELSON W., *Congress and the Presidency* (Prentice-Hall, 1971).

———— (ed.), *The Modern Presidency* (Random House, 1973).

POLSBY, NELSON W., and AARON WILDAVSKY, *Presidential Elections* (Scribners, 1968).

POPPER, FRANK, *The President's Commissions* (Twentieth Century Fund, 1970).

REEDY, GEORGE E., *The Presidency in Flux* (Columbia University Press, 1973).

————, *The Twilight of the Presidency* (World, 1970).

ROSSITER, CLINTON, *Constitutional Dictatorship* (Harcourt, Brace, 1948).

————, *The American Presidency* (Harcourt, Brace and World, 1960).

ROURKE, FRANCIS E., *Bureaucracy, Politics and Public Policy* (Little, Brown, 1969).

SCHLESINGER, ARTHUR M., JR., *A Thousand Days: John F. Kennedy in the White House* (Houghton Mifflin, 1965).

————, *The Imperial Presidency* (Houghton Mifflin, 1973).

SCHLESINGER, ARTHUR M., JR., and ALFRED DE GRAZIA, *Congress and the Presidency: Their Role in Modern Times* (American Enterprise Institute, 1967).

SCHUBERT, GLENDON, *The Presidency in the Courts* (University of Minnesota Press, 1957).

SCIGLIANO, ROBERT, *The Supreme Court and the Presidency* (Free Press, 1971).

SORENSEN, THEODORE C., *Decision-Making in the White House* (Columbia University Press, 1963).

————, *Kennedy* (Harper and Row, 1965).

STRUM, PHILIPPA, *Presidential Power and American Democracy* (Goodyear, 1972).

SULZNER, GEORGE, and STANLEY BACH (eds.), *Perspectives on the Presidency* (Heath, 1974).

SUNDQUIST, JAMES L., *Politics and Policy: The Eisenhower, Kennedy and Johnson Years* (Brookings Institution, 1968).

THACH, CHARLES C., JR., *The Creation of the Presidency, 1775–1789* (DeCapo Press, 1969).

THOMAS, NORMAN C., and HANS W. BAADE (eds.) , *The Institutionalized Presidency* (Oceana, 1972).

THOMPSON, HUNTER S., *Fear and Loathing: On the Campaign Trail '72* (Straight Arrow Press, 1973).

TUGWELL, REXFORD G., *How They Became President* (Simon and Schuster, 1965) .

————, *The Democratic Roosevelt* (Doubleday, 1957).

————, *The Enlargement of the Presidency* (Doubleday, 1960).

VINYARD, DALE, *The Presidency* (Scribners, 1971) .

WANN, A. J., *The President as Chief Administrator* (Public Affairs Press, 1968).

WHITE, THEODORE H., *The Making of the President 1960* (Atheneum, 1961).

————. *The Making of the President 1964* (Atheneum, 1965).

————. *The Making of the President 1968* (Antheneum, 1969).

————. *The Making of the President 1972* (Antheneum, 1973).

WILDAVSKY, AARON (ed.) , *The Presidency* (Little Brown, 1974).

WILLS, GARRY, *Nixon Agonistes* (Houghton Mifflin, 1970).

WISE, SIDNEY, and RICHARD F. SCHIER, *The Presidential Office* (Crowell, 1968).

YOUNG, JAMES S., *The Washington Community, 1800–1820* (Columbia University Press, 1966).

Index

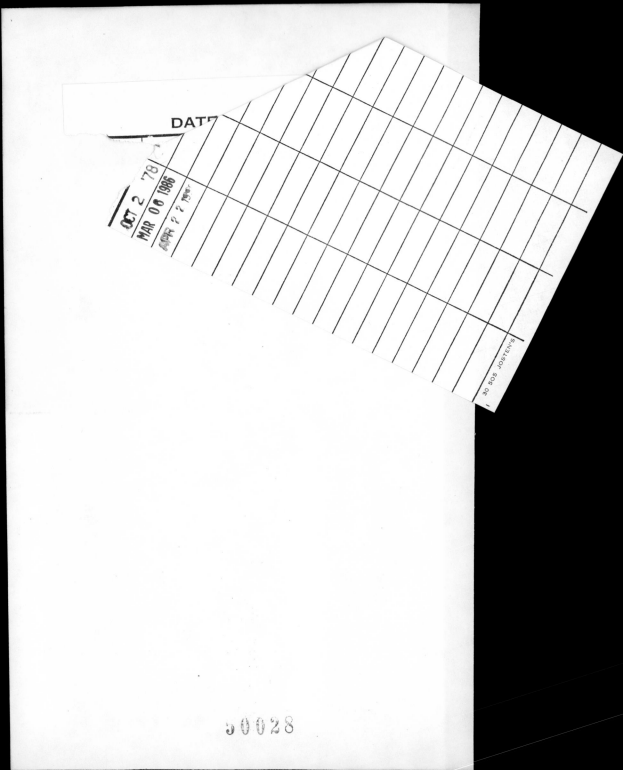

DATE